AF775946

The Idea of a China Arrest Warrant

The Idea of a China Arrest Warrant

Surrender of Fugitive Offenders between Mainland China, Hong Kong, and Macau

Yanhong Yin

HKU PRESS
香港大學出版社

Hong Kong University Press
The University of Hong Kong
Pok Fu Lam Road
Hong Kong
https://hkupress.hku.hk

© 2025 Hong Kong University Press

ISBN 978-988-8876-83-9 (*Hardback*)

All rights reserved. No portion of this publication may be reproduced or transmitted in any form or by any means, electronic or mechanical, including photocopying, recording, or any information storage or retrieval system, without prior permission in writing from the publisher.

British Library Cataloguing-in-Publication Data
A catalogue record for this book is available from the British Library.

Digitally printed

To my parents for their unconditional love.

To the magical world we are living in.

Contents

Figures and Tables

Figures

Tables

Preface

No agreement on the surrender of fugitive offenders between mainland China, Hong Kong, and Macau has been concluded, even though the two Special Administrative Regions (SARs) were returned to the People's Republic of China (PRC) more than twenty years ago. Numerous serious efforts have been made to help realize such a surrender arrangement, however no consensus has yet been reached. My study aims to investigate this problem in order to ascertain the basic principles with which the three regions should comply in reaching an arrangement. I do this mainly by referring to the legislation and practice of the European arrest warrant system which applies in the European Union (EU).

In addition to intensive bibliographical study, the research for this book relies on comparative analysis and cases studies. It undertakes comparisons between the EU and China along horizontal and vertical lines and from external and internal perspectives. These comparisons, both general and particular, are designed to provide background or context to the book's core research on the surrender system. Detailed analysis of the similarities and differences between the EU surrender system and the Chinese domestic surrender system runs through the entire narrative. The EU's development from old extradition system to the present-day European arrest warrant dates back to the 1950s and applies from the EU level to the Member States level. In China, I analyze the separate (joint) legislative domains and practices in mainland China, Hong Kong, and Macau in order to identify the common basis for, and possible obstacles to, the construction of a close surrender system. The cases studied come from the Court of Justice of the European Union (CJEU), the European Court of Human Rights (ECtHR), and the courts of mainland China, Hong Kong, and Macau.

This study concludes that mainland China, Hong Kong, and Macau need a new system for the surrender of fugitive offenders that is closer and more efficient than the current traditional form of international extradition, while also being based on the principle of human rights protection. Scrutinizing the European arrest warrant in practice, in light of the actual needs of a mainland, Hong Kong, and Macau surrender system, the EU model does offer inspiration. This study shows that a China arrest warrant system inspired mainly by its EU counterpart could be established between mainland China, Hong Kong, and Macau. The mutual recognition principle that is the cornerstone of the European arrest warrant system could be applied to the three Chinese regions, as well as most of the system's other concrete surrender principles. At the same time, some adjustment should be made in line with the lessons learned and the political and legal situations in mainland China, Hong Kong, and Macau.

Acknowledgments

Thanks to Professor Vagelis Papakonstantinou, who has offered patience and timely assistance and meaningful guidance on my research, especially its methodology. Thanks also to Professor Paul De Hert; his comments during PhD seminars pushed me to go deeper into my research topic, and his thinking on criminal law is an inspiration to young researchers. Professor John Vervaele first offered me academic assistance years ago, and his expertise on European criminal law and enthusiasm with students greatly benefited me, for which I am deeply grateful. Gratitude is owed to Professor Simon Young, a knowledgeable and gentle professor from China's Hong Kong SAR, whose comments on several of my publications enriched my knowledge about the details of Hong Kong's common law system. Also, thanks to my jury members, Professor Stefaa Smis and Dr Maarton Colette.

In addition, Professor Eleftheria Neframi, a kind, serious, and very helpful European law professor, deserves my thanks for leading me through my European law program during the early stage of research and widening my perspective on European public law. Professor Katalin Ligeti generously guided me through the complications of the European arrest warrant and Chinese extradition, for which I am truly grateful. Thanks to Professor Silvia Allegrezza; her comments on my research paper proved both useful and inspiring. Professor Huang Feng offered indispensable guidance during the earlier stages of my research, earning my heartfelt thanks. Thanks to Wayne Walsh and Cristina Ferreira, their research findings also inspire me a lot. And Professors Albert Hong Yee Chen and Richard Cullen greatly inspired my thinking about Chinese law with socialist characteristics and Hong Kong's common law. Thanks to judge and Professor Christine Van den Wyngaert; her research on the political offence exception to extradition greatly inspired my thinking on China's domestic surrender issue. Thanks to Mr. Larse Bay Larsen, judge of the Court of Justice of the European Union; his trial experience on European arrest warrant cases directly enriched my knowledge of European arrest warrant. Professor Andre Klip's research on European arrest warrant updated my understanding of EU law and Professor Paulo Pinto de Albuquerque deepened my understanding of human rights protection in judicial cooperation in criminal matters. Thanks to all of them.

Deep gratitude is owed for the assistance I received from so many young and excellent researchers. These include Irene Weicker, a tutor as well as a friend, whom I met many years ago, and Auke Willemas, whose expertise in the European arrest warrant and in US interstate rendition enriched my knowledge greatly. Special thanks for the assistance I received from Maxime Lassal, Angelo, Stanislaw, Michela, and others. And thanks to my colleagues in the Vrije Universiteit Brussel Fundamental Rights and Research Centre.

During my PhD study, I also visited Cambridge and UCLA as an exchange student and visiting researcher. Thanks to Professor John Spencer and Professor Barry Rider, who made my Cambridge trip both meaningful and useful. I greatly appreciate the guidance that Professor Maximo Langer gave me during my time at UCLA. Thanks to Professor Daniel Charles Richman of Columbia University, who lent me books and assisted me in studying American Law. Thanks to the Centre for Comparative and Public Law at the University of Hong Kong; I benefitted tremendously from its online seminars and conferences on Hong Kong public law. Also, thanks for the privilege of participating in academic associations like the European Criminal Law Network and the International Association of Penal Law, whose interesting conferences and workshops offered me opportunities to learn EU and international criminal law.

Regarding the publication of this book by Hong Kong University Press, thanks to Yasmine Hung for her great work on the project. Thanks to the great team at Hong Kong University Press.

Finally, sincere thanks should be given to my wonderful parents. Without their patience, love, and selfless help I could never have focused so thoroughly on my research as I did. Thanks to my younger sister and her lovely family, who instilled in me great optimism for my future. Special thanks to my grandmother; I will never forget the time we spent together during the book writing. Last, thanks to my aunts, uncles, cousins and neighbors, who helped so much to guarantee a peaceful and quiet study environment over the years.

Abbreviations

CAW	China arrest warrant
CFR	Charter of Fundamental Rights of the European Union
CISA	Convention Implementing the Schengen Agreement
CJEU	Court of Justice of the European Union
CPT	European Committee for the Prevention of Torture and Inhuman or Degrading Treatment or Punishment
EAW	European arrest warrant
ECHR	European Convention on Human Rights
ECtHR	European Court of Human Rights
EU	European Union
FD	Framework Decision
FOO	Hong Kong Fugitive Offenders Ordinance
ICCPR	International Covenant on Civil and Political Rights
ICESCR	International Convention on Economic, Social and Cultural Rights
ICPO	International Criminal Police Organization
ICTR	International Tribunal for Rwanda
ICTY	International Criminal Tribunal for the Former Yugoslavia
MS	Member State
MSs	Member States
NAW	Nordic arrest warrant
NPCSC	Standing Committee of the National People's Congress
PRC	People's Republic of China
SAR	Special Administrative Region
TEU	Treaty on European Union

TFEU	Treaty on the Functioning of the European Union
UK	United Kingdom
UN	United Nations
UNHRC	UN Human Rights Committee
US	United States of America

Introduction

1 Identifying the topic and the problem

Historically, Hong Kong was a colonized territory of Britain while Macau was a colony of Portugal. In those times, the reciprocal extradition of fugitive offenders vis-à-vis the People's Republic of China (PRC) and as between Hong Kong and Macau were usually matters for international diplomacy and agreement.[1] Hong Kong and Macau were returned to the PRC in 1997 and 1999 respectively. They were constituted as special administrative regions (SARs) of the PRC governed by the "one country, two systems" policy.[2] The surrender of fugitive offenders would now become an internal matter of the PRC to be settled in accordance with the high degree of autonomy granted to the two SARs. However, at the time of the respective handovers, the issue of "extradition" between Hong Kong, Macau and mainland China was highly controversial given differences in the legal systems and concerns about the death penalty applied in mainland China. All that could be agreed was that the issue be deferred for consideration in the future. Indeed, when the Hong Kong SAR and Macau SAR passed local laws to provide for the surrender of fugitive offenders, both laws clearly stated they would not apply to other parts of the PRC.[3]

The change in terminology from "extradition" to "surrender" also reflects the evolution in the constitutional orders of Hong Kong and Macau. In substance, extradition and surrender have the same meaning, i.e. the legal transfer of a person from place A to place B to face a criminal charge (or serve a sentence). But as "extradition" connotes relations between two sovereign states while "surrender" does not, those

1. Miguel Manero de Lemos and Simon N.M. Young, "Regional Judicial Cooperation in Criminal Matters: Mainland China, Hong Kong and Macau," in *Elgar Encyclopedia of Crime and Criminal Justice*, ed. P Caeiro and others (Cheltenham: Edward Elgar, July 2023).
2. See Basic Law of Hong Kong, Preamble; Basic Law of Macau, Preamble.
3. See Hong Kong's Fugitive Offenders Ordinance (Cap 503), s 2(1) (definition of "arrangements for the surrender of fugitive offenders") and Macau's Mutual Legal Assistance in Criminal Matters Law (No. 6/2006), art. 1(1).

overseeing the external relations of the SARs opted for the latter term to describe the SAR's arrangements with other states.

The surrender problem with the SARs can be contrasted with the established procedures for the interprovincial arrest and detention of fugitives in mainland China. A wanted order issued by a public prosecutor's office or a judgment given by a court is legally binding in the whole of the Mainland, and the arrest and detention of offenders is directly achieved through police cooperation in accordance with the Criminal Procedure Law of China.[4] Essentially, the arrest and "surrender" of fugitive offenders in the Mainland interprovincial system is a system of police cooperation within a single jurisdiction. In contrast with this, under the "one country, two systems" policy, the surrender of fugitive offenders between the Mainland, Hong Kong, and Macau is conceived of as a form of judicial cooperation in criminal matters between three different jurisdictions. The judicial cooperation between these three jurisdictions should be based on legal arrangements consistent with the Basic Laws of the two SARs.[5] In this regard, Article 95 of the Hong Kong Basic Law and Article 93 of the Macau Basic Law are significant; they provide that the SARs "may, through consultations and in accordance with law, maintain juridical relations with the judicial organs of other parts of the country, and they may render assistance to each other."

While agreements on judicial cooperation in civil matters have been concluded between the SARs and the Mainland, agreements in criminal matters remain underdeveloped. Negotiation on the surrender of fugitive offenders[6] between the Mainland, Hong Kong, and Macau has been underway for some time,[7] but little progress has been made to date. The three regions cannot reach consensus on the application of traditional extradition principles, including the non-surrender for offences subject to the death penalty, non-surrender of nationals (residents), non-surrender for political offences, and the double criminality principle.[8]

4. See Criminal Procedure Law of the People's Republic of China (amended in 2018), arts. 83 and 155.
5. See Hong Kong Basic Law, art. 95 and Macau Basic Law, art. 93.
6. In this research, the scope of "fugitive offenders" includes both persons requested for prosecution and persons requested for imposition or enforcement of sentence or detention order. Regarding the idiomatic usage of "fugitive offenders," see Hong Kong Fugitive Offenders Ordinance; see also Macau Surrender Agreement with South Korea.
7. See Wayne Walsh, *Cross-Border Crime in Hong Kong: Extradition, Mutual Assistance, Financial Sanctions* (Hong Kong: LexisNexis, 2020), 237.
8. Zhao Guoqiang 赵国强, "Lun 'Yiguo liangzhi' xiade yijiao taofan jizhi" 论"一国两制"下的移交逃犯机制 [Discussion on the surrender of fugitive offenders mechanism under "one country, two systems"], *Xingzheng* 行政 20, no. 78 (2007): 1050. See also Chau Pak-kwan and Stephen Lam, "Research Study on the Agreement between Hong Kong and Mainland Concerning Surrender of Fugitive Offenders" [March 2001], Legislative Council Secretariat, Research and Library Services Division and Legal Service Division, Hong Kong, https://www.legco.gov.hk/yr00-01/english/library/erp05.pdf.

Despite the inability to construct a complete domestic surrender system, mainland China, Hong Kong and Macau have signed extradition treaties and surrender agreements with foreign countries based on the traditional international extradition framework.[9] The Extradition Law of the People's Republic of China was promulgated on 28 December 2000 but does not apply to Hong Kong and Macau. The constitutional bases for Hong Kong and Macau to have surrender agreements with other foreign jurisdictions are found in Basic Law articles, which provide that "with the assistance or authorization of the Central People's Government, the SAR may make appropriate arrangements with foreign states for reciprocal judicial assistance."[10]

In 2019, the Hong Kong government attempted to amend its Fugitive Offenders Ordinance (FOO) (Hong Kong's extradition law) so that it might apply to the case of Chan Tong-kai, a Hong Kong permanent resident who killed his girlfriend in Taiwan.[11] As Hong Kong did not have a surrender arrangement with Taiwan (nor could one be agreed and applied without amending the FOO), the government feared Chan could return to Hong Kong and escape any legal consequences for the homicide, which he did not deny.[12] If the FOO was amended as proposed, the surrender of fugitive offenders between Hong Kong, Macau and other parts of China (including Taiwan) could be practiced on a case-by-case basis.[13] However, the proposal was aborted in the face of highly vocal and sustained public protests.[14]

The prolonged protest demonstrated the strong feelings of many Hong Kong people who were concerned about possible extradition of Hong Kong permanent residents to face trial in mainland China. However, as the protests escalated and became more violent, destructive, and disruptive, legal loopholes in protecting Hong Kong's social order and Chinese national security became exposed. This provoked the Central Government to enact The Law of the People's Republic of China on Safeguarding National Security in the Hong Kong Special Administrative

---

9. The chapters that follow will successively detail the principles or techniques used in these extradition treaties or agreements.
10. See Hong Kong Basic Law, art. 96; Macau Basic Law, art. 94.
11. Duncan DeAeth, "Hong Kong Man Who Killed Girlfriend in Taiwan May Never Be Charged for Murder," *Taiwan News*, March 18, 2018, https://www.taiwannews.com.tw/en/news/3384825.
12. Zen Soo, "Hong Kong Murder Suspect Plans to Turn Himself to Taiwan," *AP News*, October 2, 2020, https://apnews.com/general-news-5d1f55a53879bc34ec37fd2d7617804f.
13. Jiachao Li, "Statement Given by Secretary of HK Security Bureau on the Amendment of Hong Kong Fugitive Offender Ordinance," May 30, 2019, https://www.info.gov.hk/gia/general/201905/30/P2019053000811.htm. The text of the amendment is available at https://www.legco.gov.hk/yr18-19/english/bills/b201903291.pdf.
14. *SCMP* Reporters, "Hong Kong Leader Carrie Lam Announces Formal Withdrawal of the Extradition Bill and Sets Up a Platform to Look into Key Causes of Protest Crisis," *South China Morning Post*, September 4, 2019, https://www.scmp.com/news/hong-kong/politics/article/3025641/hong-kong-leader-carrie-lam-announce-formal-withdrawal.

Region, commonly known as the National Security Law (NSL), on 30 June 2020, promulgated in Hong Kong on the same day.[15] The political and legal relations between the three regions have actually strengthened since the law's enactment.[16] The new law defines categories of offences, including secession, subversion, terrorist activities, and collusion with foreign forces to endanger national security. Even though the legislation does not address the surrender of fugitive offenders between mainland China and Hong Kong, it does provide for an exceptional power where the Mainland authorities could apply Mainland law in Hong Kong to assume direct jurisdiction over a case.[17] It does not alter existing rules contained in agreements signed between Hong Kong and Western countries restricting the re-surrender of offenders to the Mainland, e.g. the specialty rule, the double criminality principle and other principles. The Hong Kong NSL will likely affect the application of the political offence exception as well as other principles in the surrender system between the three regions, as will be discussed later in this book.[18]

After the enactment of the Hong Kong NSL, a number of Western countries suspended their surrender agreements with Hong Kong to demonstrate their opposition to the newly enacted law and concerns about the state of judicial independence and human rights in Hong Kong.[19] However, the Western suspension of surrender agreements with Hong Kong should neither adversely affect nor raise concerns about the construction of a system of surrender of fugitive offenders between mainland China, Hong Kong, and Macau. International extradition is meant to cater to or limit the political interests of different sovereign states.[20] The surrender between mainland China, Hong Kong, and Macau occurs within one sovereign country, the PRC. It involves a domestic surrender system serving domestic interests. The

15. Hua Xia, "National Security Law Effective in Restoring Stability in Hong Kong: Official," *Xin Hua*, September 15, 2020, http://www.xinhuanet.com/english/2020-09/15/c_139370779.htm.
16. Under the National Security Law, both the Hong Kong government and the Hong Kong public have the obligation to protect the national security and national interest of People's Republic of China. For the text of the legislation, see https://hongkongfp.com/2020/07/01/in-full-english-translation-of-the-hong-kong-national-security-law/.
17. Under Article 55 of the NSL, suspects can be investigated, prosecuted, and tried by Mainland authorities, but that is direct implementation of governance power from the Central Government to Hong Kong on just four categories of offences relating to national security. It is not a surrender arrangement by nature.
18. The details appear in the following chapters.
19. William James and Andy Bruce, "UK Suspends Hong Kong Extradition Treaty, Stoking China Tensions," *Reuters*, July 19, 2020, https://www.reuters.com/article/uk-britain-china-diplomacy-idUKKCN24K0AS.
20. See M. Cherif Bassiouni, *International Extradition: United States Law and Practice*, 6th ed. (Oxford: Oxford University Press, 2014), 2–3.

three regions share a common national political interest,[21] and a common legal obligation,[22] under the umbrella of one country. This marks an essential difference between China domestic surrender system and the international extradition system, politically and legally. So long as the re-surrender restrictions remain in place, the systems of international extradition and domestic surrender can be kept separate in terms of their design and application.

Against this background, it is debatable whether all the traditional extradition principles should be applied to the China domestic surrender system.[23] For instance, the political offence exception in the traditional extradition process is a double-edged sword: while it is intended to protect individual rights and personal freedom, it imposes national standards and values on other states.[24] Under the one country policy, Hong Kong and Macau must accept political and legal responsibilities that maintain the territorial unity of China and uphold the leadership and governance of the Central Government.[25] They also bear the legal obligation to tackle secession, subversion, espionage, and other traditional political offences which hamper national security and state integrity.[26] Thus, it is doubtful whether, in the future, Hong Kong should implement the political offence exception that would allow refusal of a surrender request by mainland China.[27]

Moreover, in the case of Hong Kong and Macau, after their handover in the 1990s, all their residents have been classified as either permanent or non-permanent residents subject to provisions of the respective Basic Law. It remains in question

21. The Hong Kong Special Administrative Region is charged with upholding national unity and territorial integrity while maintaining the prosperity and stability of the region. See Hong Kong Basic Law, Preamble. Similar political goals appear in the Macau Basic Law.
22. Hong Kong is an inalienable part of the People's Republic of China. Thus, the Hong Kong SAR has the obligation to safeguard national security and territorial integrity. See Hong Kong Basic Law, art. 1 and art. 23; see also the Law of the People's Republic of China on Safeguarding National Security in the Hong Kong Special Administrative Region 2020. A similar legal position is evident in the Macau Basic Law and Macau Safeguarding National Security Law 2009.
23. See Zhao, "Lun Yiguo," n 8.
24. See Bassiouni, *International Extradition,* 672 (n 20); see also Miguel João Costa, *Extradition Law: Reviewing Grounds for Refusal from the Classic Paradigm to Mutual Recognition and Beyond* (Leiden: Brill Nijhoff, 2019), 501.
25. Hong Kong, as a Special Administrative Region enjoying a high degree of autonomy, remains a local region under the control of the Central Government; see Hong Kong Basic Law, art. 12. The high degree of autonomy is neither automatic nor naturally inherent; instead, it is laid down by the National People's Congress. See Basic Law, art 2. Similar stipulations appear in Macau and the Macau Basic Law.
26. These have been regulated in the Hong Kong (Macau) Basic Law as well as the Hong Kong (Macau) Safeguarding National Security Law.
27. Yanhong Yin and Irene Wieczorek, "What Model for Extradition between Hong Kong and Mainland China? A Comparison between the 2019 (withdrawn) Amendment to Hong Kong Extradition Law and the European Arrest Warrant," *New Journal of European Criminal Law* 11, no. 4 (2020): 517.

whether and how the traditional nationality exception principle could be applied.[28] Additionally, the fact that the three regions belong to one country and that the two SAR governments are directly subordinated to the Central Government may challenge the roles of the executive and judicial authorities in the surrender procedure.[29]

The China domestic surrender system is also limited by the "two systems" reality. According to the Basic Law, Hong Kong (Macau) enjoys a high degree of autonomy, practices the common law (Macau law) system, and the Hong Kong (Macau) Court of Final Appeal has supreme judicial power.[30] Accordingly, the direct and simple interprovincial arrest cooperation practised among the provinces of mainland China cannot be applied to China domestic surrender system. In other words, traditional extradition principles still have some role to play. For instance, the double criminality principle and the non-surrender of death penalty offenders or life imprisonment offenders may still function in the surrender system, though the precise terms of the rules and their implementation may have to accord with the overarching reality of "one country."

Also of critical importance is the level of human rights protection in this China domestic surrender system. In traditional extradition, most bilateral or multilateral treaties will treat certain human rights risks as mandatory ground to refuse the extradition.[31] Under the "one country, two systems" policy, mainland China, Hong Kong, and Macau should find a constructive solution, perhaps more so than the traditional extradition grounds protecting certain interests of the requested person, while strengthening cooperation. The "human rights check" in the surrender mechanism can also be used to help promote the human rights cause in the whole of China. It is clear that the China domestic surrender issue has a background of increasing political, economic, societal, and cultural integration, which generally does not exist

28. See Yin and Wieczorek, "What Model," 519, n 27.
29. In fact, the role of the Chief Executive and the Hong Kong courts was questioned by the Hong Kong public when amending the Hong Kong Fugitive Offenders Ordinance in 2019. The Chief Executive is required to cooperate with the Central Government, and the courts are concerned about being in a disadvantageous position and unable to refuse surrender.
30. Hong Kong Basic Law, art. 2 and art. 8. See also Macau Basic Law.
31. E.g., the UN Model Treaty on Extradition specifies that extradition shall not be granted if there are grounds to believe that the request has been made to prosecute or punish a person on account of that person's race, religion, nationality, ethnic origin, political opinions, sex or status, or that the person's position may be prejudiced for any of these reasons or if the person would be subjected to torture or cruel, inhuman treatment or degrading punishment or if that person has not or would not receive the minimum guarantees in criminal proceedings as contained in the International Covenant on Civil and Political Rights: Model Treaty on Extradition, art. 3(b)(f).

in traditional forms of extradition.[32] Nevertheless, the divergence between the three regions over human rights protection cannot be overlooked.

In brief, the China domestic surrender system must rest on the fact of "one country," be responsive to its divergent legal systems, and provide sufficient human rights protection. Traditional extradition principles did not originate under these conditions and thus would need to be re-considered and possibly adapted before being applied to the surrender of fugitives within the PRC.

To gain more insights into how this domestic surrender problem could be addressed, this book has adopted a comparative approach to find possible inspiration from other countries and regions. However, finding a close comparator is difficult as few countries have chosen to employ one system of rendition in one part of the country and a different one in another part. Though the United States of America (US) has one federal jurisdiction and 50 state jurisdictions, each with their own set of criminal laws, its interstate rendition system, in which states transfer fugitive offenders to petitioning sister states, is too dissimilar to be useful. Adopting a uniform domestic surrender system, the US interstate rendition process bears little resemblance to international extradition. Having grown more heavily subject to executive control and less to traditional extradition principles, it is an efficient system of transferring wanted persons for trial based on mutual credit.[33] It is similar to the mainland China interprovincial cooperative model but does not have to address the challenging issue of surrender of fugitives to and from more autonomous regions of the country.

The system of extradition adopted for the European Union, however, does have greater potential to inspire solutions to the problem for the PRC. The European arrest warrant, as an advanced regional "extradition system" combining efficiency and human rights protection, can be the basis for theorizing a China arrest warrant that would apply to mainland China, Hong Kong and Macau. Mutual recognition is the cornerstone principle of the European arrest warrant. The principle was proposed by the United Kingdom (UK) as an alternative to harmonization, aiming to enhance judicial cooperation within the European Union while maintaining the diversity of legal systems. The purpose behind the principle resonates with the "one country, two systems" policy and can suitably underpin surrender cooperation between mainland China, Hong Kong, and Macau. Though the European Union and the PRC lie at different ends of Eurasia, the two regions are similar to each other

---

32. Hong Kong and Macau have been returned to China for more than 20 years, and so the integration with mainland China in politics, economy, and culture should be assumed, although, in practice, the degree varies.
33. Yanhong Yin, "The Surrender of Fugitive Offenders between Mainland China and Hong Kong: European Arrest Warrant," *Utrecht Journal of International and European Law* 37, no. 1 (June 6, 2022): 1.

in many ways.[34] Such similarities offer the possibility that they can teach each other how to achieve better regional cooperation and development, including in the area of surrender of fugitive offenders.[35]

2 Background and context of the China and EU analysis

2.1 Political similarities

The European Union (EU) consists of 27 Member States. All of the Member States transfer part of their sovereignty to the EU and no Member State enjoys full sovereignty.[36] After the Lisbon Treaty, the issue of judicial cooperation in criminal matters is also moved from the third pillar to the first pillar[37] and under the direct control of the EU.[38] The goal to establish an area of freedom, security, and justice was recognized, and the European arrest warrant was adopted as an important legal tool. The enforcement of judicial cooperation in criminal matters has been strengthened by the uniform political power of the EU; the accumulation of political power in criminal matters was done for the sake of the EU region as a whole.[39]

The political relationship between mainland China, Hong Kong, and Macau bears some resemblance with that between EU Member States. Under the "one country, two systems" policy, both Hong Kong and Macau are inseparable parts of the PRC. At the same time, both Hong Kong and Macau enjoy a high degree of autonomy, which is stipulated in the respective Basic Laws enacted by the National People's Congress. Each SAR has separate administrative and executive power, legislative power, independent judicial power, and final adjudication power.[40] This mixture is very similar to that which exists in the EU, where every Member State

---

34. See Eva Minarčíková, "EU-China Cooperation on Regional Policy," *Perspectives in Science* 7 (2016): 30. See also Harry Harding, "The Concept of Greater China: Themes, Variations and Reservations," *The China Quarterly* (1993): 668.
35. See Yin and Wieczorek "What Model," 504, n 27.
36. See Jacek Czaputowicz, "Sovereignty in Theories of European Integration and the Perspective of the Polish Constitutional Tribunal," *Yearbook of Polish European Studies* 17 (2014): 18.
37. According to Maastricht Treaty 1992, the first pillar is the European Communities, the second pillar is the Common Foreign and Security Policy, the third pillar is Justice and Home Affairs. The first pillar has a supranational basis, and the latter two pillars operate on intergovernmental basis. The Treaty of Lisbon 2009 abolished the three-pillar structure entirely and the old pillar structure was subsumed into the overall European Union structure.
38. See Bahadr Yakut, "Post-Lisbon Criminal Law Competency of the European Union," *Marmara Journal of European Studies* 17 (2009): 3.
39. See Mar Jimeno-Bulnes, "European Judicial Cooperation in Criminal Matters," *European Law Journal* 9, no. 5 (2003): 614. See also Fabrini Federico, "Enhanced Cooperation under Scrutiny: Revisiting the Law and Practice of Multi-Speed Integration in Light of the First Involvement of the EU Judiciary," *Legal Issues of Economic Integration* 40, no. 3 (2013): 197.
40. See Basic Law of Hong Kong and Basic Law of Macau, art. 1 and art. 2.

belongs to the EU politically, while simultaneously retaining partial sovereignty, including judicial sovereignty.[41]

The design of a China domestic surrender system can go even further to demonstrating a close political relationship among the three regions than can the EU's European arrest warrant. It is possible to conceptualize a China arrest warrant system (CAW) similar to the European arrest warrant in which judicial authorities dominate the entire surrender procedure based on enforceable judicial decisions under the mutual recognition principle.

2.2 *Economic integration*

The EU developed from the European Economic Community.[42] The relaxation of border controls between the EU Member States was originally done for the purpose of economic development.[43] The basic principles of mutual trust and mutual recognition are rooted in economic cooperation. In practice, the European arrest warrant has demonstrated that the border can be opened for both economic reasons and judicial purposes, and the principles applicable to the economic field can also be applied to the judicial field. The same is true for mainland China, Hong Kong, and Macau.

Since Hong Kong and Macau returned to China, cooperation between the three regions in the economic field has boomed. Dozens of economic arrangements have been signed to deepen and broaden cooperation, and the mutual recognition principle can be found in the concrete arrangements as well.[44] In recent years, there has been greater formal judicial cooperation in civil matters, including the mutual recognition of arbitration decisions and judicial decisions in civil proceedings.[45] Although judicial cooperation has its own developmental approach, from the experience of the EU and the reality in the mainland, Hong Kong, and Macau, it is clear that judicial cooperation can be advanced with increasing economic cooperation.[46]

---

41. See Ion M. Anghel, "European Union's Member States Sovereignty," *Annals Constantin Brancusi U Targu Jiu Juridical Sci Series* (2010): 19.
42. European Union, "History of the EU," accessed October 29, 2022, https://european-union.europa.eu/principles-countries-history/history-eu_en.
43. See Kadir Basboga, "The Role of Open Borders and Cross-border Cooperation in Regional Growth across Europe," *Regional Studies, Regional Science* 7, no. 1 (2020): 532.
44. As to economic arrangements and the mutual recognition principle, which are used in economic cooperation, see chapter 1 on mutual recognition where this will be analyzed in detail.
45. See Department of Justice of Hong Kong, "Mainland and Macau SAR Related Topics," accessed October 29, 2022, https://www.doj.gov.hk/tc/mainland_and_macao/RRECCJ.html.
46. The situation in mainland China, Hong Kong, and Macau is that most of the judicial cooperation between the three jurisdictions relates to economic cooperation.

Therefore, the similar histories of economic integration and subsequent judicial cooperation in both the European Union and mainland China, Hong Kong, and Macau suggest that the judicial cooperation mechanisms in EU criminal law, such as the European arrest warrant, can offer useful experience to guide the establishment of a China arrest warrant system.

2.3 Geographical closeness

Mainland China, Hong Kong, and Macau lie geographically close to each other, in a similar way to the 27 Member States of the EU. The physical closeness means mainland China, Hong Kong, and Macau will share and be familiar with each other's social, political, and cultural context and be involved in each other's development. Cooperation in different fields, which naturally flows from this closeness, creates opportunities for cooperation in dealing with cross-border crime.[47] When compared to judicial cooperation with distant areas or countries, the three geographically proximate partners should enjoy an advantage in communication and co-ordination when coping with more frequent movement of criminal suspects.

2.4 Legal diversity

The diversity of legal systems and the problems resulting from diversity exist not only in the European Union but also in mainland China, Hong Kong, and Macau. Since their handovers, Hong Kong and Macau have maintained their original legal systems, based on common law and Portuguese law respectively. The legal system in mainland China is a special socialist legal system mainly influenced by Russian, German, and Japanese law.[48] Thus, the Mainland, Hong Kong, and Macau practice three different legal systems. This undoubtedly affects the design of any kind of surrender system, in areas such as conflict of criminal jurisdiction, double criminality, the death penalty, or life imprisonment.

Similar complications have arisen in developing and managing the European arrest warrant system. Among the EU's Member States, Ireland (and the United Kingdom before Brexit) belongs to the common law system, but most of the other EU countries apply civil law, which can differ in concrete legal rules between

47. See Sonny Shiu-Hing Lo, *The Politics of Cross-border Crime in Greater China: Case Studies of Mainland China, Hong Kong, and Macau* (New York: Routledge, 2009), 1–5.
48. See Albert H.Y. Chen, *The Changing Legal Orders in Hong Kong and Mainland China: Essays on "One Country, Two Systems"* (Hong Kong: City University of Hong Kong Press, 2021), 238–52.

countries.[49] For instance, Portugal has abolished life imprisonment, while most of the other civil law EU countries maintain it. The definition and regulation of rebellion also differ among different countries.[50] The EU is finding solutions to the problems that arise from the diversity of law as it affects the European arrest warrant mechanism. Thus, in addressing the legal diversity issue, which arises also in the design of a China domestic surrender system, the European Union can still offer inspiration to mainland China, Hong Kong, and Macau.

2.5 The human rights situation

Human rights protection matters in the surrender of fugitive offenders. Mainland China has been criticized for its bad record on human rights protection, and the gap between mainland China, Hong Kong, and Macau in human rights protection is clear.[51] How to address this divergence in surrender cooperation becomes another crucial question. Here, too, instructive experiences of the European arrest warrant can be found. Generally, the European Union is regarded as a region in which human rights are better protected than in others. This is a true story, but not a complete one. In fact, citizens of the Member States do not share the same level of human rights protection, the impact of which challenges the implementation and development of the union's arrest warrant system.[52] This complicated situation corresponds well to the one found today in the Mainland, Hong Kong, and Macau. Some meaningful experiences and lessons can be taken from it.

3 Research aim

The main aim of this book is to identify the specific type of surrender relationship that might be instituted between mainland China, Hong Kong, and Macau under the "one country, two systems" policy, and to articulate the basic principles and

---

49. See Julia Sievers, "Too Different to Trust? First Experiences with the Application of the European Arrest Warrant," in *Security Versus Justice? Police and Judicial Cooperation*, ed. Elspeth Guild and Florian Geyer (London: Routledge, 2008), 102–6.
50. See Frauke Holmer, "Matter Carles Puigdemont: The Extradition for the Accusation of Embezzlement of Public Funds is Admissible: An Extradition for the Accusation of Rebellion is Inadmissible. Carles Puigdemont Remains Free," The Press Department of the Oberlandesgericht for the State of Schleswig-Holstein, July 12, 2018, https://www.schleswig-holstein.de/DE/Justiz/OLG/Presse/PI/201806Puigdemontenglisch.html.
51. See Marsha Wellknown Yee, "Hong Kong's Legal Obligation to Require Fair Trial for Rendition," *Columbia Law Review* 102, no. 5 (2002): 1373.
52. See Auke Willems, *The Principle of Mutual Trust in EU Criminal Law* (Oxford: Hart, 2021), 111. As to the divergence of EU Member States in human rights protection, chapter 10 on human rights protection will offer a more comprehensive discussion.

rules for its establishment, while making reference to the European arrest warrant experience. Once accomplished, a blueprint for the establishment of a China arrest warrant system can be drawn.

Regarding the system's implementation, questions, for example, of whether there should be a Mainland–Hong Kong agreement, Macau-Hong Kong agreement, Mainland–Macau agreement, a three-way agreement, or something else are not a topic for discussion in this book. In general, whichever mode of implementation is adopted for the three China regions, the same or similar principles and procedures should be applied. These principles and procedures are decided by the nature of the China domestic surrender system, which will not be substantively influenced or challenged by the implementation mode(s) chosen. This book also does not discuss two other possible solutions to the problem. The first is to extend the interprovincial arrest and detention procedures applied in mainland China to Hong Kong and Macau. The second is to apply a Mainland direct enforcement mechanism, as seen in Hong Kong's NSL, to other crimes in Hong Kong and Macau. Both these solutions are not arrangements for the surrender of fugitive offenders and are at variance, if applied generally, with the "one country, two systems" policy, which respects the autonomy of the SARs and contemplates that cross-border juridical relations and mutual assistance will be based on consultations and be in accordance with the law.

4 Research questions and hypothesis

The book's main research questions ask: What should the China domestic surrender system be? To what extent can features of the European arrest warrant inform a China arrest warrant system applied to Hong Kong, Macau, and mainland China? Sub-research questions ask: Can the mutual recognition principle and the depoliticization of the surrender procedure be practiced in a surrender system designed for the three China regions, and if so, how? How can we best realize the settlement of criminal jurisdictional conflicts? How should traditional extradition principles—including the double criminality principle, non-surrender for political offences, the non-surrender of death penalty offenders and life imprisonment offenders, and human rights protection—be applied, if at all, in the China arrest warrant system, having regard to the European arrest warrant experience?

A fundamental claim of this book is that the China domestic surrender system, governed by the "one country, two systems" policy, is distinct from but not alien to traditional international extradition. The European arrest warrant, an efficient and advanced surrender system which functions well within the European Union, offers inspiration to policymakers and officials in mainland China, Hong Kong, and Macau to create a similarly capable China arrest warrant system. Of course, the extent of the

European Union's inspiration (and transplantation) should be compatible with the political and legal realities of the three China regions.

5 Research methodology

Intensive bibliographical work underpins this book. Efforts are made to survey a wide range of relevant official documents, including the EU extradition convention, its protocols and relevant explanatory reports, the European Arrest Warrant Framework Decision and its proposals, and other official documents from the UN as well as other regions such as the Inter-American region. Regarding mainland China, Hong Kong, and Macau, a comprehensive study is undertaken on the China Extradition Law, extradition treaties that China has signed, the Hong Kong Fugitive Offenders Ordinance, surrender agreements Hong Kong has signed, Macau surrender agreements with other countries, the Macau Law on Mutual Legal Assistance in Criminal Matters, and others. Moreover, studies are made of the criminal law and criminal procedure law in the three regions, the Basic Law in both Hong Kong and Macau, and China's Constitution in order to analyze the extradition or surrender law and practice in the three regions.

A comparative study between the region of the EU and the region of mainland China, Hong Kong, and Macau is conducted. The study considers if a comparison is appropriate on specific topics such as extradition to face the death penalty, life imprisonment, a political offence prosecution, and others. The comparative study also extends within the EU region, and within the mainland China, Hong Kong, and Macau region.

The horizonal comparison of the European Union focuses mainly on cooperation in the economic and judicial fields to demonstrate that some important principles like mutual trust and mutual recognition can be applied across different fields. At the same time, a vertical comparison within the EU also exists, which mainly refers to the comparison between the EU extradition system as it existed 50 years ago with its present-day arrest warrant mechanism. This comparison aims to detect the evolution of the European arrest warrant and its relevant advantages. For mainland China, Hong Kong, and Macau, the comparison is mainly horizontal. Understanding which kinds of extradition or surrender systems developed between mainland China, Hong Kong, or Macau with other countries helps one predict the construction of the China domestic surrender system.

The case study of the European arrest warrant system relies mainly on the analysis of cases from the Court of Justice of the European Union (CJEU) and European Court of Human Rights (ECtHR). Cases from these courts discuss problems regarding the implementation of the European arrest warrant and how they are solved in practice through the CJEU and ECtHR. In the sections on mainland

China, Hong Kong, and Macau, relevant cases from the local courts of the three systems are analyzed to explore the application of certain concrete legal principles, like *ne bis in idem*, the settlement of conflict of criminal jurisdiction. This will offer the most direct legal basis for the design of a China arrest warrant system.

To obtain more original information about the implementation of the European arrest warrant, a judge of the CJEU was interviewed. In addition, interviews were done with senior officials in Beijing and Macau, as well as lawyers in Hong Kong familiar with surrender cases, to gain an understanding of the obstacles to constructing a China domestic surrender system.

6 Book structure

Chapter One addresses the application of the mutual recognition principle, which will form the basis of the proposed China arrest warrant system. Chapter Two examines the role of judicial authority in the surrender procedure. It explores the possibility of assigning judicial authority as the main authority in charge of the surrender issue. It also discusses the delimitation of judicial authority in the China arrest warrant system. Chapter Three looks at the settlement of conflicts of criminal jurisdiction. It explores how criminal jurisdiction can be determined, how conflict can be resolved in practice, and which organizations can be utilized. After a discussion of the above basic problems, the subsequent seven chapters address the applicability of principles which are generally written into extradition or surrender systems. These include the application of the *ne bis in idem* principle; the design of the double criminality principle; the surrender of nationals or residents; surrender for political offences; the surrender of death penalty offenders; the surrender of life imprisonment offenders; and the application of the human rights ground.

1

The Principle of Mutual Recognition

1 Introduction

A China domestic surrender system has been under discussion for more than 20 years, since the two Special Administrative Regions (SARs) returned to the PRC in 1997 (Hong Kong) and 1999 (Macau).[1] There are heated debates about whether the surrender system should follow the international extradition model,[2] which includes exceptions for political offences, death penalty offenders, nationals (residents), the double criminality principle, and human rights grounds. Whether to adopt these concrete designs depends on which basic guiding principle[3] (or no guiding principle) the China domestic surrender system is based on.

In previous academic research, besides the "one country, two systems" policy being proposed as a basic principle of judicial cooperation between mainland China, Hong Kong, and Macau,[4] seldom are more specific and tailored principles studied to guide the China domestic surrender system.[5] This has greatly hindered progress in the construction of the surrender system between the three regions. Fortunately, as

---

1. Wayne Walsh, *Cross-Border Crime in Hong Kong* (Hong Kong: LexisNexis, 2018), 219.
2. Ibid.
3. In the global context, guiding principles include reciprocity, mutual trust, and mutual recognition. In the UN Model Extradition Treaty, no guiding principle is found. Under different guiding principles or the model of no guiding principle, the design of concrete extradition principles also differs. The details appear in the following section.
4. See Wang Zhongxing 王仲兴 and Guo Tianwu 郭天武, *Neidi yu Xianggang xingshi sifa hezuo yanjjiu* 内地与香港刑事司法合作研究 [Research on criminal juridical cooperation between Hong Kong and mainland China] (Beijing: Beijing daxue chubanshe, 2008), 217.
5. Other proposed principles include mutual respect, maximum cooperation, simplicity and efficiency, and human rights protection. As to these principles, see Huang Feng 黄风, *Yindu wenti yanjiu* 引渡问题研究 [Study on extradition] (Beijing: Zhongguo zhengfa daxue chubanshe, 2006), 223–26. See also Wang and Guo, *Neidi*, 222–27, n 4.

time has passed, other models based on international, regional, and even domestic extradition (such as titled surrender or, sometimes, rendition) have come into existence and offer examples in terms of their application of guiding principles.[6] Among these models, the principle of mutual recognition is the most inspiring due to its innovative and successful application within the European Union (EU) under the European Arrest Warrant Framework Decision (EAW FD).

In this chapter, firstly, I discuss generally why other principles or the model of no specific principle should not be applied to the China domestic surrender system, and why the principle of mutual recognition can be considered the most applicable. Secondly, I address how the mutual recognition principle is practiced within the EU criminal justice system and summarize its main characteristics. Thirdly, I explain why the mutual recognition principle can guide the surrender system between mainland China, Hong Kong, and Macau. Finally, I propose how mutual recognition could be applied.

2 Reciprocity, mutual trust, mutual recognition, or none?

Under international law, the principle of reciprocity provides that every act of favor, respect, benefit, or penalty that a country bestows on the citizens or legal entities of another country should be returned (reciprocated) in the same manner.[7] As far as extradition is concerned, the principle of reciprocity asserts that the territorial state must extradite the accused persons or convicts in exchange for any diplomatic kindness shown by the requesting state.[8] Most states hold the view that the duty to extradite arises by virtue of a treaty, national legislation, or both. In the absence of an international duty, states can and do rely on reciprocity and comity, which are grounded in international principles of friendly cooperation among nations.[9] In fact, even where a treaty is in place, the reciprocity principle can still be used as a guiding principle, such as in the series of extradition treaties concluded between the PRC and foreign countries.[10] It can also be used to guide specific factors in an extradition

6. These models could develop from international extradition, US interstate rendition, the EU-UK surrender arrangement, the EU-Nordic countries surrender agreement, and the European arrest warrant, as discussed in the following section 2.
7. See J. Jerusha Melanie, "Extradition in International Law," *Pleaders, Intelligent Legal Solutions*, June 13, 2022, https://blog.ipleaders.in/extradition-in-international-law/.
8. Melanie, "Extradition," n 7.
9. See M. Cherif Bassiouni, *International Extradition: United States Law and Practice*, 6th ed. (Oxford: Oxford University Press, 2014), 43.
10. Examples of the use of reciprocity as a guiding principle include the Extradition Treaty between China and South Korea, China and Thailand, China and Portugal, China and Russia, China and Spain. The China Extradition Law of 2002 also confirms that the extradition with foreign countries should be based on reciprocity: see China Extradition Law, art. 3.

treaty or a surrender agreement, such as in the surrender agreement between the EU and the United Kingdom (UK) relating to the political offence exception[11] and the nationality exception.[12]

However, it is not suggested that the reciprocity principle applies to the case of the China domestic surrender system. This is so mainly because the reciprocity principle is interest-based and too discretionary.[13] Reciprocity permits cooperation in a state of nature in which no overarching legal authority possessing compulsory jurisdiction exists to enforce agreements.[14] Its application is easily understood in the context of international extradition. But it is difficult to accept it in the case of mainland China, Hong Kong, and Macau, where the separate regional interests, common obligations to the PRC, and the cultural connection between mainland China, Hong Kong, and Macau as sister regions are entangled.[15] Reciprocity is too simplistic to handle so complicated a form of surrender relations as exists between these three regions.[16]

Additionally, mutual trust is also an important principle in extradition, even in the domestic rendition system. Trust constitutes a conviction that other parties will comply with agreed-upon rules.[17] The surrender agreement between the EU, Norway, and Iceland, for example, is based on their mutual confidence in the structure and functioning of their legal systems and the ability of all contracting parties to guarantee a fair trial.[18] The Nordic arrest warrant (NAW) offers another example of mutual trust; that is to say, the foundation of the Nordic system rests on mutual trust in the national legal systems of everyone involved.[19] Interstate rendition in the

11. See EU and UK Trade and Cooperation Agreement, art.LAW.SURR.82.
12. See EU and UK Trade and Cooperation Agreement, art.LAW.SURR.83.
13. See M. Neymark, E. Petuchov, and K. Sinkin, "Proper Observance of the Principle of Reciprocity as a Guarantee for the Sustainable Development of Cooperation between the Subjects of Cross-Border Territories in the Field of Criminal Justice: The Moral and Legal Aspects," *Advances in Social Science, Education and Humanities Research* 364 (2019): 471.
14. See Francesco Paris and Nita Ghei, "The Role of Reciprocity in International Law," *Cornell International Law Journal* 36, no. 1 (2003): 93.
15. See Wai-man Lam, "Promoting Hybridity: The Politics of the New Macau Identity," *The China Quarterly* 203 (2010): 656. See also Cora Chan, "Reconceptualising the Relationship between the Mainland Chinese Legal System and the Hong Kong Legal System," *Asian Journal of Comparative Law* 6 (2011): 1.
16. See Christine Loh, "Hong Kong's Relations with China: The Future of 'One Country, Two Systems,'" *Social Research* 73, no. 1 (2006): 293.
17. See Aleksandra Sulima, "The Normativity of the Principle of Mutual Trust between EU Member States within the Emerging European Criminal Area," *Wroclaw Review of Law, Administration & Economics* 3, no. 1 (2013): 72.
18. See Agreement between the European Union and the Republic of Iceland and the Kingdom of Norway on the Surrender Procedure between the Member States of the European Union and Iceland and Norway, Preamble.
19. See Gjermund Mathisen, "Nordic Cooperation and European Arrest Warrant: Intra-Nordic

United States (US) is also based on the mutual trust of sister states as regulated by the US Constitution, which holds that full faith and credit shall be given in each state to the public acts, records, and judicial proceedings of every other state.[20] Neither the Treaty on European Union (TEU), the Treaty on the Functioning of the European Union (TFEU), nor any other internal treaty explains what is mutual trust.[21] However, mutual trust is founded on a presumption of compliance with fundamental rights obligations, and has been recognized as comparatively more subjective, more flexible, and less binding.[22] In the abovementioned extradition or rendition systems, mutual trust works well and cooperation is actually much closer than it is in other countries or regions.

However, the mutual trust principle is not suggested for mainland China, Hong Kong, and Macau.[23] The levels of mutual trust may decide the breadth and depth of judicial cooperation between the parties concerned.[24] The mutual trust between mainland China, Hong Kong, and Macau remains at a low level, but this does not mean that there is no real need for close judicial cooperation.[25] The lack of mutual trust mainly matters in that there will be insufficient motivation and willingness to carry out surrender cooperation even when there is an actual necessity or moral obligation.[26] In this situation, mutual trust cannot be relied upon to guide the surrender system when surrender can be practiced first to foster mutual trust,[27] then mutual trust could act to nurture more mutual trust. Such a virtuous circle should be initiated by mutual recognition as a comparatively hard and binding principle, rather

Examination, the Nordic Arrest Warrant and Beyond," *Nordic Journal of International Law* 79, no. 1 (2010): 1, 5–7. See also Bassiouni, *International Extradition* 40, n 9.

20. See US Constitution, art. IV, §1.
21. See Leandro Mancano, "Trust Thy Neighbour? Compliance and Proximity to the EU through the Lens of Extradition," *Yearbook of European Law* 40, no. 1 (2021): 475.
22. See Oskar Losy and Anna Podolska, "The Principle of Mutual Trust in the Area of Freedom, Security and Justice: Analysis of Selected Case Law," *Adam Mickiewicz University Law Review* (2018): 188.
23. Especially mutual trust as a single guiding principle for Mainland China, Hong Kong, and Macau; however, if mutual trust combines with mutual recognition as the guiding principle, this is feasible, but the key will still be the function of mutual recognition as analyzed in this chapter.
24. See Mancano, "Trust Thy Neighbour?," 475, n 21.
25. See Li Shuo, "Legal Instruments for the Integration and Cooperation in the Guangdong-Hong Kong-Macau Greater Bay Area (GBA): Better Implementation of the SDGs," *2021 Sustainability* 2, 6, accessed 30 October, 2022, https://www.mdpi.com/2071-1050/13/22/12485.
26. In 2019, the Hong Kong government, in order to surrender a Hong Konger who had murdered his girlfriend in Taiwan, proposed to amend local extradition law. After this amendment, extradition could also be done between Hong Kong and mainland China; however, the proposal was withdrawn due to the year-long protest by the Hong Kong public. Simply put, the Hong Kong public lacked faith in the legal system in mainland China. See Suzanne Pepper, "The Trust Deficit: Why Hong Kongers Simply Don't Believe Gov't Reassurances over its China Extradition Law," *Hong Kong Free Press*, April 44, 2019, https://hongkongfp.com/2019/04/04/trust-deficit-hongkongers-simply-dont-believe-govt-reassurances-china-extradition-law/.
27. See Auke Willems, *The Principle of Mutual Trust in EU Criminal Law* (Oxford: Hart, 2021), 72.

than mutual trust.[28] Mutual trust can still be used as necessary filler to flesh out in the skeleton of the mutual recognition system as analyzed in the following sections.

Before we turn to discuss mutual recognition, we should mention that the absence of a guiding principle is also common in traditional extradition treaties. Even the UN Extradition Model Treaty does not recognize any guiding principle behind extradition. But this chapter does not suggest this model either. It is usually applied to cases of international extradition and cannot reflect the specific relations between mainland China, Hong Kong, and Macau under the "one country, two systems" formula. Neither can the no-guiding-principle model contribute to the efficient and precise implementation of the surrender agreement.

Finally, and comparably, the mutual recognition principle has greater potential to guide the China domestic surrender system. The European Commission, in its 2000 Communication to the Council and the European Parliament, stated that mutual recognition is a principle widely understood as being based on the idea that, while another state may not deal with a certain matter in the same or even a similar way as one's own state does, the results will be such that they are accepted as equivalent to decisions made by one's own state.[29] In the evaluation report on the implementation of the European arrest warrant (EAW) in Belgium, the Belgian Minister of Justice defined mutual recognition as follows: When a decision has been handed down by a judicial authority which has competence under the law of the Member State in which it is situated, in accordance with the law of that state, the decision becomes fully and directly effective throughout the territory of the Union, and the competent authorities in the Member States (MSs) in the territory where the decision may be enforced assist in the enforcement of the decision as if it were a decision handed down by a competent authority in that state.[30]

The mutual recognition principle is recommended to be applied to judicial cooperation between mainland China, Hong Kong, and Macau. Its characteristics, demonstrated by its practice in the EU, show great potential and adaptability. It is

28. See Nathan Cambien, "Mutual Recognition and Mutual Trust in the Internal Market," *European Papers* 2 (2017): 93.

29. European Commission, "Communication from the Commission to the Council and the European Parliament: Mutual Recognition of Final Decisions in Criminal Matters," COM (2000) 495 final, p. 4.

30. Council of the European Union, "Evaluation Report on the Fourth Round of Mutual Evaluations, 'Practical Application of the European Arrest Warrant and Corresponding Surrender Procedures between Member States': Report on Belgium," no. 16454/1/06 REV1 RESTREINT UE, March 19, 2007, p. 21, https://data.consilium.europa.eu/doc/document/ST-16454-2006-REV-2/en/pdf. See also Gisèle Vernimmen-Van Tiggelen and Laura Surano, "Final Report: Analysis of the Future of Mutual Recognition in Criminal Matters in the European Union," p. 23, Institute for European Studies, Université Libre de Bruxelles and European Criminal Law Academic Network, November 20, 2008, https://www.advokatsamfundet.se/globalassets/Advokatsamfundet_sv/Nyheter/Slutrapport_mutual_recognition_eng.pdf.

compatible with the political and legal situations of mainland China, Hong Kong, and Macau. The following chapters offer more detailed analysis of this claim. The mutual recognition principle practiced in the EAW system originated in the EU internal market. Before it was introduced to the practice of judicial cooperation in criminal matters, it had enjoyed successful and longstanding practice in the EU internal market.[31] This offered both experience and an accumulation of mutual trust for implementation in the criminal field at a later time.

3 Mutual recognition in the European Union

3.1 The mutual recognition principle in the EU internal market

In the Cassis de Dijon judgment, the Court of Justice of the European Union (CJEU) stated that there was no valid reason why, provided that "they have been lawfully produced and marketed in one of the Member States, alcoholic beverages should not be introduced into any other Member State."[32] It is generally acknowledged that with this famous statement, the CJEU introduced the principle of mutual recognition of goods into the free movement of goods area.

In the Sager case, the CJEU ordered the abolition of any restriction, even if it applied without distinction to national providers of services and to those of other Member States, if it was liable to prohibit or otherwise impede the activities of a provider of services established in another Member State where similar services had been provided lawfully.[33] Thus, the mutual recognition principle led to freedom of services.

It was in the early 1990s that the CJEU clarified and generalized the meaning of the duty of mutual recognition in the free movement of person area through the mutual recognition of diploma.[34]

It was only with the coming into force of the Treaty of Maastricht that freedom of capital was enshrined.[35] The mutual recognition mechanism ultimately amounted to a duty to recognize other Member States' regulations on the goods, services, or persons concerned, indicating the largely regulatory nature of the object of the mutual recognition mechanism.[36]

---

31. See S. Lavenex, "Mutual Recognition and the Monopoly of Force: Limits of the Single Market Analogy," *Journal of European Public Policy* 14 (2007): 764.
32. Case 120/78, *Rewe-Zentral AG v. Bundesmonopolverwaltung für Branntwein* [1979] ECR 649, ¶14.
33. Case C-76/90, *Manfred Säger v. Dennemeyer & Co., Ltd* [1991] ECR I-4221, ¶12.
34. Case C-340/89, *Irene Vlassopoulou v. Ministerium fÜr justiz, Bundes-und Europaangelegenheiten Baden-Württemberg* [1991] ECR I-2357.
35. Treaty on the Function of the European Union (TFEU), art. 63.
36. See Christine Janssens, *The Principle of Mutual Recognition in EU Law* (Oxford: Oxford University Press, 2013), 125.

It appeared when the internal market integration process was being hampered by a demanding unanimity requirement within the European Council, and when a non-discriminatory approach to technicalities barring free movement provisions proved insufficient in tackling hindrances from divergent national legislation, that the principle of mutual recognition was intended to breathe new life into the internal market project.[37] But the principle of mutual recognition was flexible enough that the proportionality test could be applied to the mutual recognition system as well. Sometimes mutual recognition will be balanced against considerations of non-economic interests such as public health or human life.[38] This balancing or limiting of the application of mutual recognition principle in the internal market field also offers experience for its application in the criminal justice field.

3.2 The mutual recognition principle in the European criminal justice area

3.2.1 The establishment of mutual recognition in the criminal justice field

In the Tampere European Council of 1999, it was decided that the principle of mutual recognition should become a cornerstone of judicial cooperation in both civil and criminal matters within the EU. The European Commission argued, in its first communication, for the introduction of the principle that "borrowing from concepts that have worked very well in the creation of the Single Market, the idea was born that judicial cooperation might also benefit from the concept of mutual recognition."[39] Since the coming into force of the Treaty of Lisbon, the principle of mutual recognition has gained an explicit legal basis, imposing a duty on Member States to recognize judgments and judicial decisions.[40] Mutual recognition has become an important tool for achieving the regional goals of freedom, security, and justice, and to a large degree it has eased the pressure of harmonization by demonstrating greater respect for the diversity of legal systems among the Member States.[41] The principle of mutual recognition in the criminal justice field mainly appears in the form of framework decisions, and the European Union has also

37. On this subject, see Roland Bieber et al., eds., *1992: One European Market?* (Baden-Baden: Nomos 1988). See also Janssens, *The Principle*,11, n 36.
38. See Janssens, *The Principle*, 126, n 36.
39. See European Communication, "Mutual Recognition," n 29.
40. TFEU, art. 82(1).
41. See Willems, *The Principle*, 189–93, n 27.

enacted directives[42] to implement mutual recognition. The European arrest warrant Framework Decision is the first such instrument.[43]

3.2.2 Mutual recognition in the European arrest warrant

3.2.2.1 *Mutual recognition and the double criminality principle*

The double criminality principle of extradition or surrender law contains two conditions. Firstly, the act for which the extradition is pursued should constitute a crime in both the requesting and executing states. Secondly, the criminal act in both the requesting and the executing states should meet the relevant threshold: for prosecution, the maximum period for imprisonment or detention is above 12 months; for executing the sentence, the maximum period is above 6 months, according to the UN extradition model[44] and to the previous extradition conventions in Europe.[45]

Under the mutual recognition principle in the European arrest warrant system, the double criminality principle is partially abolished. For 32 categories of offences, if the acts should be punishable in the issuing Member State by a custodial sentence or a detention order for a maximum period of at least three years, the European arrest warrant will give rise to surrender without verification of double criminality of the act.[46] On the other hand, mutual recognition is balanced by a proportionality check.[47] The factors to be considered mainly include the seriousness of the offence, the likely penalty imposed if the person is found guilty of the alleged offence, the likelihood of a person's detention in the issuing Member State after surrender, the

42. The Framework Decision is similar to the Directive in the way that it binds Member States to the result achieved but reserves the choice of form and method to national level; the main difference with the Directive is that it cannot have direct effect but only indirect effect.
43. See Jannemieke Ouwerkerk, "Balancing Mutual Trust and Fundamental Rights Protection in the Context of the European Arrest Warrant," *European Journal of Crime, Criminal Law and Criminal Justice* 26 (2018): 103.
44. See the UN Model Treaty on Extradition, art. 2(1).
45. See, for example, the European Convention on Extradition 1957, art. 2.
46. EAW FD, art. 2(2).
47. The background may be that Member States have increasingly reported cases in which EAWs have not been issued for serious offences but instead for harmless and minor ones. Example of minor offences include: the theft of a piglet from the 2007 Council report of the European Union; the theft of a bottle of beer (Caldwell 2009, ¶12); and the theft of ten chickens from the British High Court of Justice in 2007. Across Europe, theft is defined in such a way that the offence fulfils the requirement of a maximum penalty of at least 12 months—meaning that, in principle, an EAW can be issued for any case of theft regardless of scale, from the great train robbery to a piece of minor shoplifting. See Joachim Vogel and J.R. Spencer, "Proportionality and the European Arrest Warrant," *Criminal Law Review* 6 (2010): 518.

interests of victims of the offence, and whether less coercive alternative measures can be used.[48] Thus we see that mutual recognition is not absolute.[49]

3.2.2.2 *Mutual recognition and the surrender of nationals*

The principle that a state will not extradite one of its own nationals has been generally practiced in the international extradition system, especially in civil law systems.[50] But following the mutual recognition principle, the European arrest warrant regards the surrender of a national as a rule.[51] That is to say, a European arrest warrant cannot be rejected simply on the ground of nationality. It also actively responds to the concept of European citizenship, which means the protection of nationals in the home state should be regarded the same as that in the host state.[52]

In some situations, the mutual recognition principle relating to the surrender of nationals can be balanced.[53] For instance, if the European arrest warrant has been issued for the purpose of execution, and the person requested is staying in or is a national or a resident of the executing Member State, then the surrender can be rejected if the executing Member State undertakes to execute the sentence or detention order in accordance with its domestic law.[54] When a European arrest warrant is issued for prosecution, if the requested person is a national or resident of the executing Member State, surrender may be subject to the condition that the person, after being heard, is returned to the executing Member State in order to serve the custodial sentence or detention order passed against him in the issuing Member State.[55]

---

48. Commission Notice, Handbook on How to Issue and Execute a European Arrest Warrant [2017] OJ C335/01, p. 14.
49. Stefano Montaldo, "On A Collision Course! Mutual Recognition, Mutual Trust and the Protection of Fundamental Rights in the Recent Case-Law of the Court of Justice," *European Papers* 1, no. 3 (2016): 967.
50. Generally, in common law system, countries or regions apply the territorial principle which does not prohibit the extradition of nationals. In civil law system, the nationality principle weighs more heavily. Further discussion of this can be found in chapter 3 on conflict of criminal jurisdiction.
51. See Hans G. Nilsson, "From Classical Judicial Cooperation to Mutual Recognition," *Revenue Internationale De Droit Péna* 77, no. 1–2 (2006): 53.
52. See European Commission, "Proposal for a Council Framework Decision on the European Arrest Warrant and the Surrender Procedures between the Member States, COM (2001) 522, Preamble (12).
53. See Anne Pieter van der Mei, "The European Arrest Warrant System: Recent Developments in the Case Law of the Court of Justice," *Maastricht Journal of European and Comparative Law* 24, no. 6 (2017): 882.
54. EAW FD, art. 4(6).
55. EAW FD, art. 5(3).

3.2.2.3 *Mutual recognition and the human rights ground*

Traditionally, human rights concern is also a mandatory ground for refusal of extradition.[56] However, under the European arrest warrant system, practicing mutual recognition also means abolishing human rights as a ground, especially as a mandatory ground, for refusing surrender.[57] However, the mutual recognition principle *per se* does not absolutely break away from the application of the human rights check. The EAW Framework Decision clearly states that "nothing in this Framework Decision may be interpreted as prohibiting refusal to surrender a person for whom a European arrest warrant has been issued when there are reasons to believe, on the basis of objective elements, that the said arrest warrant has been issued for the purpose of prosecuting or punishing a person on the grounds of his or her sex, race, religion, ethnic origin, nationality, language, political opinions or sexual orientation, or that that person's position may be prejudiced for any of these reasons."[58] The CJEU has made preliminary rulings where the execution of the European arrest warrant has been scrutinized for reasons of prison conditions[59] or judicial independence.[60] It is clear, however, that the Court remains optimistic and proposes procedures through which it is possible to build mutual trust beyond initial doubt through communication and the exchange of information between the competent authorities of the concerned Member State.[61]

At the same time, we also find in the latest mutual recognition instruments that human rights have been inscribed as an optional ground to refuse cooperation.[62] This development may not be regarded as a move against the principle of mutual recognition, but rather as a demonstration of the principle's flexibility, balancing judicial cooperation with human rights protection.[63]

---

56. See John Dugard and Christine Van den Wyngaert, "Reconciling Extradition with Human Rights," *The American Journal of International Law* 92, no. 2 (1998): 187.
57. In the following case study on rights protection in the implementation of the European arrest warrant, we find that the ground of specific rights, including prison conditions, can still be used to refuse surrender.
58. EAW FD, Preamble (12).
59. See Case C-399/11, *Stefano Melloni v. Ministerio Fiscal* [Judgment of the Court, 26 February 2013]; joined Cases C-404/15 and C-659/15 PPU, Aranyosi and Caldararu [Judgment of the Court, 5 April 2016].
60. See Case C-216/18 PPU, LM [Judgment of the Court, 25 July 2018].
61. See Daniel Flore, "The Issue of Mutual Trust and the Needed Balance Between Diversity and Unity," in *The Needed Balances in EU Criminal Law: Past, Present and Future*, ed. Chloe Briere and Anne Weyembergh (Oxford: Hart, 2018), 192.
62. See Directive 2014/41/EU of 3 April 2014 regarding the European Investigation Order in Criminal Matters [2014] OJ L130/1, art. 11(f).
63. See Helmut Satzger, "Is Mutual Recognition a Viable General Path for Cooperation?" *New Journal of European Criminal Law* 10, no. 1 (2019): 44.

3.2.2.4 *Mutual recognition balanced by other mandatory and optional refusal grounds*

The mutual recognition principle is practiced conditionally throughout the European Union's internal market.[64] It is balanced by other public or private interests.[65] In the EAW mechanism, the mutual recognition principle also encounters mandatory and optional grounds for refusal, including double jeopardy, amnesty, and age (grounds for mandatory non-execution);[66] and on-going criminal proceedings in the executing Member State, that final judgment has been passed in another third state, and others (grounds for optional non-execution).[67]

3.2.2.5 *Main characteristics of mutual recognition under the European arrest warrant*

Firstly, mutual recognition is functional by nature.[68] In the EU criminal justice context, the principle of mutual recognition can be regarded as an important tool for establishing an area of freedom, security, and justice.[69] This necessitates the performance of a careful balancing act involving each of the three objectives (freedom, security, and justice).[70] The mutual recognition principle pursues the free movement of judicial decisions, though not at the expense of the other valuable interests. This characteristic reveals that mutual recognition is not the end *per se,* but rather the means by which a higher and more far-reaching goal can be achieved. Such a trait can respond to the basic political and legal situations of mainland China, Hong Kong, and Macau.

64. See Stephen Weatherill, "Comparative Internal Market Law: The UK and the EU," *Yearbook of European Law* 40 (2021): 431.
65. See the above section 3.1 on mutual recognition in the EU internal market.
66. EAW FD, art. 4.
67. EAW FD, art. 5.
68. See Matteo Ortino, "The Role and Functioning of Mutual Recognition in the European Market of Financial Services," *International and Comparative Law Quarterly* 56, no. 2 (2007): 309. See also Rebecka Krönmark, "Limits of Mutual Recognition in Criminal Matters" (Master's thesis, Lund University 2010), 12, https://lup.lub.lu.se/luur/download?func=downloadFile&recordOId=1710141&fileOId=1712723.
69. Koen Lenaerts, "The Principle of Mutual Recognition in the Area of Freedom, Security and Justice" (the Fourth Annual Sir Jeremy Lever Lecture, All Souls College, University of Oxford, January 30, 2015). https://www.law.ox.ac.uk/sites/files/oxlaw/the_principle_of_mutual_recognition_in_the_area_of_freedom_judge_lenaerts.pdf.
70. See Janssens, *The Principle,* 253, n 36.

Secondly, the principle of mutual recognition is flexible.[71] Mutual recognition can vary from full recognition to partial recognition and no recognition, to balance key values including freedom, human rights, security, justice, and public order. This has been shown in a series of European arrest warrant cases decided by the CJEU. Mutual recognition is not a principle of all or nothing, but rather a flexible, gradualist system which, in cases where full recognition is not feasible, holds that a little recognition is preferable to none.[72] This characteristic also reveals that the mutual recognition principle can be quite adaptable, not only to different legal documents in the EU criminal justice system but also, potentially, to the legal systems in different jurisdictions. Mainland China, Hong Kong, and Macau create just such a region.

Thirdly, mutual recognition is non-automatic.[73] Although the EAW Framework Decision has limited the grounds to refuse the execution of a EAW, it is also evident that optional and mandatory grounds for refusal still exist. Only after one has verified that these grounds do not exist may the execution be made. Thus, we can say that mutual recognition is non-automatic in nature.[74] This offers another opportunity for mainland China, Hong Kong, and Macau to make further adjustments to the mutual recognition principle.

Fourthly, the principle of mutual recognition can be resistant and reversible. This means that mutual recognition does not need a perfect situation for its setup and functioning.[75] It can be resistant to difficult situations, and its practice can be reversible or adjustable. For instance, in reality, human rights protection in EU Member States varies from country to country, and mutual trust is assumed.[76] However, this reality does not mean that mutual recognition is irrelevant. Instead, the mutual recognition principle continues to function, relying on its flexibility, non-automaticity, and functionality. Since trust is often seen as the result of a history

---

71. See Kalypso Nicolaidis, "Mutual Recognition: Promise and Denial, from Sapiens to Brexit," *Current Legal Problems* 70, no. 1 (2017): 1. See also Evgenia Ralli, "The Principle of Mutual Recognition Based on Mutual Trust and the Respect for Fundamental Rights: The Case of the Framework Decision on the European Arrest Warrant," European Law Institute, accessed October 30, 2022, https://www.europeanlawinstitute.eu/fileadmin/user_upload/p_eli/YLA_Award/Submission_ELI_Young_Lawyers_Award_Evgenia_Ralli_2017.pdf.
72. See Janssens, *The Principle*, 253, n 36.
73. See Stefano Montaldo, "On Collision Course! Mutual Recognition, Mutual Trust and the Protection of Fundamental Rights in the Recent Case-Law of the Court of Justice," *European Papers* 1, no. 3 (2016): 965.
74. Montaldo, "On Collision Course," 965, n 73.
75. Helmut Satzger, "Is Mutual Recognition a Viable General Path for Cooperation?" *New Journal of European Criminal Law* 10, no. 1 (2019): 44.
76. See T. Konstadinides, "The Europeanisation of Extradition: How Many Light Years Away to Mutual Confidence?" in *Crime Within the Area of Freedom, Security and Justice: A European Public Order*, ed. C. Eckes and T. Konstadinides (Cambridge: Cambridge University Press, 2011), 219.

of cooperation and the road to that trust a learning process,[77] the value of resistance to mutual recognition is that it provides time to cultivate and enhance mutual trust through its practice. In brief, the application of mutual recognition does not require a very high threshold; instead, it calls for procedural progress based on minimum standards.[78]

4 Introduction of the mutual recognition principle to the surrender system between mainland China, Hong Kong, and Macau

4.1 *In the internal market area*

Since Hong Kong and Macau returned to the PRC, economic cooperation between the three regions has increasingly deepened.[79] The mutual recognition principle was an important tool in the process of economic integration.

According to the Closer Economic Partnership Arrangement (CEPA),[80] place of origin is applied in the goods trade, and a certificate of the place of origin is issued to guarantee preferential measures. In 2015, agreements were made on the services trade, one between mainland China and Hong Kong and the other between the mainland China and Macau, promising more concrete and comprehensive measures to open the services market between the three regions.[81] Mainland China also signed a memorandum with the two regions on the mutual recognition of diplomas to improve cooperation in education, attaching a list of recognized universities to the Memorandum. The mutual recognition of professions was also written into

77. See Willems, *The Principle*, 72, n 27.
78. See Martyna Kusak, "Common EU Minimum Standards for Enhancing Mutual Admissibility of Evidence Gathered in Criminal Matters," *European Journal on Criminal Policy and Research* 23 (2017): 352.
79. See Tao Wang and Hong Liang, "II Economic Integration between Hong Kong SAR and Mainland China," in *Hong Kong SAR: Meeting the Challenges of Integration with the Mainland*, ed. William Lee et al. (USA: International Monetary Fund, 2004), accessed October 30, 2022, https://doi.org/10.5089/9781589062948.084.
80. See "CEPA (17 October 2003)," Economic and Technological Development Bureau of Macau SAR, accessed October 30, 2022, https://www.dsedt.gov.mo/en_US/web/public/pg_cepa_cepa_i#. See also "Mainland and Macau SAR Related Topics," Department of Justice, Government of the Hong Kong Special Administrative Region, accessed October 30, 2022, https://www.doj.gov.hk/en/mainland_and_macao/cepa.html.
81. See "Agreement on Trade in Service" Department of Justice, Government of the Hong Kong Special Administrative Region, accessed October 30, 2022, https://www.doj.gov.hk/en/mainland_and_macao/cepa.html. See also "Agreement on Trade in Service," Economic and Technological Development Bureau of Macau SAR, accessed October 30, 2022, https://www.dsedt.gov.mo/en_US/web/public/pg_cepa_cepa_acs.

CEPA and subsequent supplemental agreements.[82] Both Hong Kong and Macau can do renmimbi (RMB) business. Financial organizations in Hong Kong and Macau, such as qualified banks, securities companies, and fund management companies, are also allowed to establish branches in the Mainland.

It is clear that mainland China, Hong Kong, and Macau are on the path of economic integration, and mutual recognition is widely used to improve the free movement of goods, services, persons, and capital. The situation closely resembles that of the European Union; that is to say, mutual recognition starts from the internal market. But is mutual recognition developed to the justice field between mainland China, Hong Kong, and Macau too, as it is in the European Union? It is in its initial stage, but its prospects are bright.

4.2 Present-day mutual recognition practice in the judicial field between mainland China, Hong Kong, and Macau

4.2.1 In the non-criminal judicial area

In compliance with the Basic Law of Hong Kong,[83] on June 18, 1999, the Supreme People's Court and the Hong Kong government reached the Arrangement between the Mainland and Hong Kong on the Mutual Enforcement of Arbitral Decisions; on July 14, 2006, they reached the Arrangement on the Mutual Recognition and Enforcement of Civil and Commercial Judgments under the Agreement Jurisdiction by the Parties Involved; and in June 2017, the Supreme People's Court and the Hong Kong government signed the Arrangement on Reciprocal Recognition and Enforcement of Civil Judgments in Matrimonial and Family Cases by the Courts of the Mainland and of Hong Kong.[84] In the latest developments on the application of mutual recognition between mainland China and Hong Kong, on January 18, 2019, the Supreme People's Court and the Hong Kong government signed the Arrangement on Reciprocal Recognition and Enforcement of Civil and Commercial Judgments, and on May 14, 2021, they signed the Memorandum on Reciprocal Recognition of and Assistance to Bankruptcy Proceedings.[85]

---

82. See "Closer Economic Partnership Arrangement," Department of Justice, Government of the Hong Kong Special Administrative Region, accessed October 30, 2022, https://www.doj.gov.hk/en/mainland_and_macao/cepa.html.
83. Basic Law of Hong Kong, art. 95.
84. See "Reciprocal Recognition and Enforcement of Civil and Commercial Judgments between Hong Kong and the Mainland," Department of Justice, Government of the Hong Kong Special Administrative Region, https://www.doj.gov.hk/en/mainland_and_macao/RRECCJ.html.
85. See "Reciprocal Recognition," n 84.

In line with the Basic Law of Macau,[86] the Supreme People's Court concluded the Arrangement between the Mainland and the Macau on the Mutual Recognition and Enforcement of Civil and Commercial Judgments on February 28, 2006. The Supreme People's Court also made the Arrangement between the Mainland and Macau on the Mutual Recognition and Enforcement of Arbitral Decisions on October 30, 2007. Hong Kong and Macau also signed the Arrangement on Mutual Recognition and Enforcement of Arbitral Decisions between themselves in May 2005, and the Arrangement concerning Reciprocal Recognition and Enforcement of Arbitral Awards on January 2013; in December 2017, Hong Kong and Macau signed the Arrangement on the Mutual Service of Judicial Documents in Civil and Commercial Cases.[87]

Therefore, there is mutual recognition on civil and commercial judgments or arbitral decisions between mainland China, Hong Kong, and Macau. Although all the mutual recognition arrangements are conditional, especially between mainland China and Hong Kong, it is still a big improvement towards judicial cooperation and legal fusion in the region.

4.2.2 In the criminal justice area

No documents on mutual recognition in criminal justice exist between mainland China, Hong Kong, and Macau to date. The Hong Kong Safeguarding National Security Law provides that, under specific situations, national security cases in Hong Kong should be investigated, prosecuted, and adjudicated by the Mainland authorities in the name of the Central Government.[88] The law also stipulates that the legal documents issued by these (Mainland) authorities on their judicial decisions shall have legal force in the Hong Kong Special Administrative Region.[89] However, this is not mutual recognition but unilateral recognition grounded on the Central Government's overall jurisdiction over Hong Kong. To be clear, unilateral recognition mainly concerns relations between Hong Kong and the Central Government, not between Hong Kong and mainland China.

In brief, mutual recognition is widely applied in the market area comprising mainland China, Hong Kong, and Macau. It also has been widely practiced in

86. Basic Law of Macau, art. 93.
87. See "Arrangements with the Macao SAR," Department of Justice, Government of the Hong Kong Special Administrative Region, accessed October 30, 2022, https://www.doj.gov.hk/en/mainland_and_macao/arrangements_with_the_macao_sar.html.
88. See Law of the People's Republic of China on Safeguarding National Security in the Hong Kong Special Administrative Region (Hong Kong Safeguarding National Security Law), art. 55.
89. See Hong Kong Safeguarding National Security Law, art. 57.

judicial cooperation in civil matters. Its application in the criminal justice field is a matter of time.

4.3 The main conditions for the application of mutual recognition principle in the surrender of fugitive offenders between mainland China, Hong Kong, and Macau

4.3.1 "One country" and the mutual recognition principle

Traditional extradition takes place between different sovereign states. The European arrest warrant also functions between different sovereign states with partial sovereignty submitted to the European Union. However, the surrender of fugitive offenders between mainland China, Hong Kong, and Macau occurs within one country, the PRC. As a consequence, the China domestic surrender system should essentially differ from the traditional extradition system. This facilitates the application of mutual recognition in the three regions.

Extradition concerns not only the legal interest but also the political interest of the parties involved.[90] For instance, the non-surrender of nationals and exception for political offences are based partly on political considerations, such as a country's protective obligation to its nationals and the conflict of political values between different countries. Since the China domestic surrender system would operate within one country, theoretically, there will be no space in which to apply the abovementioned principles; or, at least, their application must be diluted to reflect the one country fact. Additionally, with reference to this fact, the China domestic surrender system will operate not only for the separate interests of the three regions but also for the common interest of the whole country.[91] For this reason, a more sincere and efficient form of cooperation than traditional extradition is called for.

The mutual recognition principle can be responsive to the abovementioned situations and to the one country fact. Although the EU cannot be recognized as a sovereign state, under the mutual recognition principle with its aim of increasing cooperation and effectiveness,[92] the European arrest warrant has overtaken traditional extradition between sovereign countries in terms of efficiency and willingness

90. See Christine Van Den Wyngaert, *The Political Offence Exception of Extradition* (Berlin: Springer, 1981), 42. See also Bassiouni, *International Extradition*, 56, n 9.

91. For instance, mainland China, Hong Kong, and Macau have all passed laws to protect the security of China. Among these laws, the highest power of interpretation belongs to the Standing Committee of the National People's Congress, the PRC's central legislative and political authority.

92. See Annika Suominen, "The Sensitive Relationship Between the Different Means of Legal Integration: Mutual Recognition and Approximation," in *The Needed Balance in EU Criminal Law: Past, Present and Future*, ed. Chloe Briere and Anne Weymbergh (Oxord: Hart, 2018), 197.

to cooperate. This is what is called for in the surrender of fugitive offenders between mainland China, Hong Kong, and Macau under one country.

4.3.2 "Two systems" and mutual recognition principle

4.3.2.1 *Difference of the legal systems requires mutual recognition*

The application of the mutual recognition principle in the European arrest warrant protects the sovereignty of Member States by easing pressure from harmonization.[93] Avoiding the harmonization of criminal law was a key reason for choosing mutual recognition as the format for cooperation.[94] Applying mutual recognition in cooperation in criminal matters enabled an efficient form of cooperation that preserved, at the same time, as much as possible of the sovereignty of the EU Member States.[95] This functionality in the mutual recognition principle for the purpose of cooperation is also compatible with the "two systems" fact between mainland China, Hong Kong, and Macau. The application of mutual recognition will become an important way to carry out close judicial cooperation while respecting the diversity among the legal systems of the three judicial territories. This is in line with both the Hong Kong Basic Law and the Macau Basic Law.

4.3.2.2 *Harmonization offers chances for mutual recognition*

The principle of mutual recognition, in a formal sense, does not require harmonization.[96] Actually, mutual recognition is regarded as an important alternative to harmonization.[97] However, some form of harmonization is both desirable and necessary in order to facilitate a common level of understanding and establish a sufficient level of trust on which mutual recognition can be effectively based.[98]

Regarding mutual recognition and the EAW, European legislators established a standard that the majority of subsequent instruments have followed: namely, the procedural approximation of *sensu lato*, specifically the approximation of rules relating to the conditions, procedures, and effects of surrender between national

93. See Willems, *The Principle*, 189, n 27.
94. See A. Suominen, *The Principle of Mutual Recognition in Cooperation in Criminal Matters: A Study of the Principle in Four Framework Decisions and in the Implementation Legislation in the Nordic Member States* (Cambridge: Intersentia, 2011), 51–52.
95. See Suominen, *The Principle*, 196, n 94.
96. See Maria Fletcher, Robin Lööf, and Bill Gilmore, *EU Criminal Law and Justice* (Cheltenham: Edward Elgar, 2008), 111.
97. See Susanne K. Schmidt, "Mutual Recognition as a New Mode of Governance," *Journal of European Public Policy* 14, no. 5 (2007): 667.
98. See A Weyembergh, "Approximation of Criminal law, the Constitutional Treaty and the Hague Programme," *Common Market Law Review* 42 (2005): 1574–77.

authorities, in combination with a cooperation mechanism based on direct contact and a duty to exchange information. A minimum substantive approximation is available with regard to some of the listed offences for which the dual criminality check has been abolished. These approximation measures can be identified in certain older framework decisions and in other former third-pillar instruments.[99]

Between mainland China, Hong Kong, and Macau, to achieve better cooperation, the application of the mutual recognition principle should consider the harmonization status quo between different legal systems,[100] given the distinctions that are in both substantive and procedural criminal laws. However, the situation in mainland China, Hong Kong, and Macau may be more optimistic than that in the EU.

Firstly, laws in the two SARs cannot contravene the Basic Law of Hong Kong or the Basic Law of Macau. Both of these are national laws enacted by the National People's Congress in Beijing. The Standing Committee of the National People's Congress (NPCSC) can supervise legislation in both jurisdictional territories; if a clash occurs, the legislation in Hong Kong and Macau is invalidated automatically. Hence, the substantive and procedural criminal laws in the three regions differ but will not conflict with each other. This undoubtedly will greatly reduce the need to harmonize.

Secondly, mainland China is undergoing judicial reform, with the aim of complying with international standards. During this period of reform, the laws of Germany, Japan, and the common law countries are being studied by mainland China.[101] Judicial interpretations are also being made on evidence gathering and application, on rights protection of suspects, and on the limited application of the death penalty. These new regulations in mainland China are gradually approaching the substantive and procedural criminal law of Hong Kong and Macau, especially on rights protection of the suspect and the victim. What's more, due to globalization and the increasing dominance of Western legal values and institutions on a global scale, the distinction between civil law and common law is becoming less significant.[102] Additionally, communication and exchanges between legal professionals in Hong Kong, Macau, and mainland China nowadays have become regular. In other words, the harmonization of criminal law is ongoing in a soft and voluntary way.

Thirdly, from the experience of the European Union, the objectives of freedom, security, and justice were primarily intended to be achieved through operational cooperation between (decentralized) domestic authorities, with rules to be used

99. See L. Moreillon and A. Willi-Jayet, *Coopération dans l'Union européenne* (Brussels: Bruylant, 2005), 34 ff.

100. As to the differences, see section 4.3.1 on mutual recognition and one country.

101. See Albert H.Y. Chen, *The Changing Legal Orders in Hong Kong and Mainland China: Essays on "One Country, Two Systems"* (Hong Kong: City University of Hong Kong Press, 2021), 246–53.

102. See Chen, *The Changing Legal Orders*, 261, n 101.

only where necessary.[103] It is the necessary harmonization that is needed, not the full harmonization. And harmonization of substantive criminal law is also just beginning in the European Union: in some areas like the age of criminal responsibility, limitation periods, and the liability of legal persons, no harmonization exists at all; nonetheless, mutual recognition is still applied. This demonstrates to mainland China, Hong Kong, and Macau that mutual recognition without full harmonization is feasible.

4.3.3 Mutual trust and mutual recognition

On the EU side, mutual trust is regarded as a principle behind the principle of mutual recognition.[104] The EAW experience shows that mutual trust is not absolute, and sometimes it exists at a low level, leading to non-mutual recognition. There are strong voices in the EU asserting that efforts should be made to enhance mutual trust.[105] However, restrictions in the European investigation order limit the application of mutual recognition rather than to abolish it.[106] This demonstrates that mutual recognition can be resistant to difficult situations. It can survive, even when there exists a low level of mutual trust. This is attributed to its flexibility, as discussed above. At the same time, mutual trust is a learning process: the more we learn about the unknown, the more we place our trust in it.[107] Last, the practice of mutual recognition can nurture and enhance mutual trust through cooperation, dialogue, and training during that process. Mutual trust and mutual recognition can mutually promote each other and behave as twin brothers.

The mutual trust that exists between mainland China, Hong Kong, and Macau has developed accumulatively through a series of cooperative actions in the internal market and through judicial cooperation in civil matters, as explained above.[108] We can say that mutual trust between mainland China, Hong Kong, and Macau has developed to a certain level on the whole. But it remains insufficient to motivate the

103. See Samuli Miettinen, "The Evolution of Competence Distribution Between the European Union and the Member States in the Criminal Field," in *The Needed Balance in EU Criminal Law: Past, Present and Future*, ed. Chloe Briere and Anne Weymbergh (Oxford: Hart, 2018), 61.
104. See Willems, *The Principle*, 86, n 27; see also Programme of Measures to Implement the Principle of Mutual Recognition of Decisions in Criminal Matters [2001] OJC 12/10, https://eur-lex.europa.eu/legal-content/EN/TXT/?uri=CELEX:32001Y0115(02).
105. See C. Morgan, "The Potential of Mutual Recognition as a Leading Policy Principle," in *The Future of Police and Judicial Cooperation in the EU*, ed. C. Fijnaut and J. Ouwerkerk (Leiden: Brill, 2010), 233.
106. The investigation order applies the proportionality check and uses human rights as a ground on which to refuse cooperation.
107. See R. Hardin, "Conception and Explanations of Trust," in *Trust in Society*, ed. K. Cook (New York: Russell Sage Foundation, 2001), 7–12.
108. See the above section 4.1 on mutual recognition in China's internal market.

three regions to proactively carry out close judicial cooperation in criminal matters. To this end, the application of mutual recognition can initiate cooperation and cultivate a higher stage of mutual trust. Considering the flexibility and resistance of the mutual recognition principle, given the mutually nurturing relations between mutual trust and the mutual recognition principle, the accumulation of mutual trust offers a condition for the application of mutual recognition principle in the China domestic surrender system.

4.3.4 Human rights and mutual recognition

On the EU side, although all Member States have joined the European Convention on Human Rights (EUHR) and Charter of Fundamental Rights (CFR), and are under the jurisdictional control of the European Court of Human Rights (ECtHR), in practice human rights protection in Member States varies from country to country.[109] The EAW regime contains a presumption that requesting Member States respect fundamental rights under the mutual recognition principle, but it is a rebuttable presumption.[110] The mutual recognition principle does not refuse the application of the human rights ground, but it limits its application.[111]

Between mainland China, Hong Kong, and Macau, human rights problems do exist, such as torture and crowded cells in the Mainland. However, human rights protection has been written into the Constitution of the PRC,[112] and the judicial system of mainland China is undergoing reform that aims to combine punishing criminal acts with protecting human rights.[113] Moreover, all three regions have joined a series of UN human rights conventions which will offer a basis for cooperation in the criminal justice field. Finally, the application of mutual recognition still permits the refusal of surrender in specific situations for the sake of human rights protection. In brief, the application of mutual recognition can be responsive to human rights situations in mainland China, Hong Kong, and Macau.

---

109. See S. Alegre and M. Leaf, "Mutual Recognition in European Judicial Cooperation: A Step Too Far Too Soon? Case Study—the European Arrest Warrant," *European Law Journal* 10 (2004): 201.
110. See Larse Bay Larsen, "Afterword(s) on Mutual Recognition and the Respect for Fundamental Rights Revisited – Following the Judgment," in *The Needed Balance in EU Criminal Law: Past, Present and Future,* ed. Aranyosi and Caldararu in Chloé Brière and Anne Weymbergh (Oxford: Hart, 2018), 486.
111. Case examples are C-216/18 PPU LM, Case C-220/18 PPU ML.
112. See the Constitution of the People's Republic of China, art. 33.
113. The development can be seen in evidence law, amendment of criminal procedure law, as well as other official documents which regulate the professional ethic and discipline of judges, prosecutors, and other legal practitioners.

5 Constructing mutual recognition in the surrender of fugitive offenders between mainland China, Hong Kong, and Macau

5.1 Maintain the mutual recognition principle with necessary balance

The principle of mutual recognition can be incorporated into the China domestic surrender system. The proportionality principle should be applied, too. This principle can function as a guarantee for human rights protection as well as saving judicial resources.[114] Flexibility is inherent to mutual recognition, and this offers room for the application of proportionality check while holding mutual recognition as a basic principle. When conditions are mature, for instance when the knowledge of each other region's legal system is more comprehensive and mutual trust reaches a higher level, we can theoretically expect the mutual recognition principle to be applied more strictly and with an expanded scope.

5.2 Apply mutual recognition and make necessary adjustments

The guiding role of the mutual recognition principle is closely related to the practice of other, more detailed surrender (extradition) principles. Differing from traditional extradition, the double criminality principle, the exception for nationals, the exception for political offences, and other grounds (mandatory or optional) to refuse surrender will be practiced anew in a China domestic surrender system under the principle of mutual recognition. The practices fall under the "one country, two systems" policy, which will offer new meaning to the principle of mutual recognition compared to its previous application in the EU region. All these practices will further concretize the main characteristic of the principle of mutual recognition, namely flexibility, non-automaticity, functionality, and resistance.

5.3 Mutual recognition supported by relevant mechanisms

From the above analysis, in addition to the "one country" political fact, we find that the basic conditions which concern the application of mutual recognition principle in the China domestic surrender system also include the "two systems" legal fact, the mutual trust level, and human rights protection. The above analysis demonstrates that the application of mutual recognition is feasible. But it is also evident

114. See Sarah Haggenmüller, "The Principle of Proportionality and the European Arrest Warrant," *Oñati Socio-legal Series* 3, no. 1 (2013): 95, https://bibliographie.uni-tuebingen.de/xmlui/bitstream/handle/10900/111326/194-1203-1-PB.pdf?sequence=1.

that the effectiveness of mutual recognition is up to the fulfillment of all the above conditions.

More legal and language training for lawyers, judges, prosecutors, and other legal professionals in mainland China, Hong Kong, and Macau should be done in order to enhance mutual understanding and mutual trust.[115] More joint work on human rights protection should also be made to further protect the interests of suspects and offenders, guarantee the rights of lawyers, and improve due process in judicial proceedings and cooperation. Some important experiences and lessons have also been learned from the application of mutual recognition in the EU.

6 Conclusion

The proposed model for the surrender of fugitive offenders between mainland China, Hong Kong, and Macau comes under "one country, two systems" with the aims to protect both regional and national interest and individual rights. This requires that its guiding principle should be distinct from that of traditional extradition models. The mutual recognition principle which has been practiced in the European arrest warrant offers this possibility.

This chapter analyzed the historical development of the mutual recognition principle from the EU internal market field to the European arrest warrant, finding it to be functional, flexible, non-automatic, and resistant. These characteristics suggest a high probability of successful transplantation to the China domestic surrender system. In the context of "one country, two systems," the mutual trust and human rights situations across the three regions are such that they satisfy the basic conditions for applying the mutual recognition principle. Thus, the mutual recognition offers a principal basis on which to build a China arrest warrant system.

The implementation of the mutual recognition principle in the China arrest warrant system can take inspiration from the European arrest warrant system but must also be adjusted for the actual political and legal situations that exist in mainland China, Hong Kong, and Macau. This will be reflected in the design of surrender principles, including the surrender of political offence and death penalty offenders, and the double criminality principle. These topics are addressed in the following chapters.

115. See Eva Storskrubb, "Mutual Trust and the Dark Horse of Civil Justice," *Cambridge Yearbook of European Legal Studies* 20 (2018): 179.

2
The Role of the Judicial Authority

1 Introduction

There has been a general practice that both judicial and executive authorities have decisive roles to play in extradition procedure.[1] There has also been the practice in domestic rendition (extradition) that the executive authorities dominate the procedure, despite the involvement of judicial authorities.[2] However, the 2019 protests in response to the amendment of the Hong Kong Fugitive Offenders Ordinance (FOO) demonstrates that the dominant role of executive authorities in the China domestic surrender system is controversial.[3]

This chapter proposes that the China domestic surrender system can follow the European arrest warrant model to depoliticize the surrender procedure by assigning the leading role to judicial authorities. According to the Hong Kong Basic Law, Hong Kong may, through consultations and in accordance with law, maintain judicial relations with the judicial organs of other parts of the country, and they may render assistance to each other.[4] The same applies to Macau under the Macau Basic Law.[5] Assigning judicial authorities the main role in the China domestic surrender system is compliant with both Basic Laws.

---

1. See William Julie, Sophie Menegon, and Juliette Fauvarque, "From a Political to Judicial Approach to Extradition: A Case for the Consolidation of the Requesting State's Rights in Domestic Extradition Procedures," *New Journal of European Criminal Law* 12, no. 3 (2021): 464.
2. This is mainly shown in US interstate rendition system. See Yale Law Journal, "Interstate Rendition: Executive Practices and the Effects of Discretion," *Yale Law Journal* 66 (1956): 97.
3. See Greg Torode and James Pomfret, "Exclusive: Hong Kong Judges See Risks in Proposed Extradition Changes," *Reuters*, May 29, 2019, https://www.reuters.com/article/us-hongkong-politics-extradition-judges-idUSKCN1SZ09U.
4. Hong Kong Basic Law, art. 95.
5. Macau Basic Law, art. 93.

In this chapter, firstly, I analyze the roles of judicial authorities and executive authorities in traditional extradition, to demonstrate that system's problems and incompatibility with the China domestic surrender system. Secondly, I analyze the role of judicial authorities in Court of Justice of the European Union (CJEU) cases and why their role is decisive in the European arrest warrant system, to demonstrate the characteristics and merits of that approach. Thirdly, I further discuss how the scope of judicial authority can be delimited for the establishment of a China arrest warrant system.

2 Departure from traditional extradition practice

Traditional extradition is between sovereign states, and to grant or deny extradition is a matter of sovereign interest.[6] In fact, the history of extradition reflects political relations between the states requesting and granting extradition.[7] This is as true of contemporary interstate relations as it was in the earliest recorded times, though there is now a clear tendency to accept the notion of commonly shared goal of combating criminality as an international duty or *civitas maxima*.[8] More technically, extradition has dual functions: legal and diplomatic. A decision to extradite is never a purely judicial matter, as it affects and is affected by questions of foreign policy.[9]

The mixed essence and double function of extradition mean that, as a general practice, both judicial authorities and executive authorities have decisive roles to play. The decisive executive role is linked to the fact that traditional extradition has not only a legal function but also a political function relating to foreign policy and state interests.[10] However, this ground is very weak in the China domestic surrender system. Under the "one country, two systems" policy, legal conflicts between the three regions do exist but the political conflicts are what should be avoided, in compliance with the Basic Law and National Security Law.[11] Heavy involvement of

---

6. See Thomas Rose, "A Delicate Balance: Extradition, Sovereignty, and Individual Rights in the United States and Canada," *The Yale Journal of International Law* 27 (2002): 193.
7. See Christine Van den Wijngaert, "The Political Offense Exception to Extradition: Defining the Issues and Searching for a Feasible Alternative," *Revue Belge De Droi't Int'le* (1983): 745–46.
8. See M. Cherif Bassiouni and Edward Wise, *Aut Dedere Aut Judicare: The Duty to Extradite or Prosecute in International Law* (Leiden: Martinus Nijhoff, 1995). See also M. Cherif Bassiouni, *International Extradition: United States Law and Practice*, 6th ed. (Oxford: Oxford University Press, 2014), 4.
9. See e.g. Christine Van Den Wyngaert, *The Political Offence Exception to Extradition: The Delicate Problem of Balancing the Rights of the Individual and the International Public Order* (Deventer: Kluwer, 1980), 39.
10. See e.g. Van Den Wyngaert, *The Political Offence Exception to Extradition*, 39, n 9.
11. See Base Study 基地研究, "Chongtu de zhengjie:xianfaxing falü wenjian quewei yinqide kunhuo" 冲突的症结：宪法性法律文件缺位引起的困惑 [The core of conflict: confusion arising from the absence of constitutional documents], China Criminal Justice 中国刑事法律网, accessed October 30, 2022, http://www.criminallaw.com.cn/article/?id=24.

executive authorities in the surrender procedure, as practiced in traditional extradition, will exaggerate the conflict of political interests.

As was expressed by the concerned Hong Kong public in 2019, the Hong Kong and Macau executive authorities likely cannot refuse a surrender request from mainland China where the Central Government is in charge.[12] Under the Basic Laws, both Hong Kong and Macau governments are accountable to the central authorities, and at the political level the power imbalance between mainland China and Hong Kong would make it difficult for Hong Kong to refuse a surrender request from the Mainland.[13]

The substantial role of the executive authorities in previous extradition practice has also exposed its inherent shortcomings. Firstly, competition between executive and judicial authorities causes a loophole on human rights protection, especially by depriving the judicial authority of the ability to scrutinize human rights in the committal court.[14] For instance, under the Hong Kong FOO, the committal court, namely the court first hearing the surrender case, has no power nor obligation to evaluate the general risk of torture; this is left to the executive authorities, including the Hong Kong Immigration Bureau and the Chief Executive. This leads to insufficient and deferred human rights protection.[15] Secondly, the substantial involvement of the executive authorities lengthens the extradition process.[16] A Hong Kong researcher has found that the tension between the executive and the judiciary in surrender proceedings and the possibilities of extended delays due to repeated judicial challenges to the executive decision-making process, along with other procedural and evidential burdens, has prompted legislative reform to streamline and simplify extradition procedures in other common law jurisdictions such as the United Kingdom.[17]

---

12. See Greg Torode and James Pomfret, "Exclusive: Hong Kong Judges See Risks in Proposed Extradition Changes," *REUTERS*, May 29, 2019, https://www.reuters.com/article/us-hongkong-politics-extradition-judges-idUSKCN1SZ09U.
13. See Cora Chan, "Demise of One Country, Two Systems: Reflections on the Hong Kong Rendition Saga," *Hong Kong Law Journal* 49, no. 2 (2019): 450.
14. See Tracey Hughes, "Extradition Reform: The Role of the Judiciary in Protecting the Rights of a Requested Individual," *Boston College International and Comparative Law Review* 9, no. 2 (1986): 293. See also Steven Lubet, "Extradition Reform: Executive Discretion and Judicial Participation in the Extradition of Political Terrorists," *Cornell International Law Journal* 15, no. 2 (1982): 247.
15. See Case on Ramanjit Singh KCMP 139 of 2018, ¶237.
16. See Sibylle Kapferer, "Legal and Protection Policy Research Series: The Interface between Extradition and Asylum," United Nations High Commissioner for Refugees, November 2003, https://www.unhcr.org/3fe84fad4.pdf. See also Poonpol Ngearndee, "Mutual Legal Assistance and Extradition in Thailand," accessed October 30, 2022, https://www.unafei.or.jp/publications/pdf/GG6/05-7_Thailand.pdf.
17. See Wayne Walsh, *Cross-border Crime in Hong Kong* (Hong Kong: LexisNexis, 2018), 115. Walsh refers to the UK experience that "the UK Extradition Act 2003 has reduced the role of the Home Secretary in the extradition process and left more decision-making powers to the court."

From the above analysis, it is clear that the China domestic surrender system should deviate from the traditional extradition model where the executive authorities have a substantive role to play. Greater powers should be given to the judicial authorities and the surrender process should be depoliticized.[18] The EAW can offer inspiration in this regard and provide an example for the China arrest warrant system to follow.

3 The European arrest warrant model

3.1 The shift from administrative authority to judicial authority

Before the EAW Framework Decision came into play, a series of extradition conventions were in force in Europe. All of the conventions highlighted the role of the administrative authorities; that is to say, extradition procedure was dominated by the administrative authorities.[19]

When the EAW Framework Decision came into force, judicial authorities begain to dominate the procedure. As specified in the EAW FD, decisions on the execution of European arrest warrant must be subject to sufficient control; a judicial authority of the Member State where the requested person has been arrested will decide on his or her surrender.[20] In accordance with this objective of "sufficient control", the executive authority merely assists the judicial authority in the European arrest warrant system.[21] "Sufficient control" also has a role to play in the issuing procedure. According to the EAW FD, the issuing judicial authority shall be the judicial authority of the issuing Member State which is competent to issue a European arrest warrant by virtue of the law of that State.[22]

The decisive role of the judicial authority can also be understood from an "efficiency" perspective.[23] As stated in the EAW FD, the introduction of a new simplified system of surrender makes it possible to remove the complexity and potential for delay inherent in the previous extradition procedures.[24] The data proves the efficiency of direct judicial cooperation. In 2018, an estimated average of 54.5% of

18. See Huang Feng 黄风, *Yindu wenti yanjiu* 引渡问题研究 [Study on extradition] (Beijing: Zhongguo zhengfa daxue chubanshe, 2006), 223.
19. These conventions are European Convention in 1957, the 1995 Convention on Simplified Extradition Procedure between Member States of the European Union, and the 1996 Convention relating to Extradition between the Member States of the European Union.
20. EAW FD, Preamble (8).
21. EAW FD, art. 7(2).
22. EAW FD, art. 6(1).
23. See Isabelle Pérignon and Constance Daucé, "The European Arrest Warrant: A Growing Success Story," *ERA Forum* 8 (2007): 203.
24. EAW FD, Preamble (5).

requested persons consented to their surrender (compared to 62.96% in 2017), with the surrender procedure lasting on average 16.41 days after the arrest; the average surrender time for those who do not consent is around 45.12 days. This in stark contrast with the lengthy extradition process that existed between Member States prior to the EAW Framework Decision.[25]

3.2 The scope of judicial authority under the European arrest warrant

The EAW Framework Decision provides that the European arrest warrant is issued by judicial authorities and the scope of their powers should be in line with the law of issuing Member States. The Court of Justice of the European Union (CJEU) has further clarified the role of the issuing judicial authority through a series of cases.

Cases have mainly involved the issuing judicial authority and judicial decisions, both at the national and the European Union levels. There are seldom disputes relating to the executing judicial authority. The courts are the designated executing judicial authorities in nearly all Member States. The traditional executive authorities such as the police and the justice minister are excluded from the scope of judicial authority. The role of public prosecutors can be mixed. Most of the relevant cases from the CJEU take the following form as shown in Table 2.1 on page 42.

3.2.1 Executive authorities are excluded

Firstly, the police should not be regarded as a judicial authority and is not qualified to issue the European arrest warrant. The CJEU has held that judicial authorities are the authorities that traditionally administer justice, as opposed to, inter alia, administrative authorities or police authorities which are within the province of the executive.[26] The principle of mutual recognition is founded on the premise that a judicial authority has intervened prior to the execution of the European arrest warrant for the purpose of exercising its review.[27] However, the issue of an arrest warrant by a non-judicial authority, such as a police service, does not provide the executing judicial authority with an assurance that the issue of that European arrest warrant has undergone judicial approval and cannot, therefore, suffice to justify the high level of confidence between the Member States.[28] It follows that the term "judicial

25. Commission, "Report on the Implementation of Council Framework Decision on European Arrest Warrant," COM (2020) 270 final, 1.
26. Case C-452/16 PPU, *Krzystof Maretk Poltorak* [Judgment of the Court, 10 November 2016], ¶35.
27. Case C-452/16, ¶44.
28. Case C-452/16, ¶45.

Table 2.1: The validity of a European arrest warrant

Case number	Country (issuing)	Purpose	Issuing organ (national decision)	Nature of organ	Nature of decision	Issuing organ (EAW)	Nature of organ	Other relevant elements	European arrest warrant (in)valid
C-627/19	Belgium	Execute sentence	Court	Judicial	Judicial	Prosecutor	Judicial	No separate remedy needed	Valid
C-648/20	Bulgaria	Prosecute	Prosecutor	Judicial	Judicial	The same prosecutor	Judicial	No review by court, insufficient judicial protection	Invalid
C-489/19	Austria	Prosecute	Prosecutor (endorsed by court)	Subject to minister of justice	Judicial	Prosecutor (endorsed by court)	Subject to minister of Justice	Judicial protection sufficient	Valid
C-477/16	Lithuania	Execute sentence	Court	Judicial	Judicial	Ministry of Justice	Executive	Insufficient judicial protection in issuing EAW	Invalid
C-241/15	Hungary	Prosecute	None	None	None	Court	Judicial	Insufficient judicial protection in national decision	Invalid
C-566/19626/ 19	France	Prosecute	Court	Judicial	Judicial	Prosecutor	judicial	Prosecutor not influenced in specific case by Ministry of Justice	Valid
C-508/1882/ 19	Germany	Prosecute	Court	Judicial	Judicial	Prosecutor	Subject to Ministry of Justice	Ineffective judicial protection	Invalid
C-453/16	Hungary	Prosecute	Police confirmed by prosecutor	Executive	Judicial	Court	Judicial	Effective judicial protection on national level	Valid
C-625/19	Sweden	Prosecute	Court	Judicial	Judicial	Prosecutor	Judicial	Court can review EAW issuance	Valid

authority" does not include police services, and a European arrest warrant issued by such services cannot be regarded as a "judicial decision" under this preliminary ruling.[29]

However, in the Hungary case demonstrated above, the national arrest warrant issued by Hungary police can be regarded as a judicial decision and it can be the basis for a valid European arrest warrant. The point is that although the Hungarian police are an executive organ and not qualified to issue a judicial decision, its arrest warrant is endorsed by the Hungarian prosecutor, a judicial authority. So the judicial protection in the national arrest warrant issuing stage is effective; it is the prosecutor that functions as the real issuing authority.[30] Nonetheless, this case still shows that executive authority alone is not qualified to issue national judicial decision and European arrest warrant.

Not only is the police office excluded from the scope of judicial authority, the ministry of justice is also not recognized as a judicial authority and is not qualified to issue a European arrest warrant. The CJEU explains that the words "judicial authorities" are not limited to designating only the judges or courts of a Member State, but may extend, more broadly, to the authorities required to participate in administering justice in the legal system concerned.[31] But the term "judicial authorities" cannot be interpreted as also covering an organ of the executive of a Member State, such as a ministry. The judiciary must be distinguished from the executive in accordance with the principle of the separation of powers which characterizes the operation of the rule of law, thus, judicial authorities are traditionally construed as the authorities that administer justice, unlike ministries or other government organs which are within the province of the executive.[32] The system of surrender is based on the principle of mutual recognition with a view to contributing to the attainment of the objective set for the European Union to become an area of freedom, security, and justice, founded on the high level of confidence which should exist between the Member States. And designating an organ of the executive as an "issuing judicial authority" would run counter to the above objectives and principles.[33]

29. Case C-452/16, ¶46.
30. *See* Case C-453/16 PPU, *Openbaar Ministerie v. Halil Ibrahim Özçelik* [Judgment of the Court, 10 November 2016], ¶12–13.
31. Case C-477/16 PPU, *Openbaar Ministerie v. Ruslanas Kovalkovas* [Judgment of the Court, 10 November 2016], ¶34.
32. Case C-477/16, ¶36.
33. Case C-477/16, ¶40–42.

3.2.2 Whether the public prosecutor can be regarded as a judicial authority

On the question of whether the public prosecutor can be regarded as a judicial authority, the answers from the CJEU are mixed, varying from country to country. To this point, CJEU cases have held that prosecutors from Hungary, Belgium, France, and Sweden can be considered to be issuing (executing) judicial authorities. However, prosecutors from Germany and the Netherland are excluded.

On June 21, 2016 the Hungary District Court issued a European arrest warrant against Mr Halil Ibrahim Özçelic, a Turkish national, in connection with criminal proceedings instituted against him in respect of two offences committed in Hungary. The request for execution of that European arrest warrant came before the Amsterdam District Court in the Netherlands. By a request for information of July 8, 2016, the referring court questioned the Hungarian authorities about the role of the public prosecutor's office and, in particular, on its independence from the executive, as well as on the implications of the confirmation by the public prosecutor's office of an arrest warrant issued by a police service. On July 14, 2016 the Hungarian authorities provided a response to that request, from which it was apparent that the public prosecutor's office was independent from the executive and that it was tasked with ensuing, during the whole of the investigation stage, that the police complied with the law and that the suspect could exercise his rights. Moreover, those authorities indicated that the member of the public prosecutor's office who confirmed a national arrest warrant issued by the police may act as a representative of the public prosecutor's office during the relevant criminal proceedings. In light of that information, the referring court expressed its doubts as to whether a national arrest warrant, issued by a police service and subsequently confirmed by a decision of a public prosecutor's office, may be classified as a "judicial decision," within the meaning of Article 8(1)(c)of the EAW Framework Decision.

The CJEU held that the confirmation by the public prosecutor's office of the arrest warrant issued by the police was a legal act by which the public prosecutor's office verified and validated the arrest warrant. Based on that confirmation, which appeared in the European arrest warrant, the public prosecutor's office was regarded as being responsible for the issue of the national arrest warrant.[34] The Court held that the term "judicial authority" must be interpreted as referring to the Member State authorities that administer criminal justice services.[35] In the light of that finding a decision of the public prosecutor's office, which constitutes a Member

34. Case C-453/16 PPU, *Openbaar Ministerie v Halil lbrahim Özçelik* [Judgment of the Court, 10 November 2016], ¶30.
35. Case C-453/16, ¶34.

State authority responsible for administering criminal justice, must be regarded as a judicial decision.[36]

However, the public prosecutors in some Member States like Germany cannot be regarded as judicial authorities and cannot issue the European arrest warrant, according to the CJEU. In two cases where the issuing authorities were the public prosecutors of Germany, the referring courts asked whether the concept of an "issuing judicial authority" must be interpreted as including the public prosecutors' offices of a Member State which are responsible for the prosecution of criminal offences and are subordinate to a body of the executive of that Member State, such as a justice minister.

The CJEU emphasized that the words "judicial authority" are not limited to designating only the judges or courts of a Member State, but must be construed as designating, more broadly, the authorities participating in the administration of criminal justice in that Member State, as distinct from, inter alia, ministries or police services which are part of the executive.[37]

However, it also emphasized that the "issuing judicial authority" must be capable of exercising its responsibilities objectively, taking into account all incriminatory and exculpatory evidence, without being exposed to the risk that its decision-making power be subject to external directions or instructions, in particular from the executive.[38] It also required that there be statutory rules and an institutional framework capable of guaranteeing that the issuing judicial authority is not exposed, when adopting a decision to issue an arrest warrant, to any risk of being subject, inter alia, to an instruction from the executive in a specific case.[39] Where the public prosecutors' offices at issue are exposed to the risk of being influenced by the executive in their decision to issue a European arrest warrant, those public prosecutors' offices do not meet the requirements for being regarded as an issuing judicial authority.[40]

At the same time, this case suggested that even where public prosecutors are judicial authorities, they may not guarantee sufficient judicial protection for requested persons if the same public prosecutors both make the national decision and issue the European arrest warrant. The CJEU confirmed that the European arrest warrant entails a dual level of protection of procedural rights and fundamental rights which must be enjoyed by the requested person; in addition to the judicial

36. Case C-453/16, ¶37.
37. See Case C-452/16 PPU, *Openbaar Ministerie v. Krzysztof Marek Poltorak* [Judgment of the Court, November 10, 2016],¶ 33,35; See also Case C-477/16 PPU, *Openbaar Ministerie v. Ruslanas Kovalkovas* [Judgment of the Court, November 10, 2016], ¶34, 36.
38. See joined Case C-508/18 and Case C-82/19 PPU, *Minister for Justice and Equality v. OG and PI* [Judgment of the Court, May 27, 2019], ¶76.
39. Joined Case C-508/18, ¶78–80.
40. Joined Case C-508/18, ¶88.

protection provided at the first level, at which a national decision such as a national arrest warrant is adopted, there is protection that must be afforded at the second level, at which a European arrest warrant is issued depending on the circumstances, shortly after the adoption of the national judicial decision.[41] The executing judicial authority may be satisfied that the decision to issue a European arrest warrant for the purposes of criminal prosecution is based on a national procedure that is subject to a review by a court.[42] And the review carried out at the time of adoption of an arrest warrant must include an examination of the observance of the conditions necessary for the issuing of that arrest warrant.[43] Austrian law provides that, both in the context of the decision to issue a national arrest warrant and in the context of the decision to issue a European arrest warrant, public prosecutors are to order an arrest by means of an arrest warrant, which must be endorsed in order that it may be transmitted by a court which is to carry out a review of the conditions of the issue and its proportionality, and the endorsement decision is subject to appeal before the court.[44] In those situations, the judicial protection is regarded as effective.

So, according to the above cases,[45] public prosecutors can be the judicial authority under the European arrest warrant system on the condition that they are not only in charge of administering justice but also free from external directions or instructions, especially from the executive. But when both the national decision maker and the European arrest warrant decision maker are the prosecutors, the decision should be subject to the judicial review of the court, in order to guarantee the sufficiency and effectiveness of judicial protection. However, the CJEU has been criticized by civil society for taking a formalistic approach towards the concept of independence in not seeking to enquire into the practice or other potential forms of influence of the executive over prosecutors.[46] There is also emphasize that there is no common standard for the independence of prosecutors;[47] however, guarantees must be provided at the level of the individual case to ensure that there is transparency concerning instructions that may be given.[48]

41. See Case C-489/19 PPU, NJ [Judgment of the Court, October 9, 2019], ¶34.
42. Case C-489/19, ¶36.
43. Case C-489/19, ¶37.
44. Case C-489/19, ¶39.
45. Relating to cases on Belgium, France, Sweden, and Netherland, see C-627/19, C-566/19 and C-626/19, C-625/19 and C-510/19.
46. See L. Baudrihaye-Gerard, "Can Belgian, French and Swedish Prosecutors Issue European Arrest Warrant? The CJEU Clarifies the Requirement for Independence Public Prosecutors," *EU Law Analysis Blog*, January 2, 2020, http://eulawanalysis.blogspot.com/2020/01/can-belgian-french-and-swedish.html.
47. Commission, "Opinion on the Draft Amendments to the Law on the State Prosecutorial Council of Serbia," CDL-AD (2014)029,§7.
48. Commission, "Interim Opinion on the Draft Law on the State Prosecution Office of Montenegro," CDL-AD (2014)042, §16.

3.2.3 Judicial independence

On February 7, 2020, a European arrest warrant was issued to the Netherlands court from Poland for the arrest and surrender of a Polish national suspected of drug trafficking and possession of false identity documents. The Dutch referring court took the opinion that Polish judges ran the risk of being subjected to disciplinary proceedings before a body whose independence was not assured. On June 23, 2020, the Amsterdam District Court received a European arrest warrant from the Poland district court for execution of custodial sentence. In this case, the Dutch referring court raised concerns that the legislation in the issuing Member State did not guarantee the independence of the court.

The CJEU recognized that judicial independence forms part of the essence of the fundamental right to a fair trial. However, it also confirmed that a Member State executing judicial authority which has evidence of systemic or generalized deficiencies in judicial independence in the issuing state, existing at the time of issue of the European arrest warrant or arising after issue, cannot deny the status of issuing judicial authority.[49] The existence of such deficiencies does not necessarily affect every decision of the courts of the issuing Member State in every case,[50] and an interpretation to the contrary would mean that no court of that Member State could still be regarded as a "court or tribunal" for the purpose of the application of other provisions of EU law.[51]

The CJEU suggests that to accept that systemic or generalized deficiencies in the independence of the issuing Member States' judiciary give rise to the presumption that there are substantial grounds for believing that that person will run a risk of breach of his or her fundamental right to a fair trial if he or she is surrendered to that Member State—which would justify the non-execution of that arrest warrant—would lead to an automatic refusal to execute any arrest warrant by that Member State.[52] However, the CJEU held that it is only if the European Council were to adopt a decision and the Council were then to suspend the EAW Framework Decision in respect of the Member State concerned that the executing judicial authority would be required to refuse automatically to execute any European arrest warrant issued by that Member State.[53] Instead, in view of the evidence of systematic or generalized deficiencies concerning the independence of the judiciary in the Member State that issues that arrest warrant, the executing judicial authority must determine whether

49. See Joined Case C-354/20 PPU and Case C-412/20 PPU, L.P. [Judgment of the Court, December 17, 2020], ¶41.
50. Joined Case C-354/20 and C-412/20, ¶42.
51. Joined Case C-354/20 and C-412/20, ¶44.
52. Joined Case C-354/20 and C-412/20, ¶59.
53. Joined Case C-354/20 and C-412/20, ¶58.

there is objective, reliable, specific, and properly updated material indicating that there is a real risk of breach of the fundamental right to a fair trial.[54] So, in this case we find that even courts with systematic deficiencies in independence can still be regarded as issuing authorities, and whether to refuse the execution of a European arrest warrant depends on more specific criteria.

In summary, in the surrender procedure, the central authority, which is often the ministry for justice, the ministry of foreign affairs or the General prosecutor's office, has lost its power to make decisions to extradite and plays the role of coordinator, while judges and public prosecutors became sole competent authorities in the surrender procedure.[55] Currently, in half of the Member States, courts or judges are solely competent to issue a European arrest warrant; in a few Member States, it is entirely up to the public prosecutor's offices to issue a European arrest warrant; and several Member States have designated both courts and public prosecutor's offices as issuing authorities.[56] There are currently few CJEU cases on the EAW executing judicial authority in Member States. But judging from the EAW cases referred to the CJEU for preliminary rulings, all the executing judicial authorities are courts in Member States, except that the Netherlands prosecutor consenting a specialty rule as executing judicial authority. However, the identity of the Netherlands prosecutor as executing judicial authority has recently been overruled by the CJEU.[57]

3.3 *Why the authority in charge changed from administrative authority to judicial authority*

3.3.1 The objective of extradition (surrender) has evolved

In the old extradition convention, the aim of the Council of Europe is said to be to achieve greater unity between its members.[58] This is a very general political objective without concrete legal implications. When it comes to the EAW Framework Decision, the objective is described to be for the Union to become an area of freedom, security, and justice in the process of abolishing traditional extradition and replacing it with a system of surrender directly between judicial authorities.[59] The aim to become an area of freedom, security, and justice has both political meaning

54. Joined Case C-354/20 and C-412/20, ¶54.
55. See Libor Klimek, *European Arrest Warrant* (Berlin: Springer, 2015), 79.
56. See Commission, "Report on the Implementation of Council Framework Decision of 13 June 2002 on the European Arrest Warrant and the Surrender Procedure between Member States," COM (2020) 270 final, 6.
57. See Case C-510/19, *Openbaar Ministerie v. AZ* [Judgment of the Court, November 24, 2020].
58. See 1957 European Convention on Extradition, Preamble.
59. EAW FD, Preamble (5).

and legal implications. Endowing the judicial authority as the main authority over the surrender procedure is compatible with the objective.

3.3.2 Compliance with the mutual recognition principle

At the Tampere European Council in 1999, it was decided that the principle of mutual recognition should become a cornerstone of judicial cooperation in both civil and criminal matters within the EU.[60] The EAW Framework Decision is the first instrument in the field of criminal law implementing the principle of mutual recognition. The change from administrative authority to judicial authority was intended to contribute to the efficiency of surrender via mutual recognition. At the same time, having the judicial authority rather than the executive authority taking charge of the surrender procedure would contribute to human rights protection and help to facilitate or guarantee the function of mutual recognition.

3.3.3 Responding to the role of CJEU

The European Convention on Extradition 1957 and 1996 Convention relating to extradition between Member States of the European Union are silent as to the role of the CJEU. More precisely, extradition in the European Union has had little to do with the CJEU; it is more of a political issue. Accordingly, absent any important role for the judicial organization (CJEU) at the European Union level relating to extradition, there will similarly be no major power entrusted to judicial authorities at the domestic level on the same issue. But when it comes to the EAW Framework Decision, we find that, from the European Union level to the Member State level, judicial authorities have the leading role. The CJEU has mainly played its role through preliminary rulings.

4 The surrender of fugitive offenders between mainland China, Hong Kong, and Macau

4.1 At present, unilateral "surrender" is handled in an administrative way

Pursuant to the Macau Criminal Procedure Code, surrendering suspects or criminals to another region or country should be based on the relevant specific law.[61] But

60. Nora Gevorgyan, "The Role, Impact and Development of the Principle of Mutual Recognition in EU Law," accessed October 30, 2022, http://ysu.am/files/08N_Gevorgyan_e.pdf.
61. Macau Criminal Procedure Code, art. 217.

both before and after the establishment of Macau Special Administrative Region, there has been no legislation or agreement on surrender between mainland China and Macau. The Macau court issued a personal protection order to one woman who was wanted by the Mainland and the Macau judicial police office released her after the protection order.[62]

Without a legal basis, surrendering the fugitive offenders back to mainland China is not legally permissible in Hong Kong. However, Mainland law enforcement has sent Hong Kong resident suspects back to Hong Kong for investigation or trial at their discretion. Over the past five years, on average two persons have been sent back to Hong Kong each year for offences including murder, injury and robbery.[63] The Mainland has transferred 248 suspects to Hong Kong to face justice since 2006.[64]

The situation is similar for Macau. Between the years 2012 and 2013, a group of criminals committed frauds to the value of 2.4 million Macau patacas and 5 million Hong Kong dollars, then fled to mainland China. The police office in Macau requested the assistance of Mainland public security authorities through the police cooperation mechanism between the two regions. Under this request, the mainland police arrested the principal criminal and handed him over to the Macau police office on May 12, 2017.[65] It has been routine for mainland police to assist their Macau counterparts by sending offenders back.[66]

In summary, at present, surrender of persons from mainland China to Hong Kong or from mainland China to Macau is done mainly through the cross-border police cooperation mechanism in a unilateral and administrative way. This is not a suitable model for a formal surrender of fugitive offenders system between mainland China, Hong Kong, and Macau.

62. The Macau Case on Personal Protection Order, Judge Viriato Manuel Pinheiro de Lima, Judgment on March 20, 2007, no. 12, 2007.
63. See Legislative Committee question 20, "Negotiation between Mainland China and Hong Kong on the Arrangement of Surrender of Fugitive Offenders," *Press Release*, February 3, 2016, http://www.info.gov.hk/gia/general/201602/03/P201602030531.htm.
64. Grenville Cross, "Fugitive Surrender: Rights and Responsibilities," *China Daily*, June 12, 2019, https://www.chinadailyhk.com/articles/186/73/64/1560307116859.html.
65. See "Police Cooperation Mechanism Proved Effective in Handover of Fugitive of Fraud by Mainland Chinese Police," the Bureau of Macau Judiciary Police, accessed November 9, 2022, https://www.pj.gov.mo/Web/Policia/201705/20170517/5899.html?lang=en.
66. Hong, Yiyi, "Guang Dong Police Handed over One Suspect to Macau Police Which Fled to Mainland China after Murdered," *Pengpai News*, March 16, 2017, https://www.thepaper.cn/newsDetail_forward_1640835.

4.2 *Why the judicial authority should have a definitive role*

4.2.1 China domestic surrender is distinct from extradition (surrender) between the three regions and other countries

Both Macau and Hong Kong have expressed the position that a different and creative approach should be taken when considering criminal cooperation within the three regions including the surrender of fugitive offenders. On July 20, 2015, the Director of the Secretariat for Administration and Justice in Macau told the Macau press that because the negotiation on criminal cooperation between Hong Kong and Macau is on the basis of "one country, two systems," the cooperative principles which should be observed will not be fully in line with those specified in the cooperation agreements with overseas countries.[67] On July 4, 2015, Guoqiang Yuan, the former Secretary for Justice in Hong Kong, delivered a speech in the first session of Chinese Justice Study Summit Forum. On criminal cooperation with mainland China, he pointed out that criminal cooperation between mainland China, Hong Kong, and Macau is regional cooperation (cooperation between regions), not international cooperation (cooperation between sovereign countries); that cooperation between different legal regions and legal systems within one sovereign country also exists internationally, for instance, in the US and in Australia; and that the European Union also set out regulations on the criminal cooperation issue.[68]

We see although Hong Kong, Macau, and mainland China all have their own criminal cooperation model with other sovereign countries, there is consensus that when the criminal cooperation is to take place between themselves, a different model should be applied. The European arrest warrant was also mentioned in Guoqiang Yuan's forum speech.[69] It was described as an inspiration for the China domestic surrender system, including in designating the judicial authority to take charge of the surrender procedure.

Following the European arrest warrant experience, such distinction given to China domestic surrender system can also be justified. Within the EU, 27 Member States practice the internal efficient surrender system, but externally, the Member States still apply traditional extradition with third countries. In this way, the EU

---

67. Legislative Committee Question 17, "Discussion between Hong Kong and Macau on the Arrangement of Surrender of Fugitive Offenders and Judicial Cooperation in Criminal Matters," *Press Releases*, February 24, 2016, http://www.info.gov.hk/gia/general/201602/24/P201602240391.htm.
68. See Yuan Guoqiang 袁国强, "Zhonghua sifa yanjiuhui chengli dahui ji shoujie zhonghua sifa yanjiu gaofeng luntan zhici" 中华司法研究会成立大会暨首届中华司法研究高峰论坛 [Speech in the first session of Chinese justice study summit forum], July 3, 2015, https://www.doj.gov.hk/sc/community_engagement/speeches/pdf/sj20150704sc.pdf.
69. Yuan, "Speech," n 68.

distinguishes internal surrender from external extradition. Mainland China, Hong Kong, and Macau can learn from this practice to design their domestic surrender system.

4.2.2 Efficiency in surrender between mainland China, Hong Kong, and Macau

The mutual recognition aspect of the European arrest warrant requires abolishing the leading role the administrative authority used to play in extradition procedure and letting the judicial authority have direct say.[70] This functions to improve efficiency. Surrender between mainland China, Hong Kong, and Macau should also satisfy the efficiency requirement. From a geographical perspective, the three regions are close to each other, and the movement of persons including criminals enjoys geographical advantages.[71] Efficiency can curb criminals' ways of fleeing. Referring to the European arrest warrant experience, removing the executive authorities from the surrender procedure has greatly enhanced the efficiency of surrender.[72]

4.2.3 Human rights protection

Under the European arrest warrant system, removing the role of the executive authorities and some public prosecutors which may be subject to the instructions of the executive authorities guarantees human rights protection, as explained above. China domestic surrender also faces the same demand for human rights to be guaranteed during the surrender process.[73] To achieve this, the judicial authorities in the three regions are strongly recommended to be assigned as the main authorities taking charge of surrender. This will reduce the political intervention and offer due protection to suspects or convicts of political crimes like subversion of government as well as other ordinary offences.

---

70. See Susie Alegre and Marisa Leaf, "Mutual Recognition in European Judicial Cooperation: A Step Too Far Too Soon? Case Study—The European Arrest Warrant," *European Law Journal* 10, no. 2 (2004): 200.
71. See Wang Zhongxing 王仲兴 and Guo Tianwu 郭天武, *Neidi yu xianggang xingshi sifa hezuo yanjiu* 内地与香港刑事司法合作研究 [Research on criminal juridical cooperation between Hong Kong and Mainland China] (Beijing: Beijing daxue chubanshe, 2008), 173.
72. Commission, "Report from the Commission to the European Parliament and the Council on the implementation since 2007 of the Council Framework Decision of 13 June 2002 on the European arrest warrant and the surrender procedures between Member States" COM (2011) 175 final, 2.
73. See Marsha Wellknown Yee, "Hong Kong's Legal Obligation to Require Fair Trial for Rendition," *Columbia Law Review* 102, no. 5 (2002): 1373.

4.3 *The scope of judicial authority under the surrender of fugitive offenders between mainland China, Hong Kong, and Macau*

4.3.1 Executive authorities should be excluded

The most important function of executive authorities in the extradition or surrender system is to safeguard sovereign interests in a diplomatic way when dealing with foreign governments.[74] However, surrender between the three regions takes place within the same sovereign state. No regional government can be regarded as a foreign government by another, none of the regions has an independent sovereign interest to protect, and thus the substantive function of the executive authority is greatly limited in the domestic surrender space. As barrister Wayne Walsh says, it is unlikely the executive will take the prominent role it does under Hong Kong's Fugitive Offenders Ordinance (FOO) when handling rendition requests from judicial and law enforcement authorities within China; in most simplified regimes for extradition or rendition, the processing of requests is carried out directly between the judicial authorities of each place without active engagement of the executive in the decision making process.[75] Thus, the Chief Executives, the police offices, the China Foreign Ministry and the State Council should be excluded from issuing a China arrest warrant.

Under the Hong Kong FOO, the Immigration Department has the responsibility to protect human rights through the torture screening mechanism in Hong Kong surrender with foreign countries. However, in the China arrest warrant system, this research does not suggest assigning such a role to the Immigration Department. Firstly, like the Chief Executive and other executive authorities, the Immigration Department's role in protecting human rights will be limited due to its subordination under the "one country" regime. It has been shown that during the surrender between Hong Kong and foreign countries, the Hong Kong Immigration Department has seldom recognized the torture risks for individuals requested for surrender.[76] Secondly, practice also demonstrates that the executive authorities do not have a real function to protect human rights despite holding the power (as discussed above) while the judicial authorities cannot perform sufficient human rights scrutiny due to their limited power of human rights protection under the

74. See John T. Parry, "International Extradition, the Rule of Non-Inquiry, and the Problem of Sovereignty," *Boston University Law Review* 90 (2010): 1973.
75. See Walsh, *Cross-Border Crime*, 224, n 17.
76. See Pui Yan Flora Lau and Lulia Gheorghiu, "Vanishing Selves under Hong Kong's Unified Screening Mechanism," *Cultural Diversity in China* 3, no. 1 (2017): 21.

Hong Kong FOO.[77] The exclusion of executive organs from the China arrest warrant system can offer more power to the judicial authorities and better protect the rights of the requested persons.

4.3.2 Public prosecutors can be included conditionally

Under European arrest warrant mechanism, public prosecutors can be the authorities to issue and execute warrant on the condition that they are in charge of administering justice and independent from external intervention, in particular from the executive.[78] The CJEU preliminary rulings also emphasize that judicial authorities under the European arrest warrant are not limited to judges or courts but can, in a broader sense, also entail authorities participating in the administration of criminal justice.[79] This research finds that public prosecutors in mainland China and Macau are judicial authorities which satisfy the requirements of the European arrest warrant, and Hong Kong public prosecutors should be endorsed by the courts when they issue local arrest warrants.

The Law of Public Prosecutors in China specifies that public prosecutors should investigate, arrest, and prosecute criminal cases on behalf of the state; should carry out public interest prosecutions; and should supervise litigation of criminal, civil, and administrative matters.[80] The independence of the public prosecutors is also confirmed. The Law specifies that the public prosecutors should fulfill their obligations in compliance with the law and free from the intervention of executive authorities, social organizations, and individuals.[81]

The Hong Kong public prosecutors are inside of the Department of Justice, and the Department of Justice is an executive authority in line with the Hong Kong Basic Law,[82] but the Basic Law confirms that the criminal prosecution work of the Department of Justice is free from any interference.[83] The Department of Justice handles the majority of prosecution work in Hong Kong; even some prosecution work assigned to the Police and the Hong Kong Independent Commission against Corruption is completed under the guidance and supervision of Department of

77. Case KCMP 139 of 2018, Ruling in the matter of the request for surrender of Mr. Ramanjit Singh to the Republic of India, ¶237, 240.
78. See Case C-452/16, n37 and joined case C-508/18 and C-82/19, n 38.
79. See Chad Heimrich, "European Arrest Warrants and the Independence of the Issuing Judicial Authority—How Much Independence Is Required?" *New Journal of European Criminal Law* 10 (2019): 2.
80. See Law of Public Prosecutors in China, art. 7.
81. See Law of Public Prosecutors in China, art. 6.
82. Hong Kong Basic Law, art. 60.
83. Hong Kong Basic Law, art. 63.

Justice.[84] There are scholarly views that judicial authorities under the Basic Law should be interpreted broadly,[85] but that does not align with the CJEU ruling relating to the nature of judicial authority.[86] It is better to say that Hong Kong public prosecutors in the Department of Justice can still prosecute and do prosecution-related work during the China arrest warrant issuing procedure, but their decisions should be endorsed by the courts in order to guarantee that judicial protection given to the persons subject to warrants.

When it comes to Macau, although prosecutors should generally be nominated by the Macau Chief Executive and approved by the Central Government,[87] the Basic Law not only includes the public prosecutors' office in the judicial authority chapter but also confirms that the Macau public prosecutor's office should carry out prosecutions independently and free from any interference.[88] The independence of prosecutors is also confirmed by local Macau law.[89] So Macau public prosecutors can be regarded as judicial authorities, the same as public prosecutors in mainland China.

4.3.3 The judicial independence of the courts should be recognized

Concerns have been raised as to the judicial independence of courts in mainland China. Although the external intervention in individual cases has reduced in recent years, research has shown that judicial independence has been systematically breached by one-party rule.[90] However, despite the systematic deficiency of judicial independence in mainland China, we cannot take it for granted that all requested persons' judicial rights will be breached and all the courts of mainland China suffer from a lack of judicial independence. The European arrest warrant has offered important inspiration on this.[91]

84. See Wang and Guo, *Neidi*, 112, n 71.
85. See Zhao Guoqiang 赵国强, *Jibenfa yu quji sifa xiezhu* 基本法与区际司法协助 [Basic law and regional judicial cooperation] (Beijing: Zhongguo shehui kexue chubanshe, 2000), 168.
86. See Case C-452/16 PPU, *Openbaar Ministerie v. Krzysztof Marek Poltorak* (Judgment of the Court, 10 November 2016), ¶ 33, 35. See also Case C-477/16 PPU, *Openbaar Ministerie v. Ruslanas Kovalkovas* [Judgment of the Court, 10 November 2016], ¶34, 36.
87. See Zhao Linlin 赵琳琳, *Oulu chuantong yu bendi yishi: aomen xingshifa gaige yanjiu* 欧陆传统与本地意识：澳门刑事法改革研究 [European continental tradition and local consciousness: research on the reform of Macau criminal laws] (Beijing: Falü chubanshe, 2017), 194.
88. Macau Basic Law, art. 90.
89. See the Organic Law on Judicial Organization of Macau Special Administrative Region, art. 1, art. 2, and art. 55. See also Zhao, *Jibenfa*, 128, n 85.
90. He Xin, "Pressures on Chinese Judges under Xi," *The China Journal* 85 (2021): 25.
91. See Joined Case C-354/20 and C-412/20 PPU L and P [Judgment of the Court, December 17, 2020].

Cases from the CJEU have dealt with the relationship between judges' independence and the parties or the political leaders who appoint them. On April 25, 2019 Repubblika (a legal person in Malta) brought an action to the Malta Constitutional Court. Repubblika claimed that the Prime Minister's discretion to appoint members of the judiciary raised doubts as to the independence of those judges and magistrates, and it submitted that a number of members of the judiciary appointed since 2013 were very active in the Labour Party, which was in government, or had been appointed in such a way as to give rise to suspicion of political interference in the judiciary.[92] The Malta Constitution Court referred the case to the CJEU for a preliminary ruling. The CJEU held that the mere fact that judges were appointed by the President of a Member State did not give rise to the subordination of those judges to the latter, or to doubts as to the judges' impartiality, if, once appointed, they were free from influence or pressure when carrying out their role.[93]

In mainland China, judicial independence should be evaluated in the same way. Although the appointment and promotion of judges may be a feature of one-party rule in China, the independence or impartiality of judges when they carry out their duties may not necessarily be influenced externally and illegally.[94] This can be inferred from CJEU case. The CJEU has offered further meaningful and far-reaching guidance on the judicial independence issue relating to the qualifications of domestic courts referring to the CJEU. When a body forms part of the judicial structure of a Member State, and when there are sufficient rules under national law to guarantee the impartiality and independence of that body, Advocate General Wahl has argued that the court's analysis should not go any further when assessing compliance with the requirement of independence.[95]

Adopting this perspective, mainland China has legislation to protect judicial independence. The Criminal Procedure Law stipulates that the People's Courts follow legal provisions to independently exercise the power of adjudication, while the People's Public Prosecution Offices follow legal provisions to independently exercise prosecution powers and will not be interfered with by administrative organs, social groups, or individuals.[96] Specifically, in order to protect judicial independence and avoid the intervention of external or internal senior officials, the Central Leading Team for Comprehensively Deepening Reform approved the Regulation on Recording, Notification and Accountability of Officials' Intervening Judicial

92. See Case C-896/19, *Repubblika v. II-Prim Ministru* [Judgment of the Court, April 20, 2021], ¶10.
93. Case C-896/19, ¶56.
94. The Criminal Procedure Law and other legal documents which guarantee judicial independence will be discussed below: see infra, n 96–99.
95. Charlotte Reyns, "Saving Judicial Independence: A Threat to the Preliminary Ruling Mechanism?" *European Constitutional Law Review* 17 (2021): 19.
96. China Criminal Procedure Law, art. 5.

Activities and/or Handling Specific Cases in 2015.[97] Following that, the Supreme People's Court issued the Implementation Measures to implement the Regulation.[98] There has been a series of cases reported since the enforcement of the Regulation.[99]

The instances of courts which can be authorized should not be unduly limited. Under the European arrest warrant mechanism, we find that courts of appeal, district courts, and supreme courts can all oversee European arrest warrant cases.[100] In Hong Kong, it is the magistrates' court that is entrusted to handle surrender cases.[101] For the China arrest warrant system, this research recommends the most direct cooperation between the courts concerned. Thus, the Hong Kong magistrates' court can still be the executing or issuing authority of the surrender request. Accordingly, on the mainland China and Macau side, there should also be no limitations on the levels of judicial authorities. But in some comparatively undeveloped regions (such as Tibet and Xinjiang), for practical reasons, it can still be the intermediate courts that take charge of the surrender of fugitive offenders cases.[102]

4.3.4 Summarizing the roles of authorities in the surrender procedure

The China arrest warrant executing authorities should be judges in mainland China, Hong Kong, and Macau. The judges' role in executing surrender request has been fully proven to be effective in the EAW mechanism. In the European arrest warrant system, issuing judicial authorities are not limited to judges to respect the discretion of Member States, but this has increased complexity and disputes in reality. Since in the China arrest warrant system there are only three regions, for the simplicity of the surrender procedure and for the sufficient judicial protection of individuals, all of the China arrest warrant issuing authority can be judges. This can be found in Table 2.2 on page 58.

97. Relating to the text, see The First Circuit Court of the Supreme People's Court of the People's Republic of China, "Regulation on Recording, Notification and Accountability of Officials' Intervening Judicial Activities and/or Handling Specific Cases," December 30, 2020, http://www.court.gov.cn/xunhui1/xiangqing-282221.html.

98. Relating to the texts, see The First Circuit Court of the Supreme People's Court of the People's Republic of China, "Implementation Measures to implement the Regulation on Recording, Notification and Accountability of Officials' Intervening Judicial Activities and/or Handling Specific Cases," December 30, 2020, https://www.court.gov.cn/xunhui1/xiangqing-282241.html.

99. Chen Guangzhong 陈光中 et al., eds. *Zhongguo xiandai sifa zhidu* 中国现代司法制度 [China modern judicial system] (Beijing: Beijing daxue chubanshe, 2020), 217.

100. See Klimek, *European Arrest Warrant*, 79, n 55. See also Commission, "Report" 7, n 72.

101. Hong Kong Fugitive Offenders Ordinance, s. 2 pt. 1.

102. Regarding the problems the primary courts face in the foreign-related criminal case trials, see Project Team of People's Court in Huang Pu District, Shanghai 上海市黄浦区人民法院课题组, "Jiceng fayuan shenli shewai xingshi anjian jizhi de wanshan" 基层法院审理涉外刑事案件机制的完善 [The perfection of foreign-related criminal cases trial in primary courts], *Renmin sifa (Yingyong)* 15 (2015).

Table 2.2: The validity of a China arrest warrant

Region	Purpose	Issuing organ (regional decision)	Issuing organ (China arrest warrant)	China arrest warrant	Executing organ
Mainland China	Prosecute	Prosecutor or judge or police endorsed by the two above	Judge	Valid	Judge
	Execute, sentence, and detention order	Prosecutor or judge or police endorsed by the two above	Judge	Valid	Judge
Hong Kong	Prosecute	Prosecutor endorsed by court or judge or police endorsed by judge	Judge	Valid	Judge
	Execute, sentence, and detention order	Prosecutor endorsed by court or judge or police endorsed by judge	Judge	Valid	Judge
Macau	Prosecute	Prosecutor or judge or police endorsed by the two above	Judge	Valid	Judge
	Execute, sentence, and detention order	Prosecutor or judge or police endorsed by the two above	Judge	Valid	Judge

However, for issuing regional (local) arrest warrants or other regional (local) enforceable decisions on which the China arrest warrant is based, in principle, either prosecutors or judges can have power in line with the regional (local) laws. But if the decision is made by Hong Kong prosecutors, it should be endorsed by a Hong Kong court due to the fact that Hong Kong public prosecutors are affiliated to executive authorities. And, indeed, following the experience of the European arrest warrant, there is also the possibility that the police may issue regional (local) arrest warrants which must be endorsed by judicial authorities like courts or prosecutors. But whether the police has the duty to request or issue local arrest warrants or relevant decisions is still dependent on the regional (local) laws of the three regions.

5 Joint court needed

In the European arrest warrant system, the CJEU has an important role to play through its preliminary rulings. This offers an important guarantee of the protection of human rights in the surrender procedure. It also directly facilitates the role of judicial authorities.

From the CJEU experience, a joint court formed by judges from mainland China, Hong Kong, and Macau is needed. The establishment of a joint court is mainly based on the fact that the surrender of fugitive offenders issue goes beyond the individual interests of Hong Kong, Macau, or mainland China. The surrender concerns all the three regions as well as China on the whole. The judicial authorities from all the three regions should have a say when it comes to dispute settlement. The joint court can be based in Guangzhou (Guangdong Province), as a mainland capital city close to both Hong Kong and Macau which enjoys the geographical advantage being the location closest to the site of cross-border cases. This joint court can function as a "Regional Supreme Court" when a case concerns the surrender of persons between mainland China, Hong Kong, and Macau. With more domestic cooperation agreements concluded in future, the joint court can function to the full.

6 Conclusion

From the European Union experience, depoliticizing the surrender procedure speeds up cooperation and contributes to human rights protection. Combining these learnings with the political and legal reality in mainland China, Hong Kong, and Macau, this chapter finds that judicial authorities should be assigned the leading role in the China domestic surrender system. Following the general criteria applied in the European arrest warrant system, the courts in mainland China, Hong Kong, and Macau fall within the scope of judicial authorities and should take charge of issuing and executing China arrest warrants. The public prosecutors in mainland

China and Macau are also judicial authorities who may issue regional (local) judicial decisions which the China arrest warrant can be based on. The decision of Hong Kong public prosecutors as well as of the police in all the three regions should be endorsed by local judicial authorities before being valid in the China arrest warrant procedure. This research also suggests an institution, a joint court, can be set up to handle conflicts relating to the implementation of the China arrest warrant.

3
Conflicts of Criminal Jurisdiction

1 Introduction

Jurisdiction is the power of a sovereign to affect the rights of persons, whether by legislation, executive decree, or court judgment.[1] Criminal jurisdiction generally refers to the right of a state to prosecute, adjudicate, and punish crimes occurring within its sovereign domain.[2] Whether judicial cooperation can take place in criminal matters depends on whether there is criminal jurisdiction.[3] In international extradition, if the requested state does not recognize the requesting state's jurisdiction, it may refuse the extradition request.[4] The requested state may also refuse extradition if it regards itself as having criminal jurisdiction over requested persons.[5]

The China domestic surrender system also faces the problem of criminal jurisdiction between the three regions. Timely implementation of the surrender mechanism requires the conflict over how to recognize criminal jurisdiction to be settled.[6] The issue of how to delimit the criminal jurisdiction of the Mainland, Hong Kong, and Macau within a single country must be determined according to China's domestic laws, although comparable rules of international law may also be examined

1. Joseph H. Beale, "The Jurisdiction of a Sovereign State," *Harvard Law Review* 36, no. 3 (1923): 241.
2. See Gao Mingxuan 高铭暄, *Zhongguo xingfaxue yuanli* 中国刑法学原理 [Science of China criminal law] (Beijing: Zhongguo renmin daxue chubanshe, 1993), 276.
3. See Nie Lize 聂立泽, *GangAu yu neidi xingshi falü bijiao ji xingshi sifa xiezhu yanjiu* 港澳与内地刑事法律比较及刑事司法协助研究 [Comparative research on criminal law and criminal juridical cooperation between Hong Kong, Macau, and mainland China] (Beijing: Beijing daxue chubanshe, 2009), 206.
4. See Model Treaty on Extradition, art. 4(e).
5. See Model Treaty on Extradition, art. 4(a) and art. 4(f).
6. See Nie, *GangAu*, 221, 230, n 3.

and on occasion even relied upon.[7] At this time, neither a surrender agreement nor an arrangement on the settlement of criminal jurisdiction between the three regions has been put in place. The European Union has gone many steps further than China on these issues.

In this chapter, firstly, I analyze how conflict of criminal jurisdiction takes place in mainland China, Hong Kong, and Macau. Secondly, I analyze how conflict manifests and is addressed in the EU. Thirdly, I analyze how the European experience can inspire mainland China, Hong Kong, and Macau. Considering that negative conflict of criminal jurisdiction[8] is generally not a significant obstacle to cross-border judicial cooperation compared with positive conflict of criminal jurisdiction,[9] this chapter does not address it.

2 The emergence of conflict of criminal jurisdiction between mainland China, Hong Kong, and Macau

2.1 The cross-border movement of persons

Mainland China, Hong Kong, and Macau are physically close. Since Hong Kong and Macau returned to China, the movement of persons across borders has increased. Crime, too, is dynamic and cross-border. It is reported that a high number of the cases involving drug trafficking and other crimes occurring in Shenzhen (mainland China) is related to criminal organizations and individuals from Hong Kong and Macau.[10] The cross-border fact of these crimes leads to conflict of criminal jurisdiction.

On October 30, 1998, the Intermediate People's Court in Guangzhou tried a case involving over thirty defendants for, among other crimes, illegal trading,

7. See Ling Bing, "Applicability of the PRC Criminal Law in Hong Kong and the Prospect of a Rendition Agreement between Hong Kong and the Mainland," *Hong Kong Law Journal* 29 (1999): 394.
8. Negative conflict of criminal jurisdiction mainly refers to a situation in which, among several Member States with jurisdiction over certain facts constituting a criminal offence, none is willing to exercise their jurisdiction. See European Law Institute, "Report of the European Law Institute: Draft Legislative Proposals for the Prevention and Resolution of Conflicts of Jurisdiction in Criminal Matters in the European Union," p. 6, accessed October 30, 2022, https://www.europeanlawinstitute.eu/fileadmin/user_upload/p_eli/Publications/Conflict_of_Jurisdiction_in_Criminal_Law_FINAL.pdf.
9. Positive conflict of criminal jurisdiction mainly refers two or more Member States exercising, or intending to exercise, their jurisdiction over certain facts constituting a criminal offence. See European Law Institute, "Report," p. 6, n 8.
10. See Wang Zhongxing 王仲兴 and Guo Tianwu 郭天武, *Neidi yu Xianggang xingshi sifa hezuo yanjiu* 内地与香港刑事司法合作研究 [Research on criminal juridical cooperation between Hong Kong and mainland China] (Beijing: Beijing daxue chubanshe, 2008), 175.

transporting explosives, robbery, kidnapping, and trafficking weapons and ammunition.[11] Part of the criminal activity occurred in mainland China and part in Hong Kong, and both the Mainland and Hong Kong had criminal jurisdiction; moreover, the criminals were from both mainland China and Hong Kong, so both regions could apply national (or resident) jurisdiction. This kind of case is typical.

2.2 Three equal and independent legal regions

Criminal jurisdiction is a basic national power derived from the sovereignty doctrine.[12] But the conflict of criminal jurisdiction between mainland China, Hong Kong, and Macau is different from that in the European Union in that the conflict between the three Chinese regions is not derived from the sovereignty doctrine but rather from the national policy of "one country, two systems."[13] Under the two systems policy, mainland China, Hong Kong, and Macau all operate their own legal systems. Each region enjoys autonomy and supreme judicial power in their separate legal territories. The scope of application of any state's criminal law is, first and foremost, determined by reference to the scope of its territorial sovereignty.[14] Without territorial sovereignty, Hong Kong and Macau, as two special administrative regions of China, nonetheless enjoy their own criminal jurisdiction. This offers the background for the judicial conflict.

2.3 Legislation directly leads to the conflict of criminal jurisdiction

There are four relevant principles of criminal jurisdiction: the principle of territoriality; the principle of nationality (including the passive personality principle); the principle of protection; and the universal jurisdiction principle.[15]

---

11. See Nie, *Neidi*, 217–20, n 3.
12. In general, see Ian Brownlie, *Principles of Public International Law*, 5th ed. (Oxford: Clarendon Press, 1998), 105–6.
13. Since the three regions all are parts of People's Republic of China, the surrender of fugitive offenders as well as other forms of judicial cooperation in criminal matters between the three regions is regarded as an internal issue. See Miguel Manero de Lemos and Teresa Lancy Robalo, "Judicial Cooperation in Criminal Matters in the Special Administrative Regions of Hong Kong and Macau: Through the Lens of "One Country, Two Systems" and the Surrender of Fugitive Offenders to Mainland China," *Porto Alegre* 5 (2019): 756.
14. See Ling, "Applicability," 400, n 7.
15. See generally Michael Akehurst, "Jurisdiction in International Law," in *Jurisdiction in International Law*, ed. W. Michael Reisman (Aldershot: Ashgate/Dartmouth, 1999), 145–235. See also Brownlie, *"Principles,"* ch. 15, n 12.

The territorial principle classifies jurisdiction according to territory and is recognized in China's law.[16] The principle of nationality classifies jurisdiction according to the nationality of involved person; this means that China's criminal law is applicable to any Chinese national who commits a crime outside the territory of PRC.[17] The aim of the protection principle is to protect the interests of both the country and its citizens. Under this principle, foreigners who commit a crime against China or against its citizens outside the territory of China, if the minimum sentence is above 3 years' imprisonment, are subject to the criminal law of PRC, unless the offence is not punishable in the territory where the crime was committed.[18] As to the universal jurisdiction principle, the criminal law of the PRC provides that where a person, no matter their nationality, commits a crime specified in the international conventions China has concluded or joined, the judicial authorities of China can exercise criminal jurisdiction within the scope of the convention provisions.[19]

Hong Kong courts adopt the model of territorial jurisdiction over criminal offences according to common law to adjudicate criminal cases occurring within Hong Kong.[20] The nationality jurisdiction is also applied, but it is restricted. In addition, common law allows Hong Kong courts to exercise jurisdiction over offences that occur outside Hong Kong but have an impact on Hong Kong.[21] Overall, however, the territorial jurisdiction principle dominates the jurisdictional system.

The Basic Law of Macau confirms the criminal jurisdiction of the special administrative region.[22] Territorial jurisdiction is also specified in the criminal law of Macau.[23] Macau can be regarded as the place of a crime under certain circumstances: firstly, if the criminal commits several acts, or several criminals commit a crime together, and one of the several acts or one person's act occurred in Macau; secondly, for a crime of omission, the place of the crime is the place where the obligation is to be fulfilled, so if the actor is obliged to act in the territory of Macau then the omission is against the criminal law of Macau; thirdly, in a case where the criminal act and the criminal result occur in two different places, where the criminal

16. China Criminal Law, art. 6. This law is not applicable to Hong Kong and Macau.
17. China Criminal Law, art. 7.
18. China Criminal Law, art. 8.
19. China Criminal Law, art. 9.
20. *Halsbury's Laws of Hong Kong* (1998) 408.
21. See Chau Pak-kwan and Stephen Lam, "Research Study on the Agreement between Hong Kong and the Mainland Concerning Surrender of Fugitive Offenders" [March 2001], p. 53, Legislative Council Secretariat, Research and Library Services Division and Legal Service Division, Hong Kong, https://www.legco.gov.hk/yr00-01/english/library/erp05.pdf. Cf. *HKSAR v. Wong Tak Keung* (2015) 18 HKCFAR 158.
22. See Basic Law of Macau, art. 19 (2).
23. Penal Code of Macau, art. 4.

result occurred in Macau.[24] Besides the territorial principle, Macau also confirms the nationality principle, the protection principle, and the universal jurisdiction principle.[25]

In brief, mainland China, Hong Kong, and Macau all recognize the above four criminal jurisdiction principles. Therefore, in practice, the possibility of conflict of jurisdiction is high. For instance, relating to territorial jurisdiction, if a criminal commits a crime in both mainland China and Hong Kong or Macau, there will be a possibility that all three regions can investigate or try the case in question according to their own territorial jurisdiction principle.[26] If no consensus is achieved, not only can parallel investigations be undertaken, but parallel trials are also possible. This will do serious damage to human rights protection as well as depleting judicial resources. In practice, conflicts arise from not just one but several jurisdiction principles. For instance, in a case where the crime scenes and the origins of the criminals are dispersed across the three regions, a conflict of jurisdiction arises from two principles, namely, the territorial jurisdiction principle and the nationality jurisdiction principle.

3 Conflict of criminal jurisdiction in the EU

3.1 The emergence of conflict of criminal jurisdiction

3.1.1 Sovereignty and conflict of criminal jurisdiction

The European arrest warrant is implemented by twenty-seven separate and independent sovereign countries. Jurisdiction means "Each government has general power to exercise authority over all persons and things within its territory."[27] While jurisdiction is not based on territorial power, it is nevertheless true that law generally extends the jurisdiction of a sovereign throughout its own territories.[28] Within its own territory, the jurisdiction of the sovereign is exclusive, except in so far as it may by its own will permit the exercise of jurisdiction by another sovereign.[29] Thus the

24. Penal Code of Macau, art. 7.
25. Penal Code of Macau, art. 5.
26. See Wang Xinqing 王新清, "Lun GangAu tebie xingzhengqu yu neidi xingshi guanxiaquan de chongtu yu xietiao" 论港澳特别行政区与内地刑事管辖权的冲突与协调 [On the conflict and coordination of criminal jurisdiction between inland China and the special administrative regions of Hong Kong and Macau], *Faxuejia* 法学家 6 (2000): 98.
27. *Black's Law Dictionary*, 8th ed.; see also Maria Cacho, Maria del Carmen Rebolledo, and Maria Teresa Vadell, "The Themis Project: Solving Conflicts of Jurisdiction in the European Union," May 2012, Ministerio De Justicia, https://ejtn.eu/Documents/Themis%202012/THEMIS%20 2012%20ERFURT%20DOCUMENT/written%20paper%20Spain_Team%201.pdf.
28. See Beale, "The Jurisdiction," 245, n 1.
29. See Beale, "The Jurisdiction," 245, n 1.

Member State possesses its own jurisdiction, which is mostly exclusive to that singular sovereign country and cannot be subjected to intervention by another sovereign country. Such intervention will lead to a conflict of jurisdiction, including conflict of criminal jurisdiction. To a degree, conflict of criminal jurisdiction amounts to a conflict of sovereignty.

Sovereignty and jurisdiction are closely related concepts, and exercising jurisdiction is considered to be "one of the most obvious forms of the exercise of sovereign power."[30] In general, the right to exercise jurisdiction may reach as far as, but not beyond, the limits of sovereignty.[31] This is because, "if a state assumes jurisdiction outside the limits of its sovereignty, it . . . comes into conflict with other states which need not suffer any encroachment upon their own sovereignty."[32]

However, with the loss of full sovereignty in the EU, even Member States practicing their own territorial jurisdiction may conflict with other Member States over the same crime. The increase in transnational criminal activity which impacts more than one state, and the heightened desire to prosecute international crimes often on bases of jurisdiction other than territoriality, mean this tendency is becoming more pronounced.[33]

3.1.2 Domestic and regional legislation and conflict of criminal jurisdiction

Exclusive reliance on the territorial principle has proven to be impossible for any state; as a matter of practical necessity, bases of extraterritorial jurisdiction have developed.[34] It is well recognized in international law that a state's jurisdiction to prescribe is not limited by its territorial boundaries.[35] Different national laws on competence and jurisdiction include provisions that extend the jurisdiction of Member States (MSs) to crimes committed outside their boundaries.

The principles of active nationality and passive nationality are recognized by the EU's Member States. That means if an offence has been committed in State A

30. Legal Status of Eastern Greenland, PCIJ Series A/B, No.53 [Judgment of the Permanent Court of International Justice, April 5, 1933], 48.
31. F.A. Mann, "The Doctrine of Jurisdiction in International Law," *Recueil des Cours de L'Academie de Droit International* 11 (1964): 16. See also F.A. Mann, "The Doctrine of International Jurisdiction Revisited after 20 Years," *Recueil des Cours de l'Academie de Droit International* 86 (1984): 20.
32. Mann, "Doctrine of Jurisdiction," 30, n 31.
33. See Katharine Emilia May Brookson-Morris, "Choosing the Right Forum: Competing Jurisdictional Competences in the Sphere of International, Transnational and National Crimes" (MPhil thesis, University of Birmingham, 2015), 41, https://core.ac.uk/download/pdf/42551227.pdf.
34. See Morris, "Choosing the Right Forum," 70, n 33.
35. See Ling, "Applicability," 401, n 7.

but the offender is a national of State B and the victim a national of State C, then State A, State B, and State C may all exercise jurisdiction over the case on the basis of their individual domestic laws. It is evident that where a regulation is in force in every European Member State, hundreds of cross-prosecutions could take place all over the EU.[36] This scenario has been worsened by the fact of some international instruments establishing the principle of extra-territoriality with a view to strengthening the fight against serious crime and avoiding negative conflicts of jurisdiction.[37] As a result, national authorities have universal competence on a set of offences.[38] European instruments that call upon Member States to make certain facts indictable contribute to the broadening of national court jurisdiction.[39]

3.1.3 Migration flows and conflict of criminal jurisdiction

Increased migration flows worldwide bring more concerns. The globalization phenomenon has made it much easier for people to move from one country to another for whatever reason, including tourism, study, work, or business. Unfortunately, some people have taken advantage of this shift to establish or enlarge criminal associations and operate them with several contact points.[40]

The characteristics of crime itself also worsen the situation. These include the internationalization of crime, due to the existence of criminal organizations that operate in different Member States, and the fact that a great number of crimes are committed through technological means that have connections to various jurisdictions.[41] All of these trigger conflicts of jurisdiction.

36. Willem Bas Van Bockel, "The *Ne Bis in Idem* Principle in EU Law," *Kluwer Law International BV* (2010): 37–38.
37. For a detailed overview of universal jurisdiction issues, see Amnesty International, "Universal Jurisdiction: The Duty of States to Enact and Enforce Legislation," August 31, 2001, https://www.amnesty.org/en/documents/ior53/008/2001/en/.
38. Armando A. Cottim, "Cybercrime, Cyberterrorism and Jurisdiction: An Analysis of Art. 22 of the COE Convention on Cybercrime," *European Journal of Legal Studies* 2, no. 3 (2010): 7, https://www.ejls.eu/6/78UK.pdf.
39. See Giulia Giacomelli, "*Ne Bis in Idem* Profiles in EU Criminal Law" (Master's thesis, Universita Deglistudi Firenze, 2014) 6, https://archiviodpc.dirittopenaleuomo.org/upload/1422126174full%20text%204917958%20GIACOMELLI.pdf.
40. Giacomelli, "*Ne Bis in Idem*," 6, n 39.
41. See Nathalie Isabelle Thorhauer, "Conflicts of Jurisdiction in Cross-Border Criminal Cases in the Area of Freedom, Security, and Justice: Risks and Opportunities from an Individual Rights-Oriented Perspective," *New Journal of European Criminal Law* 6, no. 1 (2015): 78.

3.2 Addressing conflicts of criminal jurisdiction

The EAW Framework Decision does not resolve conflicts of criminal jurisdiction directly. Instead, it recognizes general criminal jurisdiction principles and the existence of conflict, leaving discretion over cooperation to the requested state. For instance, surrender may be refused if the requested person is staying in, or is a national or resident of, the executing Member State (the nationality principle).[42] Surrender may also be refused if the act of the requested person has been committed in whole or in part in the executing Member State (the territoriality principle).[43] The executing Member State also has the discretion to refuse surrender if the acts have been committed outside the territory of the issuing Member State and the executing Member State does not prescribe such jurisdiction.[44] However, the question of criminal jurisdiction is not exclusive to the executing Member State, especially where conflicts between Member States occur. Certain institutions and rules have been established at the EU level to cope with the problem.

3.2.1 Eurojust: The organization addressing conflict of criminal jurisdiction

In order to reinforce the fight against serious organized crime, the Tampere European Council decided to set up a unit, Eurojust,[45] formally established in 2002.[46] Eurojust is composed of one national member seconded by each Member State in accordance with its legal system, being a prosecutor, judge, or police officer of equivalent competence.[47] The main objective of Eurojust is to stimulate and improve coordination among competent authorities of Member States in investigations and prosecutions, and to facilitate the execution of international mutual legal assistance and the implementation of extradition requests between Member States.[48] Eurojust is the main body for resolving conflicts of criminal jurisdiction, and must be informed of any case where conflicts of jurisdiction have arisen or are likely to arise. A case can be referred to Eurojust at any moment, if at least one competent authority involved in

42. See EAW FD, art. 4(6).
43. See EAW FD, art. 4(7)(a).
44. See EAW FD, art. 4(7)(b).
45. See European Parliament, "Tampere European Council 15 and 16 October 1999 Presidency Conclusions," para 46, accessed October 30, 2022, https://www.europarl.europa.eu/summits/tam_en.htm. At that time, the UK was still an EU Member State.
46. See Council Decision 2002/187/JHA of February 28, 2002, setting up Eurojust with a view to reinforcing the fight against serious crime [2002] OJ L63/1.
47. Council Decision, art. 2, n 46.
48. Council Decision, art. 3, n 46.

the direct consultations deems it appropriate.[49] Eurojust also issues guidelines that clarify which jurisdiction should prosecute in different types of conflict.[50]

3.2.2 The criteria used to address a conflict of criminal jurisdiction

Eurojust has played a key role in improving cooperation in criminal matters between Member States, and a significant aspect of this role is facilitating the execution of EAWs. Member States request the assistance of Eurojust when making decisions in the face of multiple EAW requests.[51] Eurojust has issued guidelines to settle problems of competing European arrest warrants.[52] The guidelines for deciding which jurisdiction should prosecute illustrate how Eurojust works in this regard.[53]

Regarding choice of jurisdiction, the Eurojust guideline calls for a preliminary presumption that, if possible, prosecution should take place in the jurisdiction where the majority of the criminality occurred or where the majority of the loss was sustained. The guideline also suggests that when reaching a decision, prosecutors should balance carefully and fairly all the factors both for and against commencing a prosecution in each jurisdiction where it is possible to do so. The factors which should be taken into consideration include the location of the accused, the attendance of witnesses, the interests of victims, and evidentiary problems.[54]

Besides the factors that should be considered, there are others which should not. Prosecutors must not decide to prosecute in one jurisdiction over another simply to avoid complying with legal obligations, for the sake of sentencing powers, or for more effective recovery of the proceeds of crime.[55]

49. See Council Decision 2009/948/JHA of 30 November 2009 on the prevention and settlement of conflicts of exercise of jurisdiction in criminal proceedings [2009] 0JL328/42, Preamble (14).
50. See Eurojust, "Guidelines for Deciding Which Jurisdiction Should Prosecute?" revised 2016, accessed October 30, 2022, https://www.eurojust.europa.eu/sites/default/files/Publications/Reports/2016_Jurisdiction-Guidelines_EN.pdf.
51. See EAW FD, art. 16.
52. See Eurojust, "Guidelines for deciding on competing requests for surrender and extradition," revised 2019, accessed October 30, 2022, https://www.eurojust.europa.eu/sites/default/files/Publications/Reports/2019-10_Guidelines-competing-extradition-surrender-EAW_EN.pdf.
53. See Eurojust, "Guidelines," n 50.
54. See Eurojust, "Guidelines," n 50.
55. See Eurojust, "Guidelines," n 50.

3.3 The characteristics of resolving conflicts of criminal jurisdiction

3.3.1 Flexibility

After years of practice, the Eurojust Guidelines on which jurisdiction should prosecute have proven very useful, particularly in view of their flexibility and reasonableness. As each case is different, the variety of factors allows that, in each case, the position and interests of all involved parties and all relevant aspects of the case can be taken into account.[56]

Even though "territoriality" and, in particular, the place where the majority of the criminal acts took place remains a dominant criterion, it is also clear that it is not an all-decisive factor. For instance, in cross-border cases where criminal acts take place in different Member States, other factors—such as the nationality or residence of the defendant(s) and/or victim(s), the advanced stage of the proceedings, the broader scope of the investigations, or the place where most evidence is present—often play a decisive role.[57] Even in cases in which the criminal offence takes place in a single Member State, there still can be overriding reasons to decide that another Member State is in a better position to prosecute a case. For example, if some Italian friends go to Sweden on vacation and one of them commits a crime against another, the best place to prosecute would not be Sweden but Italy. The victim, perpetrator, and witnesses are Italian, and, therefore, after discussion, coordination, and consensus, agreement could be reached to hold the trial in Italy, even though the crime was committed in another Member State.[58]

3.3.2 Flexibility needs to be balanced

Although in the majority of cases a problem can be solved without the need for a binding decision, in other cases such binding power could have prevented the conflict from arising and would have facilitated both the exchange of information and the gathering of evidence.[59] There have been proposals to create hierarchy criteria as well as binding decisions to settle conflicts of criminal jurisdiction.[60]

---

56. See Eurojust, "Guidelines," n 50.
57. See Eurojust, "Guidelines," n 50.
58. See Eurojust, "Guidelines," n 50.
59. See Catherine Deboyser, "Eurojust's Role in the Matter of Choice of Forum," in *Choice of Forum in Cooperation Against EU Financial Crimes: Freedom, Security and Justice and the Protection of Specific EU-Interests*, ed. Michiel J. J. P. Luchtman (The Hague: Eleven International Publishing, 2013): 101, 108.
60. See European Law Institute, "Report of the European Law Institute: Draft Legislative Proposals for the Prevention and Resolution of Conflicts of Jurisdiction in Criminal Matters in the European

However, flexibility is welcomed by most Member States, and Member States are clearly not in favor of a mandatory ranking order of jurisdictional rules or mandatory coordination mechanisms.[61] For now, Eurojust cannot force a resolution either. When Member States fail to reach agreement among themselves, the agency cannot compel Member States to bring criminal proceedings. But this idea can be considered by mainland China, Hong Kong, and Macau when addressing their conflicts of criminal jurisdiction.

4 The settlement of conflicts of criminal jurisdiction between mainland China, Hong Kong, and Macau

4.1 Addressing conflicts of criminal jurisdiction at present

In the China domestic surrender system, criminal jurisdiction is an unavoidable issue.[62] The prerequisite for a successful and swift surrender is that the requested region lacks criminal jurisdiction over the case involved or waives that jurisdiction and the requesting region does have criminal jurisdiction—in other words, the surrender of fugitive offenders should be based on clarification of criminal jurisdiction. Conflicts of criminal jurisdiction between mainland China, Hong Kong, and Macau have been evident in a series of actual cases as well as in legislation *per se*, so there is need for a resolution in which the EU experience can be useful.

In 1997 and 1998 a series of robberies committed by Xie Wenguang, Zhang Lizhong, and others in Macau produced several judicial cases.[63] All of the robberies took place in Macau, thus according to the territoriality principle Macau should have criminal jurisdiction.[64] However, the Supreme People's Court designated Zhuhai Intermediate Court in Guangdong Province to try the case on the grounds that one of defendants was mainland Chinese and that Mainland authorities first controlled the case in terms of investigation and trial.[65] Here, the Mainland authority prioritized

---

Union," accessed October 30, 2022, https://www.europeanlawinstitute.eu/fileadmin/user_upload/p_eli/Publications/Conflict_of_Jurisdiction_in_Criminal_Law_FINAL.pdf.

61. See Michiel Luchtman, "Choice of Forum in an Area of Freedom, Security and Justice," *Utrecht Law Review* 7 (2011): 9.
62. See Zhang Xu 张旭, *Guoji xingfa* 国际刑法 [International criminal law: Present and prospect] (Beijing: Qinghua daxue chubanshe, 2005), 338.
63. Zhong Zheping, Hung Xi, and Liu Hailing, "Yue-Au jingfang lianshou pouhuo zhuanjie dixia qianzhuang de yi Aomen heibang" [Guangdong and Macau police join hands in cracking down on the Macau gang," *Yangcheng wanbao*, November 29, 1999, http://news.sina.com.cn/china/1999-11-29/36372.html.
64. Penal Code of Macau, art. 4.
65. See Li Lepeng 李乐鹏, "Aomen xingshi guanxiaquan dulixing yanjiu" 澳门刑事管辖权独立性研究 [Discussion on the independence of the criminal jurisdiction of Macau], *Yiguo liangzhi* 4 (2012): 66.

the "nationality principle" over the territoriality principle, which went against tradition. What's more, the Mainland authority also relied on the "first control" principle to win criminal jurisdiction, notwithstanding that the jurisdiction that first prosecutes is not necessarily the jurisdiction best-placed to do so.[66]

On March 17, 2016, the Appeal Court of Macau heard a case on the recognition of criminal jurisdiction.[67] In this case, both the suspect and the victim were Macau residents and lived in Macau. The suspect injured the victim in mainland China, and both the act and the result occurred in the Mainland. The criminal law of Macau could apply to criminal acts committed beyond its territory, if the criminal had not been tried in the place where the crime occurred, or where the criminal avoided punishment there.[68] After checking that there was no judgment from the Mainland on the case, the court in Macau could assert criminal jurisdiction without violating the rule against double jeopardy.[69] In this case, although the Mainland judicial authority could have relied upon the territoriality principle to try the case, it did not.

There was also the famous "Zhang Ziqiang" case of 1998.[70] Although the main criminal act took place in Hong Kong, the High People's Court of Guangdong Province held that all of the preparatory criminal acts took place in mainland China, and the Mainland authority first controlled the case, so the court in mainland China had criminal jurisdiction.[71] In this case, the Mainland authority relied on both the territoriality and first-control principles to assert criminal jurisdiction, although Hong Kong also could rely on the territoriality and nationality (resident identity) principles to exercise jurisdiction.

The above three cases show that sometimes mainland China relies on the nationality principle to implement criminal jurisdiction, as in the case of Xie Wenguang; sometimes it relies on the territoriality principle, as with Zhang Ziqiang's case; sometimes it doesn't ask for jurisdiction, even when there exists a strong basis on which to apply the territoriality principle. The criteria for the confirmation of criminal jurisdiction between the three regions have changed from case to case. There is a risk of forum shopping to the detriment of the accused; an already undesirable situation where the location for the trial is determined by coincidence would become worse if prosecution authorities had the option to freely choose a jurisdiction.[72]

66. See Giacomelli, "*Ne Bis in Idem*," 2, n 39.
67. See Macau criminal appeal, case no. 818/2012, March 17, 2016, https://www.court.gov.mo/sentence/zh/19737.
68. Penal Code of Macau, art. 6.
69. Penal Code of Macau, art. 6.
70. See An Ping, "Zhang Ziqiang's Criminal Gang Case," *People's Court News*, July 23, 2019, https://www.chinacourt.org/art./detail/2019/07/id/4200356.shtml.
71. See Nie, *GangAu*, 220, n 3.
72. See Frank Zimmermann, "Conflicts of Criminal Jurisdiction in the European Union," *Bergen Journal of Criminal Law and Criminal Justice* 3 (2015): 6.

Taking Zhang Ziqiang's case as an example, both Hong Kong and the Mainland had criminal jurisdiction. The death penalty is practiced in the Mainland but abolished in Hong Kong. If criminal jurisdiction were exercised by Hong Kong, there would be no chance that Zhang Ziqiang would be executed.[73] In the end, the settlement of this conflict of criminal jurisdiction lacked, among other things, transparency and objectivity, which aroused public suspicion of the government.[74]

4.2 Improvements in settling conflicts of criminal jurisdiction between mainland China, Hong Kong, and Macau

4.2.1 An organization should be established to address conflicts of criminal jurisdiction

In the European Union, although both the CJEU and Eurojust can address conflicts of criminal jurisdiction,[75] it is Eurojust, an independent and impartial authority, that plays the main role in settling conflicts.[76] Eurojust can stimulate and improve coordination between competent authorities in investigations and prosecutions among Member States and facilitate the implementation of extradition requests between Member States. Requesting states request guidance from Eurojust and Eurojust offers opinions which are flexible and non-binding. Between mainland China, Hong Kong, and Macau, there is no such organization in place. Considering that the jurisdictions are three equal legal territories, a regional committee can be established.[77] This organization would function to speed up police cooperation between the three regions and contribute to the settlement of conflict between criminal jurisdictions, especially at the prosecutorial stage. The organization could consist of scholars as well as practitioners from the three regions. It could offer binding decisions subject to judicial review.[78] The committee can be set up as a permanent organization.

---

73. See UN006, "Zhang Ziqiang Was Executed on November 12, 1998," *People's Net*, November 12, 2011, http://news.sohu.com/20111112/n325374402.shtml.
74. "Government clarifies the reports on the Zhang Ziqiang case," *Press Release*, November 6, 1998, https://www.info.gov.hk/gia/general/199811/06/1106188.htm.
75. Mainly through the cases on *ne bis in idem*, details can be seen in Chapter 4 on *Ne Bis in Idem*.
76. See Annika Suominen, "The Past, Present and Future of Eurojust," *Maastricht Journal of European and Comparative Law* 9 (2008): 233. See also Anne-Sophie Massa, "Jurisdiction in England and Wales and in the Netherlands: A Comparative Appraisal with a European Touch," in *Substantive Criminal Law of the European Union*, ed. André Klip (Antwerpen: Maklu, 2011), 120.
77. See Nie, *GangAu*, 211, n 3.
78. Regarding this, see European Law Institute, "Report of the European Law Institute: Draft Legislative Proposal for the Prevention and Resolution of Conflicts of Jurisdiction in Criminal Matters in the European Union," accessed October 30, 2022, https://www.europeanlawinstitute.eu/fileadmin/user_upload/p_eli/Publications/Conflict_of_Jurisdiction_in_Criminal_Law_FINAL.pdf.

Resolving conflicts of jurisdiction can be one of its functions, and similarly to Eurojust, its activities can extend to addressing other criminal cooperation issues.

4.2.2 A possible framework decision on settlement of conflicts of criminal jurisdiction should be drawn

The European Union has its Framework Decision on the Settlement of Criminal Jurisdiction. Presently, mainland China, Hong Kong, and Macau address disputes over conflict of jurisdiction in a flexible, case-by-case manner, because there is no legal document they can rely on to guide their resolution. This is problematic because too much flexibility means a lack of legal certainty. Thus, it is necessary to construct a framework decision for the settlement of conflicts of criminal jurisdiction. Important decisions including in which jurisdiction a suspect will be tried should be guided by legislation to the greatest possible extent.[79] In the European Union, conflicts of jurisdiction are prevented by establishing uniform Europe-wide rules that allocate the exercise of criminal jurisdiction in the interests of freedom, security, and justice.[80]

4.2.3 Criteria to settle conflicts of criminal jurisdiction should be drafted

The framework decision contains criteria for settling conflicts of jurisdiction, such as the crime's locality, the offender's residence, and the victim's residence. Chinese scholars argue that the settlement of such conflicts between mainland China, Hong Kong, and Macau should be based on the territoriality principle.[81] In other words, criminal jurisdiction over the three regions should be delineated first by administrative territory. All criminal acts that occur Hong Kong and Macau should thus be punished by Hong Kong and Macau judicial authorities, just as crimes occurring in the Mainland should be tried by a Mainland authority, whether the criminal is mainland Chinese, a Hong Kong resident, a Macau resident, a foreigner, or a stateless person.

79. See Zimmermann, "Conflict of Criminal Jurisdiction," 6, n 72.
80. See European Law Institute, "Report," p. 18, n 60.
81. See Liu Guoxiang 刘国祥, "Zhongguo xingfa kongjian shiyong fanwei de lifa gaijin" 中国刑法空间适用范围的立法改进 [Legislative improvements on the spatial scope of application of Chinese criminal law], in *Xingfa xiugai Jianyi wenji* 刑法修改建议文集 [Collected essays on suggested changes in criminal law], ed. Gao Mingxuan (Beijing: Renmin daxue chubanshe, 1997), 201.

Similarly, the European Union suggests that the grounds for exercising jurisdiction should be based on territoriality, and that Member States should no longer exercise jurisdiction on the basis of extraterritorial jurisdiction principles, such as the active or passive nationality of the accused or victim.[82] Chinese scholars offer more detailed and practical analysis of this question by pointing out that if the preparation and actual act of a crime occur in different regions, the region that suffers the most loss should enjoy criminal jurisdiction; if regional losses do not vary much, then criminal jurisdiction should be designated for the sake of convenience in terms of getting access to witnesses and evidence.[83]

4.2.4 Specific clauses should be written within the surrender system

In the China domestic surrender system, criminal jurisdiction based on the territoriality principle can still be an optional ground on which to refuse cooperation. Although one cannot refuse surrender on the sole ground of nationality (resident identity), it can still be invoked when seeking the return of offenders to requested regions to complete their sentences there. This is done mainly for the purpose of social integration of the requested persons. The *ne bis in idem* can still be applied, but not as a tool to settle the conflict of criminal jurisdiction, rather to protect the rights of the requested person. Professor John Vervaele pointed out that the rationale behind *ne bis in idem* was not to prevent and settle conflicts of criminal jurisdiction:[84] it should be the last chance to balance the state's interest in prosecuting with the individuals' right not to face double proceedings for the same committal fact.[85] The following chapter offers more discussion on *ne bis in idem*.

5 Conclusion

As in the case of EU Member States, conflicts of criminal jurisdiction between mainland China, Hong Kong, and Macau come from legislation on criminal jurisdiction in different legal territories as well as the conjunction of criminal elements in reality. The Union's experience of settling conflicts of criminal jurisdiction offers

82. See European Law Institute, "Report," p. 27, n 60.
83. See Zhao Guoqiang 赵国强, "Lun 'Yiguo liangzhi' xiade yijiao taofan jizhi" 论"一国两制"下的移交逃犯机制 [The discussion of the surrender of fugitive-offenders mechanism under "one country, two systems"] *Xingzheng* 行政 20, no. 78 (2007): 1059.
84. See Michiel Luchtman, "Transnational Law Enforcement in the European Union and the *Ne Bis in Idem* Principle," *Review of European Administrative Law* 4 (2011): 5–29.
85. See Giacomelli, "*Ne Bis in Idem*," 2, n 39.

several important examples that mainland China, Hong Kong, and Macau can use. This research suggests that a specific organization, like the EU's Eurojust, should be established in mainland China, Hong Kong, and Macau. The Eurojust criteria to resolve conflicts of criminal jurisdiction can also be introduced to mainland China, Hong Kong, and Macau. A uniform framework decision or other legal instrument should be enacted to guarantee the legality and efficiency of criminal jurisdiction settlement.

4

The Application of *Ne Bis in Idem*

1 Introduction

Ne bis in idem,[1] the principle that no one should be prosecuted or tried twice for the same act and for the same criminal behavior,[2] is an important principle in the international extradition system. Generally, it is used as a mandatory ground for refusal of extradition.[3] In the China domestic surrender system, whether the principle of *ne bis in idem* can be applied as a ground for refusal of surrender remains open to question. The opinion exists that in the settlement of conflicts of criminal jurisdiction between mainland China, Hong Kong, and Macau *ne bis in idem* should be applied.[4] Scholars additionally argue that the application of the principle will contribute to the fight against cross-border crime.[5] How *ne bis in idem* is to be applied is also debatable.

Ne bis in idem is a principle that should be applied domestically, since mainland China, Hong Kong, and Macau all belong to the PRC. However, it is also the fact that the three regions constitute three independent legal territories, with their own bodies of criminal law and procedure in which the principle of *ne bis in idem*

1. In this book, *ne bis in idem* will not be distinguished from double jeopardy unless the two terms are respectively discussed.
2. See "Initiative of the Hellenic Republic with a View to Adopting a Council Framework Decision Concerning the Application of the 'Ne Bis in Idem' Principle" [2003] OJ C100/12, Preamble (1).
3. As to which see the following section 3.
4. See Chen Yongsheng 陈永生, "Yishi buzaili yu Zhongguo quji xingshi guanxia chongtu de jiejue" 一事不再理与中国区际刑事管辖冲突的解决 [*Ne bis in idem* and the settlement of conflict of criminal jurisdiction in the greater China region], *Yanjiusheng faxue* 1 (1988): 8.
5. See Huang Feng 黄风 and Peng Shengjuan 彭胜娟, "Cong zhouzhengyi an guanxia chongtu kan quji xingsu yiguan zhidu zhi goujian" 从周正毅案管辖冲突看区际刑诉移管制度之构建 [Construction of the system of transfer of criminal proceedings from the conflict of regional criminal jurisdiction of the Zhou Zhengyi case], *Faxue* 法学 7 (2007): 131.

is separately addressed. According to the Basic Law of Hong Kong and the Basic Law of Macau, neither mainland China's criminal law nor its procedural law can be applied in Hong Kong or Macau; accordingly, the *ne bis in idem* principle cannot be applied directly.[6] It remains unclear whether *ne bis in idem* is applicable to the China domestic surrender system, but it matters if and how it can be applied.[7]

In this chapter, I first analyze the legislative disagreement over *ne bis in idem* between the three regions. Secondly, I give a brief introduction to the domestic application of *ne bis in idem* throughout the world. Thirdly, I analyze the use of *ne bis in idem* in judicial cooperation in criminal matters globally. Fourthly, I discuss the application of *ne bis in idem* in the European Union, especially in the European arrest warrant mechanism. Fifthly, I argue that the *ne bis in idem* principle should be applied to the China domestic surrender system.

2 The dispute over *ne bis in idem* in the three legal territories

Mainland China's criminal procedural law has no rule of *ne bis in idem*.[8] Generally, a final judgment should follow two instances of court trial and the court of second instance should be the court of last instance.[9] However, mainland China law also recognizes the procedure for trial supervision, or retrial procedure. According to China Criminal Procedure Law, under certain situations the retrial procedure for the final judgment (verdict or acquittal) can be initiated. These situations include: new evidence proving that the original final judgment or ruling was wrongly issued so as to possibly affect conviction or sentencing; uncertain and insufficient evidence forming the basis of the original final judgment, which should have been excluded, and which proves contradictory facts in the main evidence; the original final judgment or ruling proving wrong in its application of the law; a breach of due process which may affect a fair trial; or corrupt judges, favoritism, or irregularities in or

6. See Basic Law of Hong Kong, art. 18, and Basic Law of Macau, art. 18.
7. See Wang Shuo 王朔, "Guanxia chongtu yu quji xietiao: shilun Zhongguo Gang-Ao diqu xingshi panjue zai Zhongguo neidi de shiyong" 管辖冲突与区际协调–试论中国港澳地区刑事判决在中国内地的适用 [Conflict of jurisdiction and regional coordination: study of the application of criminal judgment from Hong Kong and Macau to mainland China] *Fazhi shehui* 法治社会 4 (2018): 81. See also Hu Lusheng 胡陆生 and Li Jianghai 李江海, "Guonei butong fayu taofan yijiao wenti de jiejue silu" 国内不同法域逃犯移交问题的解决思路 [Train of thought behind solving the problem of transferring escaped criminals between a country's different judicial regions], *Faxue luntan* 法学论坛 5 (2009): 119.
8. See Chen Lan 陈岚 and Wang Lisha 王丽莎, "Lianxufan yu yishi buzaili yuanze de shiyong tantao" 连续犯与一事不再理原则的适用探讨 [Continuing offence and application of *ne bis in idem*], *Faxue pinglun* 法学评论 3 (2006): 130.
9. China Criminal Procedure Law, art. 10. If the judgment or ruling is issued by the Supreme People's Court, it will be the final judgment; see China Criminal Procedure Law, art. 244.

perversions of the law affecting the final judgment.[10] In recent years, the application of retrial procedure has been less frequent,[11] and the procedure has been criticized and evoked calls for reform,[12] however it retains an important role in correcting wrongful convictions.[13]

As a general practice, mainland China does not recognize foreign criminal judgments.[14] The China Criminal Law specifies that all crimes which occur beyond its borders, if accountable pursuant to this law, can be investigated even after trial in foreign territories; if a sentence has been served in a foreign territory, punishment can be waived or mitigated.[15] This has been seen as contradictory to the international *ne bis in idem* principle.[16] However, China does invoke *ne bis in idem* in extradition with foreign countries, as is discussed in the final section of this chapter.

In Hong Kong, the principle of *ne bis in idem* is well established. It is specified both in the Hong Kong Bill of Rights Ordinance and the Criminal Procedure Ordinance. The principle of *ne bis in idem* in Hong Kong means that no one shall be liable to trial or punishment twice for an offence for which he has already been finally convicted or acquitted in accordance with the law and penal procedure of Hong Kong. Certain conditions must be satisfied in order to apply this principle.[17] The present offence served to the accused must be the same offence in law as the one for which the accused has been acquitted or convicted in a previous trial; the

10. China Criminal Procedure Law, art. 253.

11. See Wang Minyuan, "Xingshi susong faxue yanjiu de zhuanxing–yi xingshi zaishen wenti weili de fenxi" 刑事诉讼法学研究的转型–以刑事再审问题为例的分析 [The transformation of criminal procedure law: analyzing the issue of criminal retrial], *Faxue yanjiu* 法学研究 5 (2011), accessed October 30, 2022, http://www.procedurallaw.cn/info/1005/2060.htm.

12. See Xiong Qiuhong 熊秋红, "Jinzhi shuangchong weixian yuanze goujian" 禁止双重危险原则构建 [The construction of double jeopardy], accessed October 30, 2022, http://iolaw.cssn.cn/zxzp/200710/t20071029_4600470.shtml.

13. See He Jiahong 何家弘 and Liu Yifan 刘译矾, "Xingshi cuo'an shensu zaishen zhidu shizheng yanjiu" 刑事错案申诉再审制度实证研究 [Empirical study of the system of retrial for wrongly convicted cases], *Guojia jianchaguan xueyuan xuebao* 国家检察官学院学报 6 (2015). See also Chen Yongsheng 陈永生 and ShaoCong 邵聪, "Yuan'an nanyi jiuzheng de zhidu fansi: yi shenpan jiandu chengxu wei zhongdian de fenxi" 冤案难以纠正的制度反思：以审判监督程序为重点的分析 [Systematic reflection on the difficulty of correcting wrongly convicted cases: a focus on the trial supervision procedure], *Bijiaofa yanjiu* 比较法研究 4 (2018), accessed October 30, 2022, https://www.thepaper.cn/newsDetail_forward_8642497.

14. See Wang Zheng 王铮, "Zhixing xingshi panjue zhong de guoji sifa hezuo" 执行刑事判决中的国际司法合作 [International judicial cooperation in executing criminal judgments], *Bijiaofa yanjiu* 比较法研究 3 (1997): 273.

15. See China Criminal Law, art. 10.

16. See Huang Baiqing 黄柏青, *Guoji xingshi sifa hezuo zhong de yishi buzaili yuanze* 国际刑事司法合作中的一事不再理原则 [Study of *ne bis in idem* in judicial cooperation in criminal matters] (Shanghai: Shanghai renmin chubanshe, 2011), 58.

17. See *Yeung Chun Pong v. Secretary for Justice* (2009) 12 HKCFAR 867; *Ubamaka Edward Wilson v. Secretary for Security* (2012) 15 HKCFAR 743; *HKSAR v. Fu Man Kit* (2021) 24 HKCFAR 253.

accused must be at real risk of being convicted of the same offence as in a previous trial; the acquittal or conviction must have been valid; and the acquittal or conviction of the previous offence must have been final.[18]

In Macau, the *ne bis in idem* rule is also applied. Macau has ratified the International Covenant on Civil and Political Rights (ICCPR), so the *ne bis in idem* principle can be implemented directly from that.[19] Macau Criminal Law also specifies for acts which have occurred outside the territory that the application of relevant laws should be limited to acts which have not been punished in the place of occurrence or for which the perpetrator has escaped from fulfilling all or partial punishment.[20] This clause clearly contrasts with Article 10 of the China Criminal Law which stipulates that acts outside mainland China can still can be investigated and tried in the Mainland.[21]

In brief, both Hong Kong and Macau apply the principle of *ne bis in idem* in their own legal territories, and mainland China does not apply the principle of *ne bis in idem* domestically but implements the accounting principle and accepts foreign criminal decisions passively. This provokes the question whether the *ne bis in idem* principle can be applied to the China domestic surrender system. In international and European law, positions on the application of *ne bis in idem* can offer inspiration to mainland China, Hong Kong, and Macau as they seek to address their domestic issue.

3 The domestic application of *ne bis in idem* around the world

3.1 The main international conventions recognizing the domestic application of ne bis in idem

Ne bis in idem is a general principle of criminal law in many national legal orders, sometimes even codified as a constitutional right. It has also been established as an individual right in international legal instruments on human rights.[22] In the common law system, the principle of double jeopardy is generally used as a human

18. See Law Reform Commission of Hong Kong, "Double Jeopardy Consultation Paper," March 2010, https://www.gov.hk/en/residents/government/publication/consultation/docs/2010/DoubleJeopardy.pdf.
19. See the Signatory Member State's Report, submitted to the UN Human Rights Committee pursuant to Article 40 of the International Covenant on Civil and Political Rights for the Sensation, Point 353.
20. See Penal Code of Macau, art. 6.
21. See China Criminal Law, art. 10.
22. John A.E. Vervaele, "The Transnational *Ne Bis in Idem* Principle in the EU: Mutual Recognition and Equivalent Protection of Human Rights," *Utrecht Law Review* 1, no. 2 (2005): 100.

rights protection measure; similarly, in the civil law system, the principle of *ne bis in idem* is used for the sake of judicial sovereignty as well as human rights protection.[23] Additionally, *ne bis in idem* can help to better achieve the benefits of litigation by reducing waste of litigation resources.[24] It is also a way to settle conflicts of criminal jurisdiction.[25] The domestic application of *ne bis in idem* has been recognized by a series of international and regional conventions.

The ICCPR specifies that no one shall be liable to be tried or punished again for an offence for which he has already been finally convicted or acquitted in accordance with the law and penal procedure of a country.[26] This provision prohibits bringing a person once convicted or acquitted of a certain offence before the same court on the same matter again. It also forbids bringing the individual before another tribunal for that same offence; thus, for example, someone acquitted by a civilian court cannot be tried again for the same offence by a military or special tribunal.[27]

However, the ICCPR does not guarantee *ne bis in idem* with respect to the national jurisdictions of two or more states.[28] For instance, in a 1986 case involving the conviction of an Italian citizen for same offence in two countries, the United Nations Human Rights Committee (UNHRC) declared that the *ne bis in idem* principle specified in the ICCPR does not guarantee *ne bis in idem* with regard to the national jurisdictions of two or more states; the committee observed that this provision prohibits double jeopardy only with regard to an offence adjudicated in a given state.[29] However, this understanding should not undermine efforts

23. See Gerard Conway, "*Ne Bis in Idem* in International Law," *International Criminal Law Review* 3 (2003): 217. See also Ann Black, "Double Jeopardy Revisited: Why Several Common Law Countries Are Tinkering with One of the Law's Most Treasured Principles," *National Judicial Academy Law Journal* 1 (2007): 121.
24. See Li Wenjian 李文健, "Zhuanxing shiqi de xingsu faxue jiqi jiazhilun" 转型时期的刑诉法学及其价值论 [Study of criminal procedure law and its value in the transformation period], *Faxue yanjiu* 法学研究 4 (1997); see also Richard A. Posner, *Falüde jingji fenxi* 法律的经济分析 [A translation of *Economic Analysis of Law*], trans. Jiang Zhaokang 蒋兆康 (Beijing: Zhongguo dabaike quanshu chubanshe, 1997), 750–51.
25. See Su Caixia 苏彩霞, *Zhongguo xingfa guojihua yanjiu* 中国刑法国际化研究 [Study of the internationalization of criminal law in China] (Beijing: Beijing daxue chubanshe, 2007), 284.
26. See International Covenant on Civil and Political Rights, art. 14(7).
27. See United Nations General Comment No. 32, International Convention on Civil and Political Rights, Article 14: Right to Equality before Courts and Tribunals and to a Fair Trial, adopted by the Human Rights Committee, ninetieth session, July 2007.
28. See Martin Wasmeier, "The Principle of *Ne Bis in Idem*," *Revue Internationale De Droit Péna* 77, no. 1–2 (2006): 121.
29. See *A.P. v. Italy*, CCPR/C/31/D/204/1986, Communication No. 204/1986 (Decision of UNCCPR, 02 November 1987), ¶7.3. See also the same interpretation in *A.R.J. v. Australia*, CCPR/C/60/D/692/1996, Communication No.692/1996 (Decision of UNCCPR, 6 February 1996), ¶6.4.

by states to prevent retrial for the same criminal offence through international conventions.[30]

Besides the ICCPR, the Inter-American Convention on Human Rights has also recognized the *ne bis in idem* principle. It specifies that an accused person acquitted by a non-appealable judgment shall not be subjected to a new trial for the same cause.[31] However, this clause simply prohibits retrial for the acquitted person, and the application scope is limited.

The European Convention on Human Rights (ECHR) also confirms the application of *ne bis in idem* principle at the domestic level.[32] In 1984, Protocol 7 was attached to this convention. It specifies that no one shall be liable to be tried or punished again in criminal proceedings under the jurisdiction of the same state for an offence for which one has already been finally acquitted or convicted in accordance with the law and penal procedures of that state.[33] The words "under the jurisdiction of the same State" limit the application of the article to the national level.[34]

3.2 *Exceptions for the domestic application of* ne bis in idem

The *ne bis in idem* principle is not an absolute human right; exceptions to its domestic application exist.[35] The ICCPR, for example, recognizes the domestic application of *ne bis in idem* but adds exceptions. It does not prohibit the resumption of a criminal trial justified by other exceptional circumstances, such as the discovery of evidence which was not available or known at the time of the acquittal.[36] And in the cases to be analyzed involving the European arrest warrant mechanism, the CJEU permitted the requesting state to surrender a person back to the requested state if he or she was prosecuted or sentenced for facts newly used but previously known.

Protocol No. 7 to the ECHR also offers exceptions while recognizing the principle of *ne bis in idem*. It asserts that *ne bis in idem* principle shall not prevent the reopening of a case in accordance with the law and penal procedures of the state concerned if there is evidence of new or newly discovered facts, or if there was a fundamental defect in the previous proceedings which could affect the outcome of

30. See "United Nations General Comment No.32," ¶57, n 27.
31. See Inter-American Convention on Human Rights, art. 8(4).
32. See Wasmeier, "The Principle," 121, n 28.
33. See Protocol No. 7 to the Convention for the Protection of Human Rights and Fundamental Freedoms, art. 4(1).
34. See Explanatory Report to Protocol No.7 in the Convention for the Protection of Human Rights and Fundamental Freedoms, ¶27.
35. See José Luis de la Guesta, "General Report: Concurrent National and International Criminal Jurisdiction and the Principle 'Ne Bis in Idem'," *Revue Internationale De Droit Pénal* 73, no. 3–4 (2002): 707.
36. See "United Nations General Comment No. 32," ¶56, n 27.

the case.[37] This article also does not prohibit the reopening of proceedings in favor of a convicted person or any other change to the judgment which benefits them.[38] In practice, we can see the possibility of appeal or review procedures in domestic criminal procedure laws.[39]

The Initiative of the Hellenic Republic with a View to Adopting a Council Framework Decision Concerning the Application of the *Ne Bis In Idem* Principle also proposed that a criminal procedure may be repeated if there is proof of new facts or circumstances which emerged after the judgment, or if there was a fundamental error in the previous procedure which could have affected the outcome of the proceedings, in accordance with the criminal law and the criminal procedure of the proceedings.[40]

The domestic application of *ne bis in idem* offers the basis for its application at the international level, that is, in the field of judicial cooperation in criminal matters.[41] However, its practice at the international level is less legally binding than it is within the domestic domain.

4 The application of *ne bis in idem* internationally

Ne bis in idem is a matter of recognizing the judicial decisions of other countries.[42] Very few countries recognize the validity of foreign judgments in criminal matters for execution or enforcement in their national legal order when lacking a treaty basis.[43] There is no mandatory rule of international law imposing an obligation to respect the *ne bis in idem* principle between states. However, we do find treaty-based *ne bis in idem* provisions, both in human rights treaties and in bilateral or multilateral treaties dealing with judicial cooperation in criminal matters.[44] Since the relevant human rights conventions are introduced in the above section, the emphasis here will be on documents on judicial cooperation, particularly on extradition.

---

37. See Protocol No.7 to the Convention for the Protection of Human Rights and Fundamental Freedoms, art. 4(2).
38. See Explanatory Report to Protocol No. 7 of the Convention for the Protection of Human Rights and Fundamental Freedoms, ¶31.
39. For instance, German Criminal Code, 373a; Peru New Code of Criminal Procedure 2004, art. III.
40. See Initiative of the Hellenic Republic with a View to Adopting a Council Framework Decision Concerning the Application of the "Ne Bis in Idem" Principle [2003] OJC 100/12, art. 2(2).
41. See De la Guesta, "General Report," n 35.
42. Koen Lenaerts, "The Principle of Mutual Recognition in the Area of Freedom, Security and Justice" Fourth Annual Sir Jeremy Lever Lecture, University of Oxford, January 30, 2015, p. 6, https://www.law.ox.ac.uk/sites/files/oxlaw/the_principle_of_mutual_recognition_in_the_area_of_freedom_judge_lenaerts.pdf.
43. See Vervaele, "The Transnational," 101, n 22.
44. See Vervaele, "The Transnational," 102, n 22.

The UN Model Treaty on Extradition provides a mandatory ground for refusal if there has been a final judgment rendered against the person in the requested state in respect of the offence for which the person's extradition is requested.[45] In regional extradition treaties, such as the Inter-American Convention on Extradition, we find similar regulations.[46] In the UN Model Treaty on Extradition, *ne bis in idem* is limited to the law of the requested country. In the Inter-American Convention on Extradition, it seems there is no limit to territory; that is, even if the final judgment is issued by third countries, *ne bis in idem* should be applied. Besides international or regional extradition treaties, we also find the application of *ne bis in idem* in international criminal court or tribunals.[47]

In brief, the *ne bis in idem* principle has a very important role to play in international judicial cooperation in criminal matters. Over the years there has been significant development in the understanding of the *ne bis in idem* principle in the European Union,[48] particularly in the case of the European arrest warrant.

5 The application of *ne bis in idem* in the European Union

5.1 The legal basis for the application of ne bis in idem *in Europe's extradition system*

5.1.1 Relevant human rights conventions

The Charter of Fundamental Rights of the European Union (CFR) specifies that no one shall be liable to be tried or punished again in criminal proceedings for an offence for which he or she has already been finally acquitted or convicted within the Union in accordance with the law.[49] In accordance with this article, the *ne bis in idem* principle applies not only within the jurisdiction of one state but also between the jurisdictions of several Member States. This guaranteed right has the same meaning and scope as the corresponding right in the ECHR.

45. See Model Treaty on Extradition, art. 3(d).
46. See Inter-American Convention on Extradition, art. 4(1).
47. Including the International Criminal Court (ICC), the International Tribunal for Rwanda (ICTR), and the International Criminal Tribunal for the Former Yugoslavia (ICTY).
48. See Zoran Buric, "*Ne Bis in Idem* in European Criminal Law: Moving in Circles?" *EU and Member States: Legal and Economic Issues* 3 (2019): 507.
49. See Charter of Fundamental Rights of European Union, art. 50.

5.1.2 The main extradition conventions or clauses regarding *ne bis in idem*

The European Convention on Extradition of 1957 specifies that extradition shall not be granted if final judgment has been passed by the competent authorities of the requested party upon the person claimed in respect of the offence or offences for which extradition is requested; extradition may be refused if the competent authorities of the requested party have decided either not to institute or to terminate proceedings in respect of the same offence or offences.[50] However, *ne bis in idem* is not an absolute right, as discussed above; if new facts or other matters affecting the verdict come to light, the above provision cannot be applied and the person must be extradited unless the requested party proceeds against him under the terms of Article 8.[51] In this convention, the case of a person proceeded against and finally acquitted or convicted was not provided for by the Committee of Experts, on the grounds that all of the Member States of the European Council have adopted the principle of *ne bis in idem* into their domestic law.[52]

To some degree, the domestic application of *ne bis in idem* forms the basis of its application in international judicial cooperation.[53] This also corresponds to its expansion from domestic application in the ECHR to cross-border application in the CFR. In the case of mainland China, we find that, even in legal territory where *ne bis in idem* is not fully recognized domestically, the principle can still be applicable to international judicial cooperation.[54] Just like in the country where the death penalty is maintained, the death penalty will not be imposed or executed if the extradition requires it.[55]

The 1975 Additional Protocol to the European Convention on Extradition states that the extradition of a person against whom a final judgment has been rendered in a third state (a contracting party to the convention) for the offence or offences in respect of which the claim was made shall not be granted if the afore-mentioned judgment resulted in his acquittal, or if the term of imprisonment or

50. See European Convention on Extradition 1957, art. 9.
51. See European Convention on Extradition – Explanatory Report 1957, COETSER 2, December 13, 1957. Article 8 of this Convention stipulates that the requested party may refuse to extradite the person claimed if the competent authorities of such a party are proceeding against him with respect to the offence or offences for which extradition is requested.
52. European Convention on Extradition – Explanatory Report 1957 COETSER 2, December 13, 1957.
53. See José Luis de la Cuesta and Albin Eser, "Concurrent National and International Criminal Jurisdiction and the Principle 'Ne Bis in Idem'," *Revue Internationale De Droit Pénal* 72, no. 3–4 (2001): 753.
54. This is the situation in mainland China, which is addressed in the following section.
55. See Bharat Malkani, "The Obligation to Refrain from Assisting the Use of the Death Penalty," *International and Comparative Law Quarterly* 62, no. 3 (2013): 523.

other measure to which he was sentenced has been completely enforced, or has been wholly or with respect to the part not enforced the subject of a pardon or an amnesty, or if the court convicted the offender without imposing a sanction.[56] There are also some exceptions: extradition may be granted if the offence in respect of which judgment has been rendered was committed against a person, an institution or anything having public status in the requesting state; or if the person on whom judgment was passed had himself a public status in the requesting state; or if the offence in respect of which judgment was passed was committed completely or partly in the territory of the requesting state or in a place treated as its territory.[57] Overall, this protocol enlarges the *ne bis in idem* effect to the final judgment of the third contracting state and also imposes extra conditions and exceptions.

5.2 **Ne bis in idem** *in the European arrest warrant system*

In the European arrest warrant Framework Decision (EAW FD), the principle of *ne bis in idem* provides a mandatory ground for refusal. Under the European arrest warrant, the executing judicial authority must refuse to execute a European arrest warrant if it is informed that the requested person has been finally judged by a Member State with respect to the same act provided that, where there has been sentence, the sentence has been served or is currently being served or may no longer be executed under the law of the sentencing Member State.[58] In addition, the executing judicial authority may also refuse to execute the European arrest warrant if the executing judicial authority is informed that the requested person has been finally judged by a third state with respect to the same act provided that, where there has been sentence, the sentence has been served or is currently being served or may no longer be executed under the law of the sentencing country.[59]

The CJEU has issued several judgments in cases on the interpretation of the *ne bis in idem* principle in relation to Article 54 of the Convention Implementing the Schengen Agreement (CISA); these judgments are applicable to the Framework Decision on EAW by virtue of the judgment in the case of Gaetano Mantello.[60] Other relevant cases relating to the execution of the European arrest warrant explain relevant concepts, such as "final decision," "same act," and "sentence has been served."

56. See the 1975 additional protocol to the European Convention on Extradition 1957, art. 2(2).
57. See 1975 additional protocol to the European Convention on Extradition 1957, art. 2(3).
58. See EAW FD, art. 3(2).
59. See EAW FD, art. 4(5).
60. Case C-261/09, *Gaetano Mantello* [2010]ECR I-11477.

5.3 Ne bis in idem *in the CJEU*

The first authority to consider is the joined cases of Huseyin Gozutok and Klaus Brugge, which relates to the scope of "final judgment" in the principle of *ne bis in idem* as regulated by Article 54 of the CISA. Since the court's interpretation of the CISA also applies to the implementation of the European arrest warrant, this case can provide guidelines for EAW cases.

In the Gozutok and Brugge case, the court held that where public prosecutors discontinue criminal proceedings against an accused once he has fulfilled certain obligations has effects laid down by a national law, further prosecution following such a procedure is definitively barred. The fact that no court is involved in such a procedure and that the decision in which the procedure culminates does not take the form of a judicial decision does not cast doubt on that interpretation; the situation is sufficient for the *ne bis in idem* principle to apply.[61]

From this case we see that the scope of final judgment goes beyond a judicial decision made by a court. It also includes a prosecutor's decision to discontinue criminal proceedings. This regulation responds positively to the delimitation of judicial authority; that is, the judicial authority can include both judges and prosecutors.[62]

The second authority, Mantello, concerns who can decide "facts" and give "final judgment." The CJEU concludes that the interpretation of "same act" cannot be left to be the discretion of the judicial authorities of each Member State on the basis of their national laws, due to the need for uniform application of EU law.[63] The concept of "same act" is also present in Article 54 of the CISA and in that context it has been interpreted as referring to the nature of acts, encompassing a set of concrete circumstances which are inextricably linked together, irrespective of the legal classification given to them or the legal interest protected.[64] In light of the shared objective of Article 54 of the CISA and Article 3(2) of the EAW FD, that a person is not prosecuted or tried more than once for the same acts, the interpretation given in the rulings concerning the CISA must be equally applied to the provision of the EAW FD.[65] Regarding "finally judged" the court held that whether a case has been "finally judged" must be determined by the law of the Member State in which judgment was delivered.[66]

61. See joined cases C-187/01 and C-385/01, *Gozutok and Brugge* [2003] ECR I-1378, ¶42.
62. See Kai Ambos, "The German Public Prosecutor as (no) Judicial Authority within the Meaning of the European Arrest Warrant: A Case Note on the CJEU's Judgment in OG (C-508/18) and PI (C 82/19 PPU)," *New Journal of European Criminal Law* 10, no. 4 (2019): 399.
63. Case C-261/09, *Gaetano Mantello* [2010] ECR I11477, ¶38.
64. Case C-261/09, ¶39.
65. Case C-261/09, ¶40.
66. Case C-261/09, ¶46.

From this CJEU judgment on the application of *ne bis in idem,* we find that the priority of EU law and the law of the requesting state are stressed. When final judgment is given by a third country, the requested state has the discretion to extradite the person to the requesting Member State, since it is just an optional ground for refusal. But if the final judgment is given by an EU Member State, it will constitute a mandatory ground to refuse the surrender. Compared to third countries, the judicial sovereignty of Member States allows greater respect and protection, which demonstrates greater trust between Member States of the European Union.

We also find an interesting provision relating to the accounting principle in the Initiative of the Hellenic Republic with a view to adopting a Council Framework Decision concerning the application of the *ne bis in idem* principle. It holds that if a new prosecution is brought against a person who has been definitively convicted for the same offence in another Member State, the period of deprivation of freedom or fine handed down by that State in respect of that offence shall be deducted from the sentence he would probably receive, as far as allowed by national law; any penalties other than deprivation of freedom which have been imposed, or penalties imposed via administrative procedures, shall also be included.[67]

So, when we return to the EAW FD on the grounds for optional non-execution of the European arrest warrant, the principle of *ne bis in idem* can be applied to safeguard territorial jurisdiction. It provides that the executing judicial authority may refuse to execute the European arrest warrant where the European arrest warrant relates to offences which are regarded by the law of the executing Member State as having been committed in whole or in part in the territory of the executing Member State or in a place treated as such.[68] This safeguard on territorial jurisdiction can be seen as necessary; this view is also justified in the Green Paper on Conflicts of Jurisdiction and the Principle of *ne bis in idem* in Criminal Proceedings. That states that because of the existing situation with conflicts of jurisdiction in criminal matters, some grounds for non-execution may be necessary; for example, this seems to be the case for grounds based on the fact that an act took place in the territory of the executing state, as e.g. in Article 4(7)(a) of the Framework Decision on the European Arrest Warrant.[69]

All these approaches to *ne bis in idem* in the European Union can offer inspiration to mainland China, Hong Kong, and Macau in constructing their own surrender system. This is analyzed in the following section.

---

67. See Initiative, art. 5, n 40.
68. See EAW FD, art. 4(7)1.
69. See Commission, "Green Paper on Conflicts of Jurisdiction and the Principle of *Ne Bis in Idem* in Criminal Proceedings," COM (2005) 696 final, point 4.

6 Application of *ne bis in idem* between mainland China, Hong Kong, and Macau

6.1 *The* ne bis in idem *principle in the extradition or surrender systems between the three Chinese territories and foreign countries*

The *ne bis in idem* principle has been written into China Extradition Law. In line with that law, an extradition request should be refused when the judicial authorities of mainland China have made a valid judgment or have concluded criminal proceedings.[70] There is no regulation on final judgment from third countries, and only the judicial sovereignty of the requesting and requested countries is taken into consideration.

We can also find the application of *ne bis in idem* in the extradition treaties between mainland China and foreign countries. Before the Extradition Law's enactment, the *ne bis in idem* principle was implemented in the extradition treaty between China and Russia. It specifies that extradition should be refused if, before receiving the extradition request, the authority in charge of the requested state has made a valid judgment or concluded criminal proceedings on the same criminal act.[71] Similar clauses can be found in other extradition treaties mainland China has signed.[72] China has concluded extradition treaties with more than 50 countries and nearly all of the treaties recognize the principle of *ne bis in idem*.[73]

In Hong Kong, the *ne bis in idem* principle is applied in its surrender cooperation with other countries. The Fugitive Offenders Ordinance (FOO) confirms that a person shall not be surrendered to a prescribed place, or committed to or kept in custody for the purpose of such surrender, if it appears to an appropriate authority that if the offence had occurred in Hong Kong, the law of Hong Kong relating to previous acquittal or conviction would preclude the prosecution, or the imposition or enforcement of a sentence, in respect of that offence.[74]

In the surrender agreements Hong Kong has signed with twenty countries, the *ne bis in idem* principle is a mandatory ground to refuse surrender. In the application of this principle, the final judgments from both the requesting party and the

---

70. See China Extradition Law 2002, art. 8(2).
71. See Extradition Treaty between China and Russia 1997, art. 3(4).
72. See Extradition Treaty between China and South Korea, art. 3(2); Extradition Treaty between China and Portugal, art. 3(6); Extradition treaty between China and Italy, art. 3(5).
73. See Zhang Xu 张旭, *Guoji xingfa: Xianzhuang yu zhanwang* 国际刑法：现状与展望 [International criminal law: present and prospect] (Beijing: Qinghua daxue chubanshe, 2005), 338.
74. See Hong Kong Fugitive Offenders Ordinance, pt. 1, s 4, art. 5(1)e.

requested party are taken into consideration. The Surrender Agreement between Hong Kong and New Zealand, for example, specifies that a person who has been finally acquitted, convicted, or pardoned under the law of the requesting or requested party, for any offence set out in the request, shall not be surrendered for that offence.[75] The clause can be found in all twenty surrender agreements Hong Kong has signed. Some of them articulate in an indirect way, like the agreement between Hong Kong and the Netherlands.[76]

Moreover, for most of the optional grounds to refuse surrender, a final judgment given by a third country is considered. However, this is seldom found in extradition treaties between mainland China and other countries. In the agreement between Hong Kong and the US, we find something different, that surrender shall not be precluded by the fact that the authorities in the requested party have decided not to prosecute the person sought for the acts for which surrender is requested or to discontinue any criminal proceedings which have been instituted against the person sought for those acts.[77]

Macau has concluded surrender agreements with Portugal and South Korea which contain the principle of *ne bis in idem*. According to the agreement with Portugal, surrender should be refused if the requested person has been acquitted, convicted, or pardoned for the offence for which the surrender is requested.[78] Like Hong Kong, in this surrender agreement Macau also takes final judgment from third countries into consideration by specifying that the request may be refused if the requested person has been acquitted or convicted for the same offence for which they are requested in third judicial territories, and, if convicted, the penalty has been fully implemented or cannot be implemented.[79] Similar clauses appear in the surrender agreement between Macau and South Korea.[80]

75. See Surrender Agreement between Hong Kong and the New Zealand, art. 6(2).
76. See Surrender Agreement between Hong Kong and the Netherlands, art 7(c). As both Hong Kong and the Netherlands have signed the International Covenant on Civil and Political Rights, *ne bis in idem* has been written into the Hong Kong Fugitive Offenders Ordinance. The Netherlands also upholds the tradition of recognizing foreign judgments. It is evident, then, that *ne bis in idem* is applicable.
77. See Surrender Agreement between Hong Kong and the US, art. 5.
78. See Surrender Agreement between Macau and Portugal, art. 6(8).
79. See Surrender Agreement between Macau and Portugal, art. 7(5).
80. See Surrender Agreement between Macau and South Korea, art. 5(4) and art. 6(6).

6.2 *Application of* ne bis in idem *in surrender between mainland China, Hong Kong, and Macau*

6.2.1 The trend towards application of *ne bis in idem* in extradition or surrender system

The principle of *ne bis in idem* is based on universal values like mutual respect for judicial sovereignty and protection of human rights and safeguarding the stability of judicial decisions.[81] Mainland China, Hong Kong, and Macau have applied the principle of *ne bis in idem* in their cooperation with foreign countries on extradition or surrender. The European Union has applied it in the EU, and the UN conventions recommend its application globally. The China domestic surrender system should follow this trend.

6.2.2 Existing domestic application of *ne bis in idem* can be applied to cross-boundary practice

From the growing practical application of *ne bis in idem,* we find that, generally speaking, the domestic application of *ne bis in idem* comes before its expanded application to cross-border judicial cooperation in criminal matters.[82] Based on this, both Hong Kong and Macau are qualified to apply this principle to the surrender with other regions (countries) as they have practiced, and there is no basis to exclude the principle in surrender arrangements with mainland China. Mainland China has not applied *ne bis in idem* domestically, but it has applied it to extradition with foreign countries. Mainland China still maintains the death penalty, but in all the extradition treaties mainland China has concluded, the death penalty issue has been solved by way of guarantees.[83] So the fact that mainland China does not apply *ne bis in idem* domestically should not be an obstacle to applying it in the surrender of fugitive offenders with Hong Kong and with Macau. Mainland China's international cooperation practices offer a basis for this.

81. See Su, *Zhongguo xingfa guojihua*, 280–83, n 25.
82. See Dionysios Spinellis, "Global Report the *Ne Bis in Idem* Principle in 'Global' Instruments," *Revue Internationale De Droit Pénal* 73, no. 3 (2002): 1149.
83. This means that the requesting country guarantees that it will not impose the death penalty on requested persons, or if imposed it will not be executed.

6.2.3 The "one country" fact requires the application of *ne bis in idem*

Ne bis in idem means mutual recognition of the law and the judicial decisions of foreign countries, and it is a requirement for mutual respect of judicial authority.[84] It is based on the decline of absolutism of sovereignty and the development of relativism of sovereignty.[85] This is evident in the principle's application in today's global world. In particular, the EU's experience demonstrates that *ne bis in idem* is not only an important principle for settling conflicts of criminal jurisdiction but also an important measure for implementing the principle of mutual recognition in judicial cooperation in criminal matters.

The less the sovereignty dispute, the more the integration will be, and the more friendly to judicial cooperation *ne bis in idem* should be. That is true for the situation between mainland China, Hong Kong, and Macau. The three regions belong to one country, and no sovereignty conflict exists between them. Their mutual recognition of law and judicial decisions aligns with the common interests of China as a whole. The three regions constitute independent legal territories, and the mutual recognition of final judicial decisions will sustain mutual respect for the distinctions of each legal system and the particular interests of each region. Under the mutual recognition of decisions and the law, the application of *ne bis in idem* will come naturally.

6.3 *Design of the* ne bis in idem *principle in the China domestic surrender system*

From the experience of the EU as well as current practice between Hong Kong, Macau, and mainland China with foreign countries, the valid final judgment or ruling for *ne bis in idem* purposes should be assessed from the law of the relevant side. As with the case of the EAW, whether something constitutes a final judgment should be decided by the law of the requesting state.[86] Especially in the mainland China situation, as analyzed above, although judgment should be final after the second instance trial, the procedure of supervision retrial is available. Therefore, whether a case should be regarded as final and whether it can be open for retrial is better left to the law of the requesting region. This respects the distinction between laws and contributes to swift resolution of requests.

In addition, the scope of final judgment and ruling cannot be limited to judicial decisions given by the court; out-of-court settlements can also be included.[87] In the

84. See Teresa Bravo, "*Ne Bis in Idem* as a Defence Right and Procedural Safeguard in the EU," *New Journal of European Criminal Law* 2, no. 4 (2011): 393.
85. See Huang, *Guoji*, 42–45, n 16.
86. See Case C-261/09, *Gaetano Mantello*, n 63.
87. See joined cases C-187/01 and C-385/01, *Gozutok and Brugge*, n 61.

earlier analysis, it was seen that public prosecutors can also be regarded as judicial authorities in the China domestic surrender system. If this is so, their valid and final rulings should also be restricted by the *ne bis in idem* principle.

At the same time, territorial jurisdiction can be a discretionary ground on which to refuse surrender. Under this ground, the requested region has the power to refuse surrender if the requested person is subject to criminal proceedings for the same act in the requested region. But dialogue and negotiation can take place to decide which jurisdiction is more suitable to take charge of the case, as discussed in the chapter on conflict of criminal jurisdiction.

Final judgments or rulings issued by third countries can be an optional ground to refuse surrender. On the one side, it has been global practice to protect human rights as well as respecting the legal authority of foreign countries. On the other side, mainland China does not fully recognize the principle of *ne bis in idem*, so acts which have been tried and punished abroad may still be tried in mainland China with the possibility of waiving or mitigating the punishment. There is a chance that the Mainland will request the surrender of persons in such situations. Taking the final judgment of third countries as optional ground on which to refuse surrender will leave room for both requesting and requested regions to negotiate and, in doing so, balance the interests of justice and human rights.

7 Conclusion

The application of *ne bis in idem* has extended from domestic practice to international judicial cooperation. Although the principle is not legally binding internationally, it has been widely written into multilateral or bilateral treaties. Functionally, this principle works to protect human rights, to settle conflicts of criminal jurisdiction, and to respect the judicial sovereignty of countries or legal territories. Judging from both international and EU experiences, combined with the present practices of Hong Kong, Macau, and mainland China in applying *ne bis in idem*, in the China domestic surrender system, the *ne bis in idem* principle should be applied. The experience from the EU of giving priority to the law of the requesting party can also be learned from.

5
The Application of the Double Criminality Principle

1 Introduction

Double criminality (also labeled dual criminality and double incrimination) refers to the characterization of a person's conduct as criminal under the laws of both the requesting and requested states in extradition and surrender. Reciprocal characterization of criminality is considered to be a substantive requirement for granting extradition.[1] It is not so much a rule of international law as a consideration based on policy and expediency;[2] thus, a fugitive cannot raise the double criminality question as a bar to extradition if the applicable treaty or statute—or both, depending upon the forum—is silent.[3] Whether it can be applied to the China domestic surrender system is open to question. It seems neither fully applying the double criminality principle nor fully abolishing the double criminality principle is ideal. The European arrest warrant, where the double criminality principle has greatly evolved, sheds some light on the double criminality issue between mainland China, Hong Kong, and Macau.

In this chapter, firstly, I analyze the problems relating to the application of the double criminality principle in the three regions. Secondly, I discuss the origin and development of the double criminality principle in international extradition. Thirdly, I analyze how the double criminality principle has been applied in the European arrest warrant system. Finally, I explore if and how the double criminality can be applied in the China domestic surrender system.

---

1. M. Cherif Bassiouni, *International Extradition: United States Law and Practice*, 6th ed. (Oxford: Oxford University Press, 2014), 500.
2. Sharon A Williams, "The Double Criminality Rule and Extradition: A Comparative Analysis," *Nova Law Review* 15 (1991): 582.
3. Williams, "The Double Criminality," 582, n 2.

2 The applicability of the double criminality principle in mainland China, Hong Kong, and Macau

2.1 The applicability of double criminality at present

2.1.1 Double criminality is recognized in the mainland China extradition system

The double criminality principle is recognized by the China Extradition Law. The Law specifies that when foreign countries submit a request for extradition, the extradition can be permitted only when two conditions are met. The first is that the act referred to by the extradition request also constitutes a crime pursuant to the law of the PRC; the second is that if the extradition is requested for prosecution, the penalty should be at least one year's imprisonment pursuant to both the law of the PRC and the requesting country; if the extradition is requested for executing a penalty, at the time the request is submitted the remaining imprisonment period must be no less than six months.[4] China has signed more than fifty extradition treaties with foreign countries and the double criminality principle is recognized in all of those on the basis of the China Extradition Law.

2.1.2 Double criminality is recognized in the Hong Kong surrender system

Double criminality in the Hong Kong Fugitive Offenders Ordinance (FOO) means that the offence is punishable under the law of the requesting place with imprisonment for at least 12 months, and the acts or omissions constituting the conduct in respect of which the person's surrender to the requesting place is sought amount to conduct which, if the conduct had occurred in Hong Kong, would constitute an offence.[5] The underlying foreign offences must come within the generic descriptions of offences in Schedule 1 of the FOO.[6] So the double criminality principle is also established qualitatively and quantitatively in the law of Hong Kong.[7] Hong

4. China Extradition Law, art. 7.
5. Fugitive Offenders Ordinance, ss. 2 pt. 1.
6. These offences, listed in the Fugitive Offenders Ordinance, include murder or manslaughter, offences of a sexual nature, kidnapping, criminal intimidation, offences against bankruptcy law or insolvency law, offences against the law relating to firearms, and others.
7. Many states deem the double criminality formula sufficient without needing to add a list of extraditable offences. See Bassiouni, *International Extradition*, 500, n 1.

Kong has concluded surrender agreements with twenty countries and all of the agreements apply the double criminality principle.[8]

2.1.3 Double criminality is confirmed in the Macau surrender system

Macau has concluded agreements on the surrender of fugitive offenders with Portugal and South Korea. The Portugal surrender agreement provides that extradition should be based on conduct which is regarded as an offence in both the requesting and requested regions and punishable by at least one year's imprisonment after trial; for execution of sentence the unserved sentence should be above six months.[9] The surrender agreement between Macau and South Korea is similar.[10] The Macau Law on Judicial Cooperation in Criminal Matters provides that only where the offences attract one year's imprisonment or more in both the requesting place and Macau can the requested person be surrendered.[11] In brief, the double criminality principle is also a basic principle of Macau's surrender system.

However, when it comes to the China domestic surrender system, the application of double criminality is a contested rather than an agreed principle.[12]

2.2 Disputes over double criminality between mainland China, Hong Kong, and Macau

2.2.1 Views on abolishing the double criminality principle

Some scholars argue that the double criminality principle should not be applied between the three regions, based mainly on the fact that double criminality is a principle applied between sovereign countries whereas Hong Kong and Macau are parts of the PRC.[13] There is also a view that this position is supported by the differences

8. The number of listed offences for surrender under the double criminality principle differs: in the arrangement with Portugal, 46 categories of offences are listed; with Indonesia, 44; with India, 33; with the Netherlands, 29; etc. In all the arrangements, there is also an overriding provision that other offences which comply with double criminality pursuant to the law in the two parties can also be subject to surrender. There are also arrangements like that with the Czech Republic, in which the offences are not listed but the double criminality principle is still applied.
9. Surrender Agreement between Macau and Portugal, art. 3.
10. Surrender Agreement between Macau and South Korea, art. 2.
11. Macau Law on Judicial Cooperation in Criminal Matters, art. 32.
12. See Yanhong Yin and Irene Wieczorek, "Extradition between Hong Kong and Mainland China: A Comment on the 2019 Amendment to the Hong Kong Fugitive Offenders Ordinance in Comparison with the European Arrest Warrant," *New Journal of European Criminal Law* 11, no. 4 (2020): 504.
13. Zhao Guoqiang 赵国强, "Guanyu neidi yu xianggang xianghu yijiao fanzui xianyiren de jidian sikao" 于内地与香港相互移交犯罪嫌疑人的几点思考［Thinkings on the surrender of fugitive

in legislated offences between mainland China, Hong Kong, and Macau.[14] For instance, abortion under certain circumstances is a criminal offence in Hong Kong and Macau, but does not constitute a crime in mainland China. There are also acts in the Mainland which constitute crimes against the customs of ethnic minorities which have no counterpart in Hong Kong or Macau criminal law. If the double criminality principle applied, these crimes may not be combated. Zhao Guoqiang also argues that if the double criminality were applied and the requested regions refused to surrender the requested persons for offences due to a lack of double criminality, the criminal jurisdiction of the requesting region would be undermined.[15] Some authors propose that double criminality should not be applied in principle but that there should be some exceptions, such as when the conduct of requested persons relates to legal rights in the requested regions.[16]

2.2.2 Views in support of the double criminality principle

The position that the double criminality principle should be maintained is mainly based on its role serving the principle of legality and protecting human rights. It is consistent with the "one country, two systems" policy, particularly showing the respect to "two systems." Huang Feng argues that domestic surrender within China aims for criminal prosecution or the execution of criminal punishment, which is closely related to criminal procedure, hence surrender should be bound by the legality principle.[17] The Hong Kong side also argues that double criminality should apply, and that persons should not be surrendered if their acts do not constitute a criminal offence under Hong Kong law; since most people understand what constitutes an offence under Hong Kong law, they need not worry about rendition to the Mainland for an unfamiliar crime.[18]

offenders between Mainland and Hong Kong], *Huadong zhengfa xueyuan xuebao* 华东政法学院学报 (2000): 32–37.

14. Guo Jia 郭佳, "Quji xingshi sifa xiezhuzhong 'shuangchong fanzui yuanze' xianzhi shiyonglun" 区际刑事司法协助中"双重犯罪原则"限制适用论 [The limited application of double criminality principle in regional judicial cooperation in criminal matters], *Zhoukou shifan xueyuan xuebao* 周口师范学院学报 34 (2017): 95.
15. See Zhao, "Guanyu," n 13.
16. See Guo, "Quji," 95, 98, n 14.
17. Huang Feng 黄风, *Yindu wenti yanjiu* 引渡问题研究 [Study on extradition] (Beijing: Zhongguo zhengfa daxue chubanshe, 2006): 222.
18. See Wayne Walsh, *Cross-Border Crime in Hong Kong: Extradition, Mutual Assistance, Financial Sanctions*, 2nd ed. (Hong Kong: LexisNexis, 2020), 119.

Some scholars suggest that double criminality should be applied in principle with some limitations.[19] As to the surrender of fugitive offenders between Macau and mainland China, Zhao Guoqiang argues that since Macau is an independent judicial territory under Basic Law of Macau, the double criminality principle can be referred to but exceptions should be made when the crimes are against national security or military interests are involved.[20] Su Caixia also holds that the complete abolition of the double criminality principle will hinder the conclusion of surrender agreements between the three regions, and that recognizing the double criminality principle with some reservations will reduce confrontations in negotiation between the regions.[21]

In summary, we find that besides human rights concerns, the debate mainly focuses on the "one country" political reality and the "two systems" legal fact. The traditional double criminality principle cannot respond to these complicated situations. In fact, the application of double criminality has also become problematic in international extradition.

3 The controversial application of double criminality principle in international extradition

Generally, when verifying the double criminality, the majority of states will evaluate whether the act is chargeable in both states as a criminal offence regardless of its likelihood of prosecution or possibility of conviction.[22] According to the UN Extradition Model Treaty, in determining whether an offence is punishable under the laws of both parties, it shall not matter whether the laws of the Parties place the acts or omissions constituting the offence within the same category of offence or denominate the offence by the same terminology;[23] nor does it matter whether under the laws of the Parties the constituent elements of the offence differ.[24]

19. See Su Caixia 苏彩霞, "Woguo quji xingshi sifa xiezhu shiyong shuangchong fanzui yuanze xinlun" 我国区际刑事司法协助适用"双重犯罪原则"新论 [The new discussion on the application of double criminality principle in the regional judicial cooperation in criminal matters], *Zhengzhi yu Falv* 政治与法律 6 (2009): 141.
20. Zhao Guoqiang 赵国强, "Yiguo liangzhi yu guoji yindu guanli-yi Aumen yu neidi xianghu yijiao taofan wei shijiao" 一国两制与国际引渡惯例—以澳门与内地相互移交逃犯为视角 [One country two systems and international extradition traditions: a perspective from the surrender of fugitive offenders between Mainland and Macau], *Aumen faxue* 澳门法学 3 (2015): 21.
21. See Su, "Woguo," 143, n 19.
22. See Bassiouni, *International Extradition*, 501, n 1.
23. Model Treaty on Extradition, art. 2 (2) (a).
24. Model Treaty on Extradition, art. 2 (2) (b).

Double criminality has an important role in securing national sovereignty and the protection function of the state; provides fair warning to potential extraditees; generates public support for the extradition of nationals; and serves to exclude non-criminal political offences and trivial requests.[25] Double criminality is based upon both a reciprocal characterization of the offence and a mutuality of obligations between states.[26] It is also based on the legality principle, which prevents a person from being restricted in his or her liberty on account of acts that are not established to be criminal.[27]

It is recognized that double criminality should be applied in a way so as not to frustrate extradition.[28] Some voices suggest that while there should be an inquiry into the nature of the proceedings the person faces in the requesting state, this does not necessarily require double criminality.[29] Based on a strong tradition of respect for territorial jurisdiction,[30] in the case of extradition with EU countries, the UK even proposed that "we consider that it was not necessary to retain the requirement for the offence to be an offence in both the requesting and requested country. This was thought to be an inappropriate judgment on the criminal justice systems of our European partners. If an offence is a crime on the statute book of our European partners then the UK should respect that."[31] This signifies openness on the part of Home Office to consider a complete abolition of dual criminality within the EU.[32]

The application of double criminality in the international field illustrates its merits but also that it has aroused debate.[33] The same merits and problems are relevant to its application in the China domestic surrender system. Here, reference can be made to the European arrest warrant, which abolishes the double criminality requirement for a list of offences and reserves it for others.

---

25. Neil Boister, "Global Simplification of Extradition: Interviews with Selected Extradition Experts in New Zealand, Canada, the US and EU," *Criminal Law Forum* 29 (2018): 351.
26. See Willams, "The Double Criminality," 582, n 2.
27. Miguel João Costa, *Extradition Law: Reviewing Grounds for Refusal from the Classic Paradigm to Mutual Recognition and Beyond* (Leiden: Brill Nijhoff, 2020), 215.
28. See Boister, "Global Simplification," 351, n 25.
29. See Boister, "Global Simplification," 351, n 25.
30. See Costa, *Extradition Law*, 218, n 27.
31. See Costa, *Extradition Law*, 218, n 27.
32. See Costa, *Extradition Law*, 218, n 27.
33. See Jonathan O. Hafen, "International Extradition: Issues Arising Under the Dual Criminality Requirement," *BYU Law Review* 1 (1992): 191.

4 Double criminality in the European arrest warrant

4.1 *The double criminality principle from the previous extradition conventions to the new EAW Framework Decision*

4.1.1 Double criminality in the 1957 European Convention on Extradition

In the 1957 European Convention on Extradition, the double criminality check includes two elements. The first is that the act constitutes a crime in both the requesting and requested states. The second is that the maximum period for detention or deprivation of liberty is at least 12 months in both the requesting and requested states.[34] This position has changed with the introduction of new instruments.[35]

4.1.2 The double criminality principle in the 1996 Convention on Extradition between Member States of the European Union

The 1996 Convention specifies that extradition shall be granted in respect of offences which are punishable under the law of the requesting Member State by deprivation of liberty or a detention order for a maximum period of at least 12 months and under the law of the requested Member State by deprivation of liberty or a detention order for a maximum period of at least six months.[36] This rule has shown a tendency to speed up the surrender process and to give priority to the law of the requesting state. This has been more evident in the twenty-first century.

Compared to the earlier extradition conventions, the double criminality principle is more restricted in the European arrest warrant system. Not only are 32 categories of offences without a double criminality check, the priority of the law of the issuing Member State is also strengthened.[37]

---

34. See Lech Gardocki, "Double Criminality in Extradition law," *Israel Law Review* 27, no. 1–2 (1993): 288.
35. European Convention on Extradition, art. 2.
36. Convention relating to Extradition between the Member States of European Union 1996, art. 2.
37. See Libor Klimek, "Surrender VS. Extradition: A Comparison Focused on Innovations of European Arrest Warrant," *International and Comparative Law Review* 11, no. 1 (2011): 145.

4.2 *Double criminality in the EAW Framework Decision*

4.2.1 No double criminality requirement for 32 categories of offences

4.2.1.1 *Neither the offence nor the penalty in the law of the requested state are relevant*

In European arrest warrant system, if the criminal act constitutes a listed offence and is punishable in the requesting country by a custodial sentence or detention order for a maximum period of at least three years, double criminality in the executing country is not required.[38] The 32 categories of offences are listed in the EAW Framework Decision. Only the penalty in the issuing country should be considered.[39] This is a significant development under the mutual recognition principle.

However, concerns exist that the exemption from the double criminality requirement for the 32 listed offences violates the principles of legality, equality, and non-discrimination.[40] The European Court of Justice has clarified that not verifying double criminality for the listed offences does not breach the principle of legality as the definition of the offence follows from the law of the issuing Member State; the aim of the EAW FD is not to harmonize the legislation of Member States with regard to criminal offences and their constitute elements nor the penalties they attract. The actual definitions of the offences and the penalties applicable are those which follow from the law of the issuing Member State.[41] Nor does the non-verification of double criminality breach the principle of equality and non-discrimination, because the seriousness of the listed offences, which harm public order and public safety, justifies their distinction from the non-listed offences; and, again, the application of the EAW is not conditional on harmonization of the criminal laws of Member States.[42]

There remains no full harmonization of the substantive criminal law of European Member States; the law varies from state to state.[43] But based on the high level of mutual trust in each other's criminal justice systems, mutual recognition of judicial decisions from other Member State is safeguarded. From a practical viewpoint, the

38. EAW FD, art. 2 (2).
39. Case C-303/05, *Advocaten voor de Wereld VZW v. Leden van de Ministerraad* [2007] ECR I-03633, ¶48–¶61.
40. In 2007, a non-profit organization, Advocaten voor de wereld, brought an action before the Belgian Constitutional Court seeking the annulment of the Belgian law transposing the EAW FD, one reason being this doubt. The Belgium court referred the question to the Court of Justice of the European Union.
41. See Case C-303/05, ¶52, n 39.
42. See Case C-303/05, ¶59, n 39.
43. See Konstantinos Zoumpoulakis, "From the Ground up: the Use of Minimum Rules in EU Procedural Criminal Law and the Question of Member States' Discretion," *European Papers* 5, no. 3 (2020): 1289.

32 categories of offences seriously endanger public order and public safety, and cover offences on which almost all the Member States have cracked down.[44]

4.2.1.2 *The 32 categories of offences*

The 32 categories include the traditional crimes of murder, grievous bodily injury, organized or armed robbery, swindling, racketeering and extortion, counterfeiting and piracy of products, forgery of administrative documents and trafficking therein, rape, arson, and sabotage. Their differences in the domestic law of various states are not significant and many jurisdictions punish them with prison sentences of over three years.

Some listed crimes are harmonized in the European Union. According to the Treaty on the Functioning of the European Union (TFEU), both the European Parliament and the Council may, by means of directives adopted in accordance with the ordinary legislative procedure, establish minimum rules concerning the definition of criminal offences and sanctions in the areas of particularly serious crime with a cross-border dimension resulting from the nature or impact of such offences or from a special need to combat them on a common basis.[45] These areas of crime include terrorism, trafficking in human beings and sexual exploitation of women and children, illicit drug trafficking, illicit arms trafficking, money laundering, corruption, counterfeiting of means of payment, computer crime, and organized crime. Most of these crimes have been regulated by the UN or international conventions which the EU and its Member States have joined.[46] The presence of minimum standards for these forms of crime and the presence of international conventions mean few difficulties in extradition and surrender.[47]

The European arrest warrant is also open to other categories of offences, and the European Council may decide at any time to add other categories of offence to the list.[48] After the enactment of the EAW Framework Decision, more crimes have been harmonized, such as corruption in the private sector[49] and violence against women

44. Sabela Oubina Barbolla, "The European Arrest Warrant in Law and in Practice: Special Reference to the Spanish Experience," *European Journal of Legal Education* 6 (2011): 10.
45. TFEU, art. 83 (1).
46. For instance, participation in a criminal organization is not only in the Council Framework Decision 2008 on the fight against organized crime, but also in the 2000 United Convention against Transnational Organized Crime; terrorism, trafficking in human beings, illicit trafficking in narcotic drugs and psychotropic substances, corruption and other crimes are also widely recognized by both the European Union and UN conventions.
47. Antonio Roma Valdes, "Mutual Recognition Principle in Criminal Matters: A Review," *ERA Forum* 16 (2015): 291.
48. EAW FD, art. 2 (3).
49. Council Framework Decision 2003/568/JHA of 22 July 2003 on Combating Corruption in the Private Sector [2003]OJ L192/54.

and domestic violence.[50] The list of offences exempted from the double criminality check may be extended.

4.2.1.3 *Potential problems with non-verification of double criminality for listed offences*

The European arrest warrant catalogue of offences has been criticized for the lack of logical order in which the offences are listed, with critics arguing that they should have been grouped together via logical criteria; for example, the legal interest being protected and/or the seriousness of the crime.[51]

Not all of the categories listed are considered crimes throughout the EU. The act for which a European arrest warrant is issued may be unlawful but may not breach the criminal law; for instance, for trafficking in cultural goods, the Convention allows the ratifying States to punish it under criminal or administrative law:[52] seventeen states in Europe punish the export as a crime.[53] Some criminal acts in the requesting Member State may be legally protected in the requested Member State: for instance, carrying out an abortion may be murder in some countries but it is completely legal in the UK, and the use of soft drugs is tolerated by the Netherlands but is considered a crime of imprisonment in Finland.

Contrary to the criticisms, the European Commission has defended the list of 32 offences, arguing that "there are no major difficulties at this stage with the transposal of the list of 32 categories of offence for which double criminality is abolished."[54]

4.2.2 Double criminality principle updated and applied

4.2.2.1 *The penalty in the requested Member State is irrelevant*

In the European arrest warrant system, if the criminal act constitutes a listed offence and is punishable in the requesting country by a custodial sentence or a detention order with a maximum period of at least three years, double criminality in the executing country need not be verified.[55] The 32 categories of offences are listed in the Framework Decision and only the relevant penalty in the issuing country should be

50. Convention on Preventing and Combating Violence against Women and Domestic Violence 2011.
51. See Barbolla, "The European Arrest Warrant," 8, n 44.
52. 1970 Convention on the Means of Prohibiting and Preventing the Illicit Import, Export and Transfer of Cultural Property, art. 8.
53. Include Greece, Italy, France, UK, Spain and so on, see Valdes, "Mutual Recognition," n 47.
54. Libor Klimek, *European Arrest Warrant* (Berlin: Springer 2015), 102.
55. EAW FD, art. 2(2).

considered,[56] making this a significant development under the principle of mutual recognition.

For offences not covered by the 32 categories, a double criminality check is still needed. A European arrest warrant may be issued for acts punishable by the law of the issuing Member State by a custodial sentence or a detention order for a maximum period of at least 12 months or, where a sentence has been passed or a detention order made, for sentences of at least four months.[57] Surrender may be subject to the condition that the acts for which the European arrest warrant has been issued constitute an offence under the law of the executing Member State, whatever the constituent elements or however it is described.[58] Under the European arrest warrant, as long as the act for which the warrant is issued also constitutes a certain offence in the requested Member State, the double criminality requirement is met and the type or the nature of the penalty is irrelevant.

In a case referred from a Dutch court,[59] the CJEU held that the EAW FD no longer took account of the levels of punishment applicable in the executing Member States.[60] This demonstrates the priority of the law of the requesting Member State. It also corresponds to the primary objective of the EAW FD of ensuring free movement of judicial decisions in criminal matters based on mutual recognition, within an area of freedom, security, and justice. A chart on the EAW double criminality check can be found in Figure 5.1 on page 105.

4.2.2.2 *A proportionality check is required in the requesting Member State*

The execution of a European arrest warrant can lead to the deprivation of the requested person's liberty and restrictions of his or her free movement, particularly as the EAW is built on the concept of mutual recognition and execution in the requested Member State is a general rule; thus a proportionality check by the requesting Member State is necessary, theoretically speaking.[61]

---

56. Case C-303/05, *Advocaten voor de Wereld VZW v. Leden van de Ministerraad* [2007] ECR I-03633, ¶48–¶61.
57. EAW FD, art. 2 (1).
58. EAW FD, art. 2 (4).
59. Case C-463/15 PPU, *Openbaar Minsterie v. A* [Order of the Court, September 25, 2015].
60. Case C-463/15,¶32, n 59.
61. See Ermioni Xanthopoulou, "The Quest for Proportionality for the European Arrest Warrant: Fundamental Rights Protection in a Mutual Recognition Environment," *New Journal of European Criminal Law* 6, no. 1 (2015): 32.

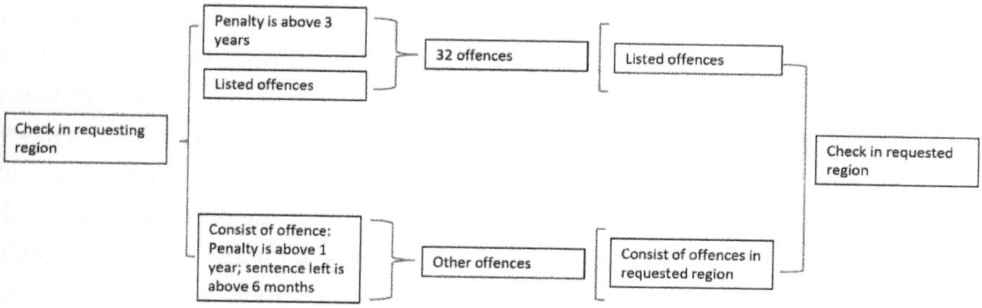

Figure 5.1: Double criminality checks in the EAW system

In recent years, Member States have increasingly reported cases in which EAWs have been issued for harmless and minor offences, such as the theft of a piglet,[62] the theft of a bottle of beer,[63] or the theft of 10 chickens.[64] Across Europe, theft is an offence that fulfills the requirement of a maximum penalty of at least 12 months, thus, in principle, an EAW can be issued for any case of theft, whether it is on the scale of the great train robbery or a piece of minor shoplifting, as described by Spencer.[65]

The Council of the European Union recommends a modification to the Handbook on how to issue a European arrest warrant, so that issuing authorities should assess the proportionality of issuing a European arrest warrant in each case before making their decisions.[66] The factors which should be assessed include the seriousness of the offence, the possibility of the suspect being detained, the likely penalty imposed if the person sought is found guilty of the alleged offence, the interests of the victims of the offence, and alternative measures which can be taken.[67]

62. Council 10975/07 Proposed subject for discussion at the experts' meeting on the application of the Framework Decision on the European arrest warrant on 17 July 2007—the proportionality principle [2007] Copen 98, accessed October 31, 2022, https://data.consilium.europa.eu/doc/document/ST-10975-2007-INIT/en/pdf.
63. See Sarah Haggenmuller, "The Principle of Proportionality and the European Arrest Warrant," Onati Socio-Legal Series 3, no. 1 (2013): 98.
64. See *Sandru v. Government of Romania* [2009] EWHC2879 (Admin), ¶5. The extradition case of *Sandru v. Romania* before the British High Court of Justice was based on the conviction of a defendant in Romania to 3 years imprisonment for stealing and killing 10 chickens.
65. See Joachim Vogel and J. R. Spencer, "Proportionality and the European Arrest Warrant," *Criminal Law Review* 6 (2010): 581.
66. Council 17195/10 Revised Version of the European Handbook on How to Issue a European Arrest Warrant [2010] Copen 275, 14.
67. Commission Notice-Handbook on How to Issue and Execute a European Arrest Warrant [2017] OJ C 335/01, 14.

Such a proportionality check should also be applied to the offences listed in the 32 categories, especially for acts like trafficking in cultural goods, carrying out abortion, using soft drugs, and euthanasia.[68] There are large differences in the nature of these acts in domestic legislation, and taking all of the factors into consideration can make the issuing of a warrant more justified. The proportionality check is mainly done by the requesting Member State[69] and the double criminality check is mainly done by the requested Member States;[70] the objectives of the two checks are different and their factors are also distinct. Thus, the two "obligations" or "rights" imposed on the requesting state and requested state can be independent from each other. The exemption from a double criminality check in requested states does not mean there is no need to comply with the proportionality principle in the requesting state.

5 The inspiration for mainland China, Hong Kong, and Macau on the double criminality principle

5.1 The double criminality principle can be compromised on in a modern society and closely related region

5.1.1 The relationship between double criminality and sovereignty

The double criminality requirement is embedded in the principles of sovereignty, reciprocity, and non-intervention, which constitute the fundamental elements of cooperation between states enshrined in instruments of public international law. Cooperation essentially aims at avoiding interference in the domestic affairs of the states involved.[71]

However, the existence of only one sovereign country does not mean that double criminality should be disapplied. Double criminality firstly means that there are two or more legal systems in which the regulation of offences and penalties differs.[72] No matter that it is one sovereign country, the existence of different legal regulations matters. Su Caixia points out that whether the double criminality principle should be applied in the China domestic surrender system has nothing or

68. See Luisa Marin, "Effective and Legitimate? Learning from the Lessons of 10 Years of Practice with the European Arrest Warrant," *New Journal of European Criminal Law* 5, no. 3 (2014): 327.
69. See Marin, "Effective," n 68.
70. See Suzanne Andrea Bloks and Ton van den Brink, "The Impact on National Sovereignty of Mutual Recognition in the AFSJ. Case-Study of the European Arrest Warrant," *German Law Journal* 22, no. 1 (2021): 45.
71. Daillier and Pellet, *Droit International Public*, 7th ed. (Paris: LGDJ, 2008), 515.
72. See Wendy De Bond, "Overcoming Offence Diversities in EU Policy Making: Needs and Feasibility Assessment" (PhD thesis, University of Gent 2012), 27–52.

at least little to do with sovereignty.[73] Nowadays, different legal regulations can occur in one country, like the US, and more complicated situations, like mainland China, Hong Kong, and Macau. As Zhao Guoqiang proposes, different legal systems and independent judicial territories are the main basis for the application of the double criminality principle.[74]

5.1.2 The relationship between double criminality and the nature of offences and penalties

The European arrest warrant experience shows that double criminality can be abolished for some categories of crime without breaching the principles of legality and foreseeability of sanctions.[75] It is the nature of the 32 listed categories of offences that determines the application of the principle.

From the 32 categories of offences,[76] we find that the traditional offences included are serious crimes on which all Member States have cracked down in criminal law. Most of the remaining offences in the 32 categories are harmonized through the European law. These offences can also be found in UN and other international conventions. Hence, regarding offences and penalties, there is a high degree of consistency between Member States. For some exceptional acts like abortion and euthanasia, a proportionality check is suggested. Overall, the principle of legality and the foreseeability of the sanctions can be guaranteed even where there is no double criminality check in the requested Member State for listed offences.

Consistency of criminal legislation can also be found in mainland China, Hong Kong, and Macau. Some traditional serious crimes are punished by all three regions, including killing, robbery, and rape. There are also UN conventions on particular crimes which all of the regions have joined, such as the UN conventions on combatting corruption, terrorism, and trafficking in human beings. All of these crimes can be considered to be exempted from the double criminality check. At the same time, the proportionality principle can still be applied to guarantee the principle of legality and foreseeability of sanctions. The following sections address those details.

73. See Su, "Woguo," 141, n 19.
74. See Zhao, "Yiguo," n 20.
75. This point is mainly worried about by the scholars and the public which insist on the retention of double criminality, the analysis in this part just to explain that abolishing the double criminality on some crimes will not breach the principle of legality and the foreseeability of sanctions.
76. Discussed in the above section 4.2.1.2.

5.1.3 The relationship between double criminality and human rights protection

In a modern society, the double criminality principle is closely related to human rights protection.[77] The principle undoubtedly contributes to human rights protection such as by excluding non-criminal political offences and trivial requests.[78] But abolishing the double criminality check for some offences will not breach human rights. Essentially, it is not the double criminality requirement that is set aside, but the requirement of its verification.[79] As mentioned above, the method for choosing the 32 categories of offences is scientific and prudent, and can guarantee the principle of legality and the foreseeability of sanctions even without the check for double criminality.

It is the same for mainland China, Hong Kong, and Macau. Abolishing the double criminality check on certain categories of offences will not necessarily endanger human rights, and the key is how the relevant offences are selected.

5.2 Designing a partial non-verification double criminality principle between mainland China, Hong Kong, and Macau

5.2.1 Double criminality as a general rule

Neither completely abolishing nor retaining the double criminality principle is ideal between mainland China, Hong Kong, and Macau. The partial abolition of the double criminality principle is the best choice. Double criminality can be used as a general principle between mainland China, Hong Kong, and Macau. But it should be emphasized that the law of the requesting region is the priority. That is, as long as the act for which the arrest warrant is issued also constitutes a crime in the requested region and the maximum penalty in the requesting region is above 12 months for prosecution or minimum six months remaining on an imposed penalty, execution of the warrant should be granted. The priority given to the law of requesting region guarantees the effectiveness of execution and the full implementation of the mutual recognition principle.

---

77. See Blaas Fey-Constanze, "Double Criminality in International Extradition Law" (LLM Thesis, University of Stellenbosch, December 2003), 19, https://core.ac.uk/download/pdf/37376692.pdf.
78. See Boister, "Global Simplification," n 25.
79. See Barbolla, "The European Arrest Warrant," n 44.

5.2.2 Categories of offences which can be beyond the double criminality principle

Partially abolishing the double criminality principle will be a new approach for the China domestic surrender system. Relevant experience can be taken from the European arrest warrant system. Firstly, traditional serious offences like murder, rape, robbery, and theft can be listed. Secondly, the offences which are specifically addressed in UN conventions or other international conventions should fall into this category too, including corruption, terrorism, trafficking in human beings, trafficking in drugs, organized crime, and unlawful seizure of aircraft. Thirdly, there are acts which constitute crimes in one region but are not criminalized in other regions;[80] if these offences seriously breach the relevant interest, culture, or customs locally and should be combated specifically, they can also be added into the list. The condition may be that the maximum penalty for that offence should be above three years in the requesting region. The list can be lengthened or shortened with time, based on a careful review by a specialized legal team.

Hong Kong,[81] Macau,[82] and mainland China[83] have all legislated on crimes against national security. It has been suggested that the double criminality check should be removed for the crimes against national security.[84] This chapter recommends that double criminality should be applied in order to enhance trust among the public in the China domestic surrender system, and also to offer more time for the judicial authorities to become familiar with the new "extradition" system.[85] Hong Kong's Safeguarding National Security Ordinance was only recently enacted and the national security awareness of the Hong Kong public remains low; hence the double criminality principle can function as a psychological safeguard and dispel tension in negotiations for surrender arrangements.[86]

80. These include racial discrimination in Macau (Macau Penal Code, art. 233 (1)), incest in Hong Kong (Crimes Ordinance, s. 47 pt. 5), and illegal use of farmland in Mainland (China Criminal Law, art. 342).
81. Hong Kong's national security law was legislated on June 30, 2020, aiming to safeguard the security of the People's Republic of China and Hong Kong.
82. Macau's national security law was legislated in 2009, aiming to safeguard the security of the People's Republic of China and Macau.
83. The relevant crimes are mainly stipulated in the China Criminal Law.
84. See Zhao, "Yiguo," n 20.
85. See Yanhong Yin, "The Surrender of Fugitive Offenders between Mainland China, Hong Kong, and Macau: Relevance of the Political Offence Exception?" *Hong Kong Law Journal* 51, no. 3 (2021): 951.
86. In this chapter, "terrorism" will be beyond the scope of the double criminality check, mainly because it has been internationally recognized as a "severe" but "non-political" crime. Combating terrorism is an international obligation confirmed in international conventions; it is not an exception for Mainland China, Hong Kong, and Macau.

5.2.3 The proportionality principle should be complied with

Human rights protection should be sufficiently guaranteed, despite the fact that the China arrest warrant system should also be based on the mutual recognition principle. The requesting region should apply the proportionality principle and make a proportionality check when issuing an arrest warrant, to guarantee that the warrant is necessary and urgent. The check elements should include the seriousness of the crime, the interests of victims, the possibility of conviction and the possible penalty. For example, in Hong Kong's common law system, the threshold for criminalization is very low: stealing 50 yuan may constitute theft. But it is doubtful that this kind of act should justify a China arrest warrant; most likely, the answer would be "no" under the proportionality principle. A manual on the application of proportionality principle should be made and distributed to the judicial authorities in the three regions, which can offer guidance and enhance consistency in implementing the principle.

At the same time, following the experience of the European arrest warrant and holding to the spirit of the mutual recognition principle, this chapter recommends that *prima facia* is not applied in the requested region and only a formality check is needed.[87] Requested regions still need to check if the relevant documents comply,[88] including as to the identity of the requested person, evidence of an enforceable judgment or arrest warrant, the nature and legal classification of the offence, the description of the circumstances in which the offence was committed, and the penalty imposed. If relevant documents are missing, more information should be offered by the requesting region, otherwise the China arrest warrant would be invalid and non-executable. See Figure 5.2 on page 111 for details.

6 Conclusion

The double criminality principle has traditionally been applied in international extradition. Its importance is still recognized but the application of the principle to avoid frustrating extradition has become a problem. This is also so for its application in the China domestic surrender system.

The experience of the partial abolition of the principle in the European arrest warrant system can offer inspiration to mainland China, Hong Kong, and Macau. In the China domestic surrender system, the three regions can maintain double criminality as a general principle but exempt some categories of offences. This will better

87. In the extradition treaties mainland China (China) has signed with foreign countries, three kinds of evidence requirement exist: *prima facia*, evidence requirement lower than *prima facia*, and no evidence check needed.
88. See EAW FD, art. 8.

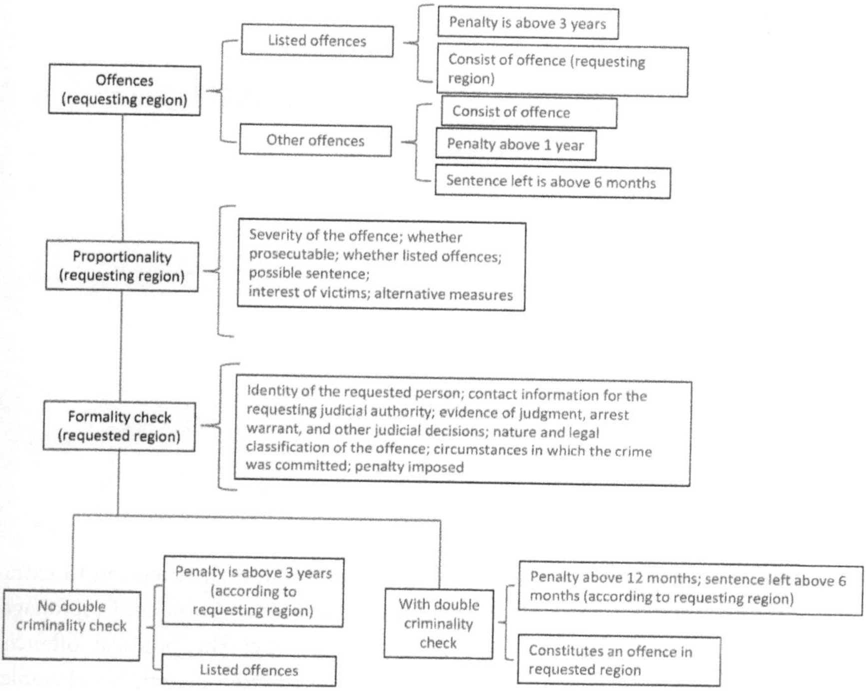

Figure 5.2: China arrest warrant checks for double criminality

respond to the "one country, two systems" policy, safeguard human rights, and at the same time improve efficiency in combating crimes.

On the whole, the double criminality principle still can be applied. Certain categories of offences should be listed for waiver of the double criminality check taking into account the local political, social, and cultural conditions. The proportionality principle should be formally recognized and applicable by the requesting region. In the requested region, no *prima facia* is needed and only a formality check can be made. In this way, partial abolition of double criminality can become an aspect of the China arrest warrant system as it has been practiced in the European arrest warrant system.

6
The Application of the Political Offences Exception

1 Introduction

The China arrest warrant system must address the traditional exception to extradition for political offences including treason, secession, sedition, and espionage. Under the "one country, two systems" policy, whether the political offences exception should be applied in a China domestic surrender system is debatable. This chapter argues that there should be no political offences exception in the China arrest warrant system. This is in line with international trends and inspired by the abolition of the political offences exception in the EU extradition system. It is also based on the political and legal realities of mainland China, Hong Kong, and Macau.

In this chapter, firstly, I introduce the current disputes over the political offences exception in mainland China, Hong Kong, and Macau. Secondly, I explore the origin and development of the exception in international extradition. Thirdly, I analyze its abolition in the EU extradition and European arrest warrant systems. Finally, I analyze why the political offences exception should not be applied to the China arrest warrant system.

2 Disputes over the political offences exception between mainland China, Hong Kong, and Macau

The view has been expressed that because both mainland China and Hong Kong (Macau) have the obligation to prohibit acts against national security, the concept of political offences should not be recognized and the refusal of a surrender request on the ground of the political offences exception should not be permitted.[1] It has also been suggested that the primary objective of the political offences exception is to maintain the sovereignty and political system of a country (the requested country); since Hong Kong and mainland China belong to the same country, the principle should not apply.[2] There are also views that Hong Kong and mainland China have different political systems and different protection of citizens' political rights; Hong Kong has its own legislation on crimes of treason, sedition, and the like; the application of the political offences exception in China's domestic surrender system contributes to the guarantee of Hong Kong's (Macau's) legal system and way of life under the Basic Law.[3]

However, after scrutinizing the application of the political offences exception in international extradition and in the European arrest warrant system, we see that the exception does not function effectively and is not an inevitable rule in closely related regions. This offers clear guidance for the China arrest warrant system.

3 The political offences exception internationally

3.1 Origin and controversy

The practice of extradition dates back to at least 13 BCE, when an extradition treaty was signed between an Egyptian Pharaoh and a Hittite King.[4] Extradition treaties were later used by European monarchs to gain custody over fugitive political offenders.[5] The primary purpose of these treaties was to protect the standing of the monarchy by ensuring the state's ability to punish those who could endanger its status.[6] In light of this goal, many of the treaties concluded during the eighteenth and early nineteenth centuries were concerned with the return of military deserters,

1. Zhao Guoqiang 赵国强, "Lun yiguo liangzhi xiade yijiao taofan jizhi" 论 "一国两制"下的移交逃犯机制 [The discussion on the surrender of fugitive offenders mechanism under "one country, two systems"], *Xingzheng* 行政 20, no. 78 (2007): 1050.
2. See Zhao Yongcheng, "Analysis of the Constitutional Basis of Chinese Judicial Assistance" (Academic Conference on Judicial Cooperation under One Country Two Systems, Faculty of Law of the University of Hong Kong, 1999), 5.
3. Chau Pak-kwan and Stephen Lam, "Research Study on the Agreement between Hong Kong and Mainland Concerning Surrender of Fugitive Offenders" [March 2001] 85, Legislative Council Secretariat, Research and Library Services Division and Legal Service Division, Hong Kong, https://www.legco.gov.hk/yr00-01/english/library/erp05.pdf.
4. Ivan Anthony Shearer, *Extradition in International Law* (Manchester: Manchester University Press, 1971), 5.
5. M. Cherif Bassiouni, *International Extradition and World Public Order* (Leiden: Sijthoff, 1974), 4–5.
6. Bassiouni, *International Extradition*, n 5.

which facilitated maintenance of the national war machine.[7] The political offences exception first appeared in the Belgian Extradition Act of October 1, 1833.[8] Other Western governments soon followed. Four things can account for this choice: (1) recognition of the legitimacy of political dissent; (2) the desire to protect political offenders from summary execution or delivery to a biased tribunal; (3) the belief that the extraditing state should remain detached from the internal affairs of the requesting state;[9] and (4) it was preferable not to incur the wrath of an insurgent group since there was a chance that it might form the next government.[10]

Political offences fit into two broad categories: pure and relative offences. A pure political offence is a crime that is directed against the "security and structure of the state" or "the regime of official power" and that contains none of the elements of a common crime.[11] This category of offences is limited to treason, espionage, and sedition.[12] Relative political offences are common crimes, such as murder or theft, which are connected with a political act. These offences may qualify for the political offences exception.

But the concept of "political offence" is ill-defined, and there are practical difficulties with putting appropriate evidence before a court to establish the exception.[13] There is also an argument that the political offences exception has provided a basis for unfair and discriminatory treatment between domestic and foreign political offenders. In the event that a political offence was committed within a state's own borders, the perpetrator would be punished according to the laws of the state. By contrast, in cases where the crime was committed in another state, the perpetrator could remain free due to the political offences exception.[14] The neutrality argument

---

7. Eric W. McNeil, "Comments: The Political Offense Exception: An Historical Analysis and Model for the Future," *Tulane Law Review* 64 (1989): 1196.
8. See Harvard Research in International Law: Draft Convention on Extradition 1935 (29), *The American Journal of International Law* 29 (1935): 362–63.
9. See McNeil, "Comments," 1197, n 7.
10. Christine Van Den Wyngaert, *The Political Offence Exception to Extradition* (Berlin: Springer, 1981), 22. See also Francis A. Allen, *The Crimes of Politics: Political Dimensions of Criminal Justice* (Cambridge, MA: Harvard University Press, 1974), 26.
11. See McNeil, "Comments," n 7.
12. See Lora L. Deere, "Political Offenses in the Law and Practice of Extradition," *American Journal of International Law* 27 (1933): 247; see also Manuel R. Garcia-Mora, "Treason, Sedition and Espionage as Political Offenses under the Law of Extradition," *University of Pittsburgh Law Review* 26 (1964): 65.
13. See Gavan Griffith and Claire Harris, "Recent Development in the Law of Extradition," *Melbourne Journal of International Law* 6, no. 1 (2005): 33–54.
14. J. Reuben Clark Jr., Fredrick R. Coudert, and Julian Mack, "The Nature and a Definition of Political Offence in International Extradition Discussion," *Proceedings of American Society of International Law* 3 (1909): 140.

used in favor of the political offences exception is also weak.[15] It provides states with the possibility of supporting rebellious action in enemy states without engaging in open war.[16] Bassiouni further points out that the denial of extradition disrupts the global political order, as it causes turmoil in relations between states, and allows states to abstain from prosecuting offenders regardless of their duty to do so.[17] Time has seen the political offences exception declining in importance and practical operation.[18]

3.2 Development of the international extradition treaties: Limiting the exception

The UN Model Treaty on Extradition provides that extradition shall not be granted if the offence for which extradition is requested is regarded by the requested state as an offence of a political nature.[19] However, it adds that "reference to an offence of a political nature shall not include any offence in respect of which the parties have assumed an obligation, pursuant to any multilateral convention, to take prosecutorial action where they do not extradite, or any other offence that the parties have agreed is not an offence of a political character for the purposes of extradition."[20] It further explains that countries may wish to exclude certain conduct, e.g., acts of violence, such as serious offences involving an act of violence against the life, physical integrity, and liberty of a person, from the concept of a political offence.[21] We also find limits on the political offences exception in other UN treaties.[22]

The trend against the political offences exception is most pronounced in the EU, particularly in the European arrest warrant system. However, the European arrest warrant system is not the only one to reject the political offences exception.

---

15. Miguel João Costa, *Extradition Law: Reviewing Grounds for Refusal from Classic Paradigm to Mutual Recognition and Beyond* (Leiden: Brill Nijhoff, 2020), 6.
16. Julia Jansson, *Terrorism, Criminal Law and Politics: The Decline of the Political Offence Exception to Extradition* (Oxford: Routledge, 2020), 75.
17. M. Cherif Bassiouni, *Criminal Law and Its Processes: The Law of Public Order* (New York: Thomas Press, 1969), 234.
18. See Griffith and Harris, "Recent Development," n 13.
19. UN Model Treaty on Extradition, art. 3(a).
20. UN Model Treaty on Extradition, art. 3(a).
21. See Model Treaty on Extradition, cited in its footnote 8.
22. The offences excluded from the political offence can be found in Convention for the Suppression of Unlawful Seizure of Aircraft, the Convention for the Suppression of Unlawful Acts against the Safety of Civil Aviation, Convention on the Prevention and Punishment of Crimes against Internationally Protected Persons, International Convention for the Suppression of Terrorism Bombings, International Convention for the Suppression of the Financing of Terrorism.

The Nordic arrest warrant (NAW) mechanism,[23] the EU Surrender Agreement with Iceland and Norway,[24] the EU-US Extradition Agreement, and the UK-US Extradition treaty all do the same. These new practices reveal that the political offences exception is not an indispensable part of extradition.[25]

4 Application of the political offences exception in the EU

4.1 Abolishment of the political offences exception in the EU extradition system

4.1.1 The history from the political offences exception to its abolition

The 1957 European Convention on Extradition provides for the political offences exception. It states that extradition shall not be granted if the offence in respect of which it is requested is regarded by the requested party as a political offence or as an offence connected with a political offence.[26] The Convention also excludes some offences from the political offences category.[27] In 1975 the Additional Protocol to the European Convention on Extradition excluded yet more offences.[28] It is clear that the exclusion of some offences from the category of political offences in Europe's extradition system was influenced by international and regional conventions.[29]

In the 1996 Convention Relating to Extradition between the Member States of the European Union, all offences are excluded from the scope of political offences. The convention provides that no offence may be regarded by the requested Member State as a political offence, as an offence connected with a political offence, or as an offence inspired by political motives.[30] It also stipulates that the reservation

23. The Convention is authentic in five languages: Danish, Finnish, Icelandic, Norwegian, and Swedish. On the Convention, see e.g. Z. Deen-Racsmány, "The European Arrest Warrant and the Surrender of Nationals Revisited: The Lessons of Constitutional Challenges," *European Journal of Crime, Criminal Law and Criminal Justice* 14, no. 3 (2006): 302.
24. Agreement between the European Union and the Republic of Iceland and the Kingdom of Norway on the surrender procedure between the Member States of the European Union and Iceland and Norway [2006] OJL 292/2.
25. See Costa, *Extradition Law*, 502–6, n 15.
26. European Convention on Extradition 1957, art. 3(1).
27. European Convention on Extradition 1957, art. 3(3).
28. 1975 Protocol to the European Convention on Extradition, art. 1.
29. These include the European Convention on the Suppression of Terrorism, the Convention for the Suppression of Unlawful Seizure of Aircraft, the Convention for the Suppression of Unlawful Acts against the Safety of Civil Aviation.
30. 1996 Convention relating to Extradition between the Member States of the European Union, art. 5(1).

made pursuant to Article 13[31] of the European Convention on the Suppression of Terrorism shall not apply to extradition between Member States.[32]

Under the European arrest warrant system, there is no political offence exception.[33] The EAW Framework Decision provides three mandatory refusal grounds and seven optional refusal grounds, with no space given to the political offences exception. Still, the preamble to the EAW FD indicates concern for political persecution. Point 12 of the preamble states that nothing in the Framework Decision may be interpreted as prohibiting refusal to surrender a person for whom a European arrest warrant has been issued for the purpose of prosecuting or punishing a person on the grounds of political opinions or if the person's position may be prejudiced for any such reason. A similar clause can also be found in the old European extradition conventions.

4.1.2 The reasons for the abolition of political offences exception in the EU

4.1.2.1 The influence of international trends

As said above, there is a tendency for more and more offences to be excluded from the scope of political offences and regarded as extraditable through international conventions.[34] These offences include unlawful acts against the safety of civil aviation, unlawful seizure of aircraft, and crimes against internationally protected persons. Most of the EU countries are contracting states for these conventions, with the obligation to exclude the offences from the category of political offences.[35] This is also in line with the UN Model Treaty on Extradition.

---

31. Article 13 is the clause of European Convention on the Suppression of Terrorism regarding reservations; it provides that any state may, at the time of signature or when depositing its instrument of ratification, acceptance or approval, declare that it reserves the right to refuse extradition in respect of any offence mentioned in Article 1 which it considers to be a political offence, an offence connected with a political offence, or an offence inspired by political motives.
32. 1996 Convention relating to Extradition between the Member States of the European Union, art. 5(4).
33. See Griffith and Harris, "Recent Development," 33, n 13.
34. See Sarah L. Nagy, "Political Offense Exception to United States Extradition Policy: Aut Dedere Aut Judicare (Either Extradite or Prosecute)," *Indiana International & Comparative Law Review* 1 (1991): 109.
35. For example, Article 8(1) of the Convention stipulates that the offences shall be deemed to be included as extraditable offences in any extradition treaty existing between contracting states. Contracting states undertake to include the offences as extraditable offences in every extradition treaty to be concluded between them. Article 8(2) provides that if a contracting state which makes extradition conditional on the existence of a treaty receives a request for extradition from another contracting state with which it has no extradition treaty, it may at its option consider the Convention as the legal basis for extradition in respect of the offences. Extradition shall be subject to other conditions provided by the law of the requesting state.

4.1.2.2 The trend of EU extradition development

In the Additional Protocol to the European Convention on Extradition 1975 and the European Convention on the Suppression of Terrorism 1977, the EU restricted the application of the political offences exception by excluding crimes against humanity, violations specified in Geneva conventions, and a series of terrorist crimes from the scope of political offences. When it came to the 1996 convention, the Council directly stated that no offence may be regarded by the requested Member State as a political offence, as an offence connected with a political offence, or as an offence inspired by political motives.[36] So, before the European arrest warrant Framework Decision abolished the political offences exception completely, there was already a trend towards that abolition in Europe and a lot of preparatory work had been done. To fully abolish the political offences exception was just a matter of time.

4.1.2.3 Deepening mutual trust and EU integration

The main reason for the political offences exception is to protect a political offender from a biased tribunal; another reason is because that the extraditing state should remain detached from the internal affairs of the requesting state.[37] The European arrest warrant serves to strengthen EU political integration. Criminal justice, which used to be administered under the third pillar of the EU as an intergovernmental issue, has been moved to the first pillar as a supranational issue under the direct management of the European Community. Civil affairs and criminal affairs have become the affairs of both the Member States and the EU.[38] When it comes to political offences, neither surrender nor non-surrender can be taken as intervention in internal affairs any longer.[39]

Furthermore, all EU Member States have signed the European Convention on Human Rights (ECHR) and the Charter of Fundamental Rights of the European Union (CFR). All Member States are under the jurisdiction of Court of Justice of the European Union (CJEU) and the European Court of Human Rights (ECtHR). Under these circumstances, there is also no need to emphasize the political offences exception, which will harm mutual trust between Member States. The European arrest warrant is the first instrument to enforce the mutual recognition principle.

36. See 1996 Convention Relating to Extradition between the Member States of the European Union, art. 5.
37. See McNeil, "Comments," n 7.
38. See Finn Laursen, "The Lisbon Treaty: A First Assessment," *L'Europe En Formation* 4, no. 362 (2011): 45.
39. See Harmen van der Wilt, "The Political Offence Exception in Extradition Law: An Antidote to Prefixed Ideas about Political Integration in Europe," *Maastricht Journal of European Comparative Law* 4, no. 1 (1997): 25.

If the political offences exception was retained by Member States, the implementation of mutual recognition principle and mutual trust principle would be heavily compromised.[40]

4.2 Rights protection for political offences and European arrest warrants

4.2.1 European arrest warrant decisions are judicial

The surrender procedure in the European arrest warrant (EAW) system is guided and practiced by judicial authorities.[41] If there is a dispute on the issuance or execution of a warrant, the CJEU can offer a preliminary ruling. This can provide a positive response to the political offences controversies in the EAW system. The issue of political offences is politically sensitive, concerning diplomatic relations between countries.[42] The traditional political offences exception is closely tied to administrative discretion and impacted by the diplomatic relations between countries.[43] But the European arrest warrant is built on mutual trust of the rule of law in Member States, and the surrender procedure is under the control of the judicial authorities which can guarantee that the surrender is objective, legitimate, and in line with rule of law.[44] This offers a sound basis to abolish the political offences exception.

4.2.2 The partial double criminality principle can provide protection

In the European arrest warrant mechanism, 32 categories of offences need not be verified for double criminality, but the "pure" political offences like rebellion, sedition, and espionage are not listed in this category, so that the double criminality requirement still applies. In the Puigdemont case, Puigdemont was charged with rebellion by the Spanish Court, but under the German Criminal Law, the double criminality requirement could not be satisfied. The counterpart crime of rebellion

40. See Dace Winther, "Extradition, Asylum and Mutual Trust in the European Union: One Man's Terrorist is Another Man's Freedom of Fighter, yet Another Man's Asylum Seeker, yet Another Man's Fugitive" (Master's thesis, Lund University, 2018).
41. As to the meaning of judicial authority, see chapter 2.
42. See James J. Kinneally III, "The Political Offense Exception: Is the United States–United Kingdom Supplementary Extradition Treaty the Beginning of the End?" *American University International Law Review*2, no. 1 (1987): 203.
43. See Maria P. Imbalzano, "In Re Mackin: Is the Application of the Political Offense Exception an Extradition Issue for the Judicial or Executive Branch?" *Fordham International Law Journal* (1981): 565.
44. See Anne Pieter van der Mei, "The European Arrest Warrant System: Recent Developments in the Case Law of the Court of Justice," *Maastricht Journal of European and Comparative Law* 24, no. 6 (2017): 882.

in German law, sedition, required violence involved in the criminal act, whereas the acts of Puigdmeont were regarded as peaceful.[45] It is likely that where the double criminality principle cannot be satisfied because of diversified legislation in Member States, the surrender of offenders of "political offences" will be rejected. In this way, the double criminality principle functions to protect human rights where the political offences exception is abolished.

4.2.3 Human rights clauses can offer further protection

In the Preamble to the EAW Framework Decision, point 12 stipulates that nothing in the Framework Decision may be interpreted as prohibiting refusal to surrender a person for whom a European arrest warrant has been issued when there are reasons to believe, on the basis of objective elements, that the warrant has been issued for the purpose of prosecuting or punishing a person on the grounds of his or her political opinions, or that person's position may be prejudiced for any such reason. However, human rights are not listed as mandatory or optional grounds for non-execution of a European arrest warrant, so, in theory, their application should be exceptional. CJEU decisions show that the human rights ground can be used in exceptional cases where the human rights violation is comprehensive and systematic and the human rights risk of the requested individual is real and objective.[46]

5 The political offences issue in the surrender system between mainland China, Hong Kong, and Macau

5.1 The traditional political offences exception should not be applied

5.1.1 The origins of political offences exception: sovereignty

From the origins of the political offences exception, we can see that it is mainly used to avoid intervening in another country's internal affairs and to maintain good diplomatic relationships between requesting and requested countries.[47] Mainland China, Hong Kong, and Macau belong to one country, the PRC, and there is no basis for the application of a political offences exception from the perspective of not intervening in the internal affairs of another country. In other words, this traditional

45. See Braum Stefan, "The Carles Puigdemont Case: Europe's Criminal Law in the Crisis of Confidence," *German Law Journal* 19, no. 6 (2018): 1349.
46. See Theodora. A. Christou, "Justice and Trust: The European Arrest Warrant and Human Rights" (PhD thesis, Queen Mary University of London, June 2013).
47. As to the origin of the political offences exception see the above section 3.1.

theory supporting the political offences exception in international extradition does not apply to domestic surrender in China.

The more fundamental ground behind the political offences exception in international extradition is that different countries have different political interests, including protecting their own citizens, enhancing their international reputations and winning resources in the competition with other countries. The application of the political offences exception is one way to avoid contributing to other countries' interests while at the same time not harming its own interests. For mainland China, Hong Kong, and Macau, every region belongs to the PRC, every region shares the political interests of the country, and every region has the obligation to strive for the common interests of the country. These are reasons to disapply the political offences exception in a China arrest warrant system.

5.1.2 Joint legislation on national security

Since 1997, scholars of China criminal law have agreed that crime against national security involves conduct "intentionally endangering the national security of the PRC."[48] National security includes sovereignty, territorial integrity, and the consolidation of state power.[49] In the China Criminal Law, a special chapter on crimes against national security lists nine offences: treason; sedition and incitement to sedition; rebellion; subversion and incitement to subversion of national sovereignty; surrender to enemies; fleeing off duty; espionage; stealing, penetrating, trading, and illegally offering of State secrets and intelligence overseas; and financing enemies in war.[50] In terms of subversion of national sovereignty, the intention, the act, and the risk of subversion are required.[51] With regard to sedition, in China law and legal practice, mainland China has allowed criticism of government but has stopped short of allowing incitement by public expressions of disaffection against the state.[52] Public critiques or expressions of anger against the state or the local government for concrete errors, mistakes, or flaws in the state government, or their functionary personnel—no matter whether the criticism is warranted or not—shall not be defined as the crime of sedition so long as violence is not involved.[53]

48. Yang Chunxi 杨春喜 and Yang Dunxian 杨敦先, eds., *Zhongguo xingfa lun* 中国刑法论 [Study on China criminal law], 2nd ed. (Beijing: Beijing daxue chubanshe, 2001), 211.
49. Shizhou Wang, "China Crimes Against National Security," *UMKC Law Review* 82, no. 4 (2014): 1043.
50. China Criminal Law, art. 102 and art. 112.
51. See Jia Yu, "Crack Down Crimes against National Sovereignty and Safeguard National Security," *People's Net*, August 5, 2016, http://news.jcrb.com/jxsw/201608/t20160805_1639884.html.
52. See Wang, "China Crimes," 1047, n 49.
53. Zhou Daoluan 周道鸾 and Zhang Jun 张军, eds., *Xingfa zuiming jingshi* 刑法罪名精释 [Elaboration on criminal charges], 3rd ed. (Beijing: Renmin fayuan chubanshe, 2007), 43.

National security legislation is established not only in mainland China; Hong Kong and Macau have followed suit. In 2009, Macau enacted Law on Safeguarding National Security, which enumerated seven offences including treason; secession; subversion of the Central Government; rebellion; stealing national secrets; membership of foreign political organisations or bodies endangering the national security; and membership of Macau local political organisations or bodies establishing ties with the foreign counterparts to endanger national security,[54] in order to comply with the requirement of the Basic Law of the Macau Special Administrative Region. To date, no national security case has been reported in Macau.[55]

On June 30, 2020, the Law of the People's Republic of China on Safeguarding National Security in the Hong Kong Special Administrative Region came into effect. This law listed four offences including secession, subversion of national sovereignty, terrorism, and colluding with foreign forces to endanger national security.[56] This legislation has been criticised for its vagueness. As Johannes Chan wrote, "the law should define precisely what constitutes an act of subversion or sedition, including making clear that such acts must involve violence and have an actual, substantial effect."[57] It is likely that this will be left to the Hong Kong courts to address when dealing with cases in practice. However, where there is ambiguity in a provision of the National Security Law "which permits both an interpretation that is consistent with the Basic Law and an interpretation that is inconsistent with it, the former interpretation should probably be preferred."[58] In addition, Hong Kong still has an obligation to legislate on the other offences listed in Article 23 of the Hong Kong Basic Law.[59]

In summary, national security legislation in mainland China, Hong Kong, and Macau has enacted offences against national security; there is no crime specifically titled a "political offence." It is illogical that the offence of sedition in Hong Kong, which seeks to protect the sovereignty of the PRC, will be regarded as a "notorious political offence" by mainland China, and vice versa, when this offence in two regions is actually serving the same purpose for the same sovereign country. All the national security laws are under the ultimate interpretational power of the Standing

54. See the Macau Law on Safeguarding National Security.
55. See AFP, "National Security Law: Whether Macau Can be Model of Hong Kong," *BBC News*, May 28, 2020, https://www.bbc.com/zhongwen/simp/chinese-news-52817548.
56. The Law of the People's Republic of China on Safeguarding National Security in the Hong Kong Special Administrative Region, arts. 20–35.
57. See Johannes Chan, "Details Vital for New Security Law," *RTHK*, June 14, 2020, https://news.rthk.hk/rthk/en/component/k2/1531974-20200614.htm.
58. Albert H.Y. Chen, "Constitutional Controversies in the Aftermath of the Anti-Extradition Movement 2019," *Hong Kong Law Journal* 50 (2020): 630.
59. Legislative Council Question 6, "Legislation on Article 23 of Basic Law," *Press Release*, May 20, 2020, https://www.info.gov.hk/gia/general/202005/27/P2020052700520.htm.

Committee of National People's Congress (NPCSC). As Simon Young stated, there should be "some degree of harmonization between the national security laws at the national and regional levels. This is not to say that they should be the same but that they should at least be consistent and not diametrically opposed to each other."[60] In practice, there should be no major risk of conflict on the implementation of national security laws in the three regions.

5.1.3 The international trend towards abolishing the political offences exception

From the analysis of international extradition, we see that there is a decline of political offences exception around the world. More and more offences have been excluded from the scope of political offences. And in some closely related regions, like the European Union, the political offences exception has been abolished completely. This development is not only based on the need to combat international and cross-border crimes, but also on the condition that more and more trust is built up among these countries. To mainland China, Hong Kong, and Macau, abolishing the political offences exception in the China arrest warrant system will be a positive response to the international trend as well as to the political integration reality of the country, the PRC.

Another factor should be taken into account when choosing to abolish the political offences exception is that the levels of protection of political rights and freedoms are different in the three regions. Looking at the implementation of the national Constitution, the Basic Law of Hong Kong, and the Basic Law of Macau, we see that the fundamental rights of individuals are different in the three regions, and obviously Hong Kong residents and Macau residents enjoy rights of greater scope. For example, according to the Basic Law of Hong Kong, the International Covenant on Civil and Political Rights (ICCPR) and the International Convention on Economic , Social, and Cultural Rights (ICESCR) remain valid in Hong Kong and are applied through legislation of the Hong Kong government.[61] The same clause can be found in the Basic Law of Macau.[62] But no similar clause exists in the national Constitution and the ICCPR has not been ratified by the National People's Congress. It is self-evident that the political rights enumerated in the ICCPR are not sufficiently guaranteed in mainland China. In practice we find that torture is still

---

60. Simon N.M. Young, "Old Law in New Bottles: Reintroducing National Security Legislation in Hong Kong," in *China's National Security: Endangering Hong Kong's Rule of Law*, ed. Cora Chan and Fiona de Londras (Oxford: Hart, 2020), 218.
61. See Basic Law of Hong Kong, art. 39.
62. See Basic Law of Macau, art. 40.

applied in mainland China, although it is illegal according to the China Criminal Procedure Law.[63]

The divergence on rights protection in the three regions may have the result that some acts which have been criminalized in mainland China are legally protected in Hong Kong and Macau. This also leads to the lack of trust of Hong Kong and Macau in mainland China's judicial system, and concerns remain about potential political persecution in the Mainland. In view of these concerns, the following safeguards are suggested.[64]

5.2 Safeguards for the non-application of the political offences exception between mainland China, Hong Kong, and Macau

5.2.1 The human rights ground can be used to reject surrender in exceptional situations

Human rights checks can function to protect the rights of requested persons in the China arrest warrant system which lacks the political offences exception. With reference to human rights scrutiny in the EAW system, prior to rejecting a surrender request, at least two assessments should be made. The first is to evaluate the general recent human rights situation in the requesting region. The second is to assess the risk of human rights violations in respect of the requested person in the specific court according to concrete and objectively obtained information. The requesting region could be asked to provide further documentation to prove the real judicial or detention situation the requested person would face after surrender. Under certain situations, the requested region could require the requesting region to offer guarantees or assurances to protect the human rights of the requested person. And a monitoring system after surrender, institutional restrictions, or sanctions for breach of assurances by the local executive organ or law enforcement organs could be negotiated by the requested region.

5.2.2 The role of judicial authorities should be emphasized

The judicial authorities of the three regions should play the dominant role in China domestic surrender, to guarantee functional rights protection in the China arrest warrant system. This should avoid or reduce political interference with the surrender procedure and protect offenders' rights to a fair trial, particularly when offenders

63. See China Criminal Procedure Law, art. 56.

64. Yanhong Yin, "The Surrender of Fugitive Offenders between Mainland China, Hong Kong and Macau: Relevance of the Political Offence Exception?" *Hong Kong Law Journal* 51, no. 3 (2021): 951.

commit "political offences." Under the Hong Kong FOO, the courts' role in human rights protection is curtailed as the Chief Executive shares part of that power. This research suggests that the courts can play a fuller role in human rights scrutiny. While there is still concern that in mainland China the courts are dictated to by the Chinese Communist Party, it is still best to assign the role to the courts rather than the administrative authorities. Executive officials in Hong Kong and Macau are subordinated to the Central Government and their independence is less guaranteed than that of their judicial counterparts.

5.2.3 Application of double criminality

The double criminality requirement can also function as an important tool for the protection of human rights. Although the legislation on national security in the three regions protects the same interests under the same ultimate interpretative power, and even legislated by the same institution,[65] there are different judicial systems protecting national security. This means that double criminality can function as a safeguard for human rights. For example, if a person in mainland China desecrated a political figure's image and fled to Hong Kong, and thereafter were wanted by the Mainland for the charge of subverting the Central Government or state sovereignty, the double criminality check can be applied by the Hong Kong courts. If the act does not fall within the definition of a crime on the Hong Kong side, surrender can be refused. The rights of the individuals can be protected under a double criminality check in a way that is more definite and less controversial than applying the political offences exception. Besides the double criminality check, human rights scrutiny also has an important role to play due to its greater flexibility and responsiveness as discussed above.

Summarising the above analysis, the reasons to abolish the political offences exception and the safeguards after the abolition are shown in Figure 6.1 on page 126.

6 Conclusion

From the European experience we see that the abolition of the political offences exception reflected the international cooperative tendency to combat serious and cross-border crimes as well as the increasing political and legal integration of the European Union. The political offences exception can also be excluded in the China arrest warrant system. This is not only because the principle *per se* is controversial and is declining in its application to international extradition, but also because surrender between mainland China, Hong Kong, and Macau occurs within a sovereign

65. The Standing Committee of the National People's Congress.

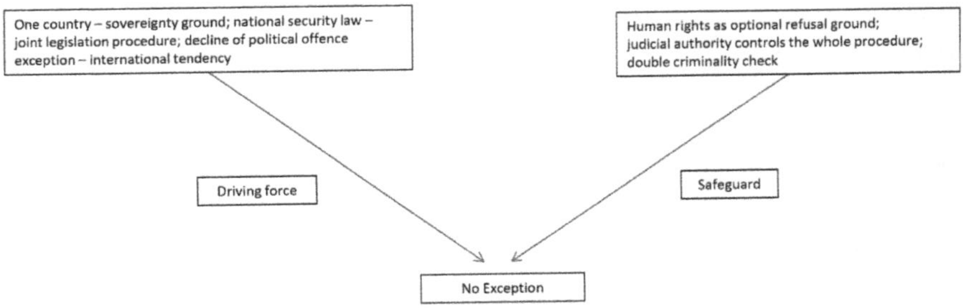

Figure 6.1: The political offences exception

country. The three regions have the same political and legal obligations to protect the same sovereign interests and national security of the PRC. From the perspective of human rights protection, the political offences exception is not irreplaceable. After its exclusion, the double criminality check and human rights scrutiny can be applied to guarantee the rights of requested persons; courts are suggested to take a more important role in the surrender procedure to strengthen human rights protection.

7

The Application of the Nationality Exception

1 Introduction

The non-extradition of one's own nationals, or the nationality exception, is a principle of the traditional extradition system.[1] In many states the prohibition on extraditing nationals even constitutes a constitutional guarantee.[2] However, the application of the principle has declined and become doubtful with globalization. The Model Treaty on Extradition provides for a nationality exception, but makes it an optional rather than a mandatory feature.[3] Whether and how the principle can be applied in the China domestic surrender system, is open to question.[4]

Surrender in China's three legal territories is different from international extradition in that it occurs in one country of which the majority of residents share the same nationality.[5] At the same time, the three legal territories have independent power to govern their residents. It is doubtful that the traditional nationality exception principle can be fully applied between mainland China, Hong Kong, and Macau as in international extradition. Meanwhile, the nationality exception has evolved in

1. This is especially the case in civil law system: all of the more than 50 extradition treaties China has concluded with foreign countries include the nationality exception.
2. See Miguel João Costa, *Extradition Law: Reviewing Grounds for Refusal from the Classic Paradigm to Mutual Recognition and Beyond* (Leiden: Brill Nijhoff, 2020), 552.
3. See Costa, *Extradition Law* 256, n 2. See also Model Treaty on Extradition, art. 4(a).
4. See Wang Zhongxing 王仲兴 and Guo Tianwu 郭天武, *Neidi yu xianggang xingshi sifa hezuo yanjiu* 内地与香港刑事司法合作研究 [Study on judicial cooperation in criminal matters between mainland China and Hong Kong] (Beijing: Beijing daxue chubanshe, 2008), 221. See also Huang Feng 黄风, Yindu wenti yanjiu 引渡问题研究 [Study on extradition] (Beijing: Zhongguo zhengfa daxue chubanshe, 2006), 224.
5. See Chen Duanhong 陈端洪, "Lijie xianggang zhengzhi" 理解香港政治 [To understand Hong Kong politics], *Zhongwai faxue qikan* 中外法学期刊 28, no. 5 (2016): 1125.

the European arrest warrant system and moved towards abolition.[6] This development also offers inspiration to the China domestic surrender system.

In this chapter, firstly, I explore the problems mainland China, Hong Kong, and Macau will encounter regarding applying the nationality exception principle in their surrender system. Secondly, I analyze the long-standing doubts as to questions of both "exception" and "national" in traditional extradition. Thirdly, I analyze why and how the nationality exception has evolved in the European arrest warrant (EAW) system. Finally, I explore whether and how the EAW approach can be implemented in a China arrest warrant system.

2 Problems with the surrender of nationals (residents) between mainland China, Hong Kong, and Macau

2.1 *Regulations on the surrender of nationals (residents) in the individual extradition (surrender) systems*

In extradition with other countries, mainland China recognizes the nationality exception as a civil law system with Chinese socialism characteristics.[7] The China Extradition Law provides that extradition should be rejected when extradited persons are of Chinese nationality.[8] In the extradition treaties China concludes with foreign countries, the nationality exception principle is similarly stipulated. Besides confirming the principle, these treaties also add that if extradition is rejected on the ground of the nationality exception, the requested party should submit the case to the competent domestic authority for prosecution in compliance with its domestic law.[9]

Hong Kong differs from mainland China on the Chinese nationals and Hong Kong residents[10] in surrender. The Hong Kong Fugitive Offenders Ordinance (FOO) does not rule out the surrender of Chinese nationals or Hong Kong residents. But in some of surrender agreements Hong Kong has signed with foreign

6. See Rob Blekxtoon and Zsuzsanna Deen-Racsmány, "The Decline of the Nationality Exception in European Extradition?" *European Journal of Crime, Criminal Law and Criminal Justice* 13, no. 3 (2005): 317.
7. See He Hairong 何海榕, "Shenhua duiwai kaifang beijingxia zhongguo yindu minalinde tiaozhan he yingdui" 深化对外开放背景下中国引渡面临的挑战与应对 [The challenge and response to the China extradition under the background of deepening open policy], *Renmin sifa* 人民司法 34 (2018): 76.
8. China Extradition Law, art. 8(1).
9. This point can be found in the extradition agreements between mainland China and other countries, such as with Italy, Spain, Portugal, and France.
10. In Hong Kong, residents can be classified into Chinese citizens and foreigners according to their nationality (most of the Hong Kong residents are Chinese), and can also be classified into permanent residents who have the right of abode and the non-permanent residents who do not.

countries, exceptions are stated for Chinese nationals and Hong Kong permanent residents.[11]

Macau's rules on the surrender of nationals or residents[12] can be firstly found in the Macau Cooperation Law in Criminal Matters. Under that law, it is mandatory to refuse the surrender of a person who is a non-Macau resident but has Chinese nationality[13] or a person who is a Macau resident (unless the requesting country is the country of the person's nationality or the surrender obligation is from the self-enforcement clause in the international treaties Macau has applied).[14] This ground can be found in the surrender agreements with both Portugal and South Korea.[15]

2.2 Disputes on the surrender of nationals (residents) between mainland China, Hong Kong, and Macau

Under the Hong Kong Basic Law, the Hong Kong residents are classified into permanent residents and non-permanent residents,[16] and the majority are Chinese nationals.[17] The population structure is similar in Macau.[18] Whether the nationality (residents) exception should be applied in China domestic surrender is open to question.

Some scholars take the position that mainland China and Macau have the tradition of excluding nationals (residents) in extradition (surrender), and Hong Kong has a tradition to surrender its residents under its common law system; thus between mainland China and Macau, the nationality (residents) exception can be applied, but regarding Hong Kong it can be different.[19] There is also the view that the nationality (residents) exception should not be applied between mainland China and Hong Kong, because the application of the principle is contrary to mutual respect and not intervening in each other's criminal jurisdiction; practically, Hong Kong is adjacent to mainland China and the movement of residents between the

11. See the Surrender Agreement between Hong Kong and Singapore, Surrender Agreement between Hong Kong and Canada, Surrender Agreement between Hong Kong and Portugal.
12. As in Hong Kong, Macau residents can be classified into permanent residents and non-permanent residents.
13. See the Macau Law on Judicial Cooperation in Criminal Matters, art. 33(2).
14. See the Macau Law on Judicial Cooperation in Criminal Matters, art. 33(3).
15. See Surrender Agreement between Macau and Portugal, art. 4(2); see also Surrender Agreement between Macau and South Korea, art. 3(1).
16. Basic Law of Hong Kong, art. 24.
17. See Chen, "Lijie Xianggang," n 5.
18. Basic Law of Macau, art. 24.
19. See Liu Peng 刘鹏 and Feng Weiguo 冯卫国, "Guoji yindu hezuo yuanze kuangjiaxia zhongguo quji taofan yijiao wenti yanjiu" 国际引渡合作原则框架下中国区际逃犯移交问题研究 [Study on China regional surrender of fugitive offenders under international extradition framework], *Qiusuo* 求索 2 (2015): 107.

two regions is frequent, so if the nationality (residents) exception were applied Hong Kong would become a haven for criminals.[20] Between mainland China and Macau, there is also the view that the nationality exception is the international custom, but mainland China and Macau both belong to the PRC, and China's Nationality Law is also applied in Macau, so there is no room for the nationality exception; nor should the residents' exception be applied, as it will be contrary to the "one country, two systems" policy and detrimental to the fight against crime.[21]

The debate on the application of the nationality (resident) exception is heated and no consensus has been reached. The traditional nationality exception principle cannot cope with the complicated situation in the China domestic surrender system. From an international perspective, too, the nationality exception has been controversial.

3 Nationality exception: A controversial principle *per se*

Many states are traditionally opposed to extraditing their own nationals.[22] The nationality exception principle has its origin in the sovereign authority of the ruler to control his subjects, the bond of allegiance between them, and the lack of trust in other legal systems. The reasons traditionally voiced in support of the exception include that the fugitive ought not to be withdrawn from his natural judges; that the state owes its subjects the protection of its laws; that it is impossible to have complete confidence in the justice meted out by a foreign state, especially with regard to a foreigner; and that it is disadvantageous to be tried in a foreign language, separated from friends, resources and character witnesses.[23] Under the territorial jurisdiction and nationality jurisdiction principles, a sovereign country can have criminal jurisdiction over all crimes that occur in its legal territory and also over crimes committed by its nationals overseas; extraditing its nationals to foreign countries for prosecution or execution of punishment means giving up nationality jurisdiction and the legal protection of its nationals; worse, it means giving up judicial sovereignty, so

20. See Zhao Guoqiang 赵国强, "Lun yiguo liangzhi xiade yijiao taofan jizhi" 论"一国两制"下的移交逃犯机制 [The discussion on the surrender of fugitive offenders mechanism under "one country, two systems"], *Xingzheng* 行政 20, no. 78 (2007): 1054.
21. See Zhao Guoqiang 赵国强, "Yiguo liangzhi yu guoji yindu guanli-yi Aumen yu neidi xianghu yijiao taofan wei shijiao" 一国两制与国际引渡惯例–以澳门与内地相互移交逃犯为视角 [One country two systems and international extradition traditions: a perspective from the surrender of fugitive offenders between Mainland and Macau], *Aumen faxue* 澳门法学 3 (2015): 30.
22. See I.A. Shearer, *Extradition in International Law* (Manchester: Manchester University Press, 1971), 94–132. See also M. Cherif Bassiouni, *International Extradition: United States Law and Practice* (New York: Dobbs Ferry 2002), 682–89.
23. See S.A. Williams, "Nationality, Double Jeopardy, Prescription and the Death Sentence as Bases for Refusing Extradition," *International Review of Penal law* 62 (1991): 260–61.

that extradition of nationals should be rejected.[24] Another argument against the extradition of nationals is that it will not help criminals to reintegrate into their own society and adjust to life after punishment.[25]

There are counter-arguments to the above. A court that should assert the right of jurisdiction should be the court where the crime occurred, and the criminal law to be imposed should also be that of the place of the crime, and the principle of closest connection should be applied. If trust in the foreign court is lacking, not only should the extradition of nationals be rejected, the extradition agreement itself should be abolished;[26] if nationals cannot be extradited to countries in which the territorial jurisdiction principle is practiced, criminals will avoid punishment;[27] when a case involves criminals from different countries, rejecting the extradition of one or some criminals will lead to differing judgments under different criminal law systems, which harms the justice; and, from a practical point of view, the court of the country where the crime occurs can better scruitinise evidence and have eyewitnesses at trials.[28] As to rehabilitation argument, this argument is relevant to the enforcement of a penalty but has limited validity at the prosecution stage.[29] The fact that a state bestows constitutional rank to the principle of non-extradition of nationals denotes the importance of the rule to its community, but it does not necessarily translate into the protection of any essential value.[30]

The non-extradition of nationals has somewhat declined in the modern world,[31] for several reasons. It is commonly perceived as a sovereign prerogative,

---

24. See M. Cherif Bassiouni, *International Extradition: United States Law and Practice*, 6th ed. (Oxford: Oxford University Press, 2014), 406–8.
25. See Ma Decai 马德才, "Benguo guomin buyindu yuanze de fazhan qushi tanxi" 本国国民不引渡原则的发展趋势探析 [Explore the development tendency of the principle of exception for nationals and discuss the perfection of the extradition Law in China], *Jiangxi shehui kexue* 江西社会科学 2 (2011): 166.
26. See Blekxtoon and Deen-Racsmány, "The Decline," 318, n 6.
27. Ibid.
28. See Huang Yaying 黄亚英, "Lun dui benguoren de yindu wenti" 论对本国人的引渡问题 [Explore the question on extradition of nationals], *Faxue yanjiu* 法学研究 6 (1993): 71.
29. See Costa, *Extradition Law*, 553, n 2.
30. See Costa, *Extradition Law*, 552, n 2.
31. Most likely, this kind of decline is combing with the "or extradition or prosecution" principle, such as the UN Model Treaty on Extradition 1990, article 4 on optional grounds for refusal, paragraph (a) regulates that extradition may be refused if the person whose extradition is requested is a national of the requested state. Where extradition is refused on this ground, the requested state shall, if the other state so requests, submit the case to its competent authorities with a view to taking appropriate action against the person in respect of the offence for which extradition had been requested. The UN Convention on Anti-corruption (art. 44 para. 11) does similarly; and some countries, in a smaller regional scope, such as the Extradition Agreement between Italy and US 1983, article 4 rules that the requested Member State cannot refuse the extradition on the ground of nationality, the Extradition Agreement between Italy and Canada 2005 also offers the same approach.

and the claimed decline of the importance of state sovereignty in contemporary international law and international relations may be a reason against retaining the nationality exception.[32] Information about foreign legal systems is readily available with technological advancement.[33] Globalization and increased cooperation in criminal matters have brought about the harmonization of national criminal laws, at least but not exclusively at the regional level. Foreign legal systems have become far more similar and far less unpredictable than they were at the birth of the nationality exception.[34] Concerns about and mistrust towards foreign jurisdictions are lesser.

With the decline of the nationality exception, doubts over the scope of its subjects are also growing. There is a view that in the absence of comprehensive population registers, ID-cards, and passports, the traditional determining factor for such protection must have been residence or domicile rather than the later developed romanticized notion of nationality.[35] Swart forcefully advocated that: "The traditional objections against extradition of nationals . . . are not so much based on nationality in the legal sense. Rather the emphasis is on the fact that a person has his social roots and residence in a given society . . . If there are valid reasons not to extradite a national on occasion, the same objections might be relevant to aliens who have their ordinary residence in the requested state."[36] From the social integration perspective, there has been the call to extend the scope of protection to not be limited to nationals but include all residents who have social connections with the requested country.[37]

There is also the view that rather than merely adopting an extended nationality or resident exception in extradition, the better approach would be to resort as often as possible to established models of transfer of sentenced persons, in connection with nationals as well as long term residents. This regime favors rehabilitation in the state to which the person will return after the sentence; at the same time, it could

32. See Suzanne Andrea Bloks and Ton van den Brink, "The Impact on National Sovereignty of Mutual Recognition in the AFSJ. Case-Study of the European Arrest Warrant," *German Law Journal* 22, no. 1 (2021): 45. See also Dawn L. Rothe and Christopher W. Mullins, "The Death of State Sovereignty? An Empirical Exploration," *International Journal of Comparative and Applied Criminal Justice* 34, no. 1 (2010): 79.
33. See James E. Cabral et al., "Using Technology to Enhance Access to Justice," *Harvard Journal of Law and Technology* 26, no. 1 (2010): 243.
34. Zsuzsanna Deen-Racsmány, *Active Perspective and Non-extradition of Nationals in International Criminal Law at the Dawn of the Twenty-First Century: Adapting Key Functions of Nationality to the Requirements of International Criminal Justice* (Leiden: Leiden University Press, 2007), 8–9.
35. See Zsuzsanna Deen-Racsmány, "Modernizing the Nationality Exception: Is the Non-extradition of Residents a Better Rule?" *Nordic Journal of International Law* 75 (2006): 35.
36. See A.H.J. Swart, "Refusal of Extradition and the United Nations Model Treaty on Extradition," *Netherlands Yearbook of International Law* 23 (1992): 195.
37. See Stefano Saluzzo, "EU Law and Extradition Agreements of Member States: The Petruhhin Case," *European Papers* 2, no. 1 (2017): 435.

facilitate successful prosecution in the territorial state, a double gain for criminal justice.[38]

It is clear that the grounds for refusing the extradition of nationals have been challenged over time, especially in respect of viewpoints, like sovereignty and criminal jurisdiction, which can be greatly influenced by the development of joint and separate forms of sovereignty and the development of theory on jurisdiction. Regarding practical considerations like fair trials and the integration into society of criminals, these can be scrutinized from a pragmatic perspective. Meanwhile, doubts not only focus on the "exception" but also on the meaning of "national". For human rights protection, mainly the social integration perspective, there has been a call for the scope of protection not to be limited to nationals but to include all residents who have social connections with the requested country.[39]

Against the background of these theoretical and practical challenges to the nationality exception, its application to the China arrest warrant system is questionable. Comparatively, the European arrest warrant has made fundamental change regarding the surrender of nationals.[40] This may offer inspiration to mainland China, Hong Kong, and Macau.

4 The surrender of nationals in the European arrest warrant system

4.1 The extradition (surrender) of nationals in the European extradition and EAW surrender systems

4.1.1 The traditional extradition system

The 1957 Convention on Extradition specifies that contracting parties shall have the right to refuse extradition of their nationals.[41] Nordic states and other countries defined the term "nationals" for the purpose of the nationality exception to include permanent resident aliens.[42] The Convention also provided that if a requested party did not extradite its national, it would at the request of the requesting party submit the case to its competent authorities so that proceedings may be taken if they were considered appropriate.[43]

38. See Deen-Racsmány, "Modernizing the Nationality Exception," 61, n 35.
39. See Saluzzo, "EU Law," 435, n 37.
40. See Joske Graat, *The European Arrest Warrant and EU Citizenship: EU Citizenship in Relation to Foreseeability Problems in the Surrender Procedure* (Cham: Springer, 2022), 1–12.
41. European Convention on Extradition 1957, art. 6 (1)(a).
42. See Deen-Racsmány, *Active Perspective*, 31, n 34.
43. European Convention on Extradition 1957, art. 6(2).

The 1996 Convention on Extradition between Member States of the European Union ambitiously attempted to reverse the traditional regime on the nationality exception. It provided that extradition may not be refused on the ground that the person claimed is a national of the requested Member State within the meaning of Article 6 of the European Convention on Extradition.[44] This Convention still permits contracting states to make a reservation that they will not grant extradition of their nationals or will authorize it only under certain specified conditions.[45] This was an important step towards subsequently removing one of the traditional bars to extradition among Member States.[46]

4.1.2 The EAW Framework Decision

The nationality exception is not recognized as a mandatory ground to refuse surrender in the European arrest warrant system, and surrender of nationals for prosecution has been carried out as a general rule. The nationality exception as an optional ground to refuse surrender can only be invoked under certain conditions: when the European arrest warrant has been issued for the purpose of execution of a custodial sentence or detention order, where the requested person is staying in, or is a national, or a resident of the executing Member State, and where that State undertakes to execute the sentence or detention order in accordance with its domestic law.[47] Where a person who is the subject of a European arrest warrant for the purpose of prosecution is a national or resident of the executing Member State, the execution of the European arrest warrant by the executing judicial authority may, under the law of the executing Member State, also be subject to the condition that after being heard, the person is returned to the executing Member State in order to serve there the custodial sentence or detention order passed against him in the issuing Member State.[48]

Under the EAW Framework Decision, the nationality exception cannot apply in surrender for the purpose of prosecution. But for social reintegration purposes, serving the sentence imposed by the requesting state in the executing state based on nationality is legally permitted. In addition, the social integration benefit is extended

44. Convention on Extradition between Member States of the European Union 1996, art. 7(1).
45. Convention on Extradition between Member States of the European Union 1996, art. 7(2).
46. The reasons for this development can be found in the shared values, common legal traditions and the mutual confidence in the proper functioning of the criminal justice systems of the Member States of the European Union. See Convention Relating to Extradition Between the Member States of the European Union Explanatory Report [1997], OJC 191/13.
47. EAW FD, art. 4(6).
48. EAW FD, art. 5(3).

to residents.[49] However, this approach triggered a series of legislative amendment in Member States and preliminary rulings from the CJEU.

4.2 *The practice of the European arrest warrant regarding the surrender of nationals*

4.2.1 Member States amending constitutions to comply with the surrender of nationals principle

Continental Europe, with its predominantly civil law tradition, is commonly seen as the cradle and one of the current strongholds of the non-extradition of nationals.[50] Constitutional amendments have been made by the various countries to accommodate the obligation under the EAW to surrender nationals.[51] The old German constitution prohibited the extradition of nationals,[52] and was amended in 2000 to accommodate Germany's obligations under the International Criminal Court Statute.[53] Due to developments in the EU in the sphere of judicial cooperation following the Tampere Council, the way was opened for further exceptions. Now the German constitution provides that no German may be extradited to a foreign country, but the law can provide otherwise for extradition to a Member State of the European Union or to an international court of justice, as long as the rule of law is upheld.[54]

Comparable amendments can also be found in Portugal[55] and Slovenia.[56] Other countries, like Estonia, Italy, Lithuania, Netherland, Portugal also have constitutional bans on the extradition (and/or deportation, transfer or surrender) of their nationals but provide that applicable treaties in force may limit this right.[57]

---

49. See Ester Herlin-Karnell, "European Arrest Warrant Cases and the Principles of Non-discrimination and EU Citizenship," *The Modern Law Review* 73, no. 5 (2010): 824.
50. See Zsuzsanna Deen-Racsmány, "The European Arrest Warrant and the Surrender of Nationals Revisited: The Lessons of Constitutional Challenges," *European Journal of Crime, Criminal Law and Criminal Justice* 14, no. 3 (2006): 271.
51. Countries like Germany, Poland, Italy, Estonia, the Netherlands, and Portugal do have constitutional prohibitions. See Libor Klimek, *European Arrest Warrant* (Cham: Springer, 2015), 285–304.
52. German Old Constitution, art. 16(2).
53. See "Progress Report by Germany and Appendices to Council of Europe" 2, July 20, 2001, Consult/ICC (2001) 14, https://www.coe.int/t/dlapil/cahdi/Source/ICC/ConsultICC%282001%2914E%20Germany.pdf.
54. German New Constitution, art. 16(2).
55. Portuguese Constitution, art. 33.
56. Slovenia Constitution, art. 47.
57. See Deen-Racsmany, "The European Arrest Warrant," n 50.

4.2.2 Further clarifications from the CJEU on the surrender of nationals

4.2.2.1 The definitions of "resident" and person "staying in"

As to the scope of the terms "resident" and person "staying in" in the EAW FD, the CJEU has held that the interpretations of these terms cannot be left to the assessment of each Member State: they are autonomous concepts of Union law that must be given uniform interpretation throughout the Union.

"Resident" means that the requested person has established his actual place of residence in the executing Member State. And the requested person is "staying in" the executing Member State when, following a stable period of presence in that state, he has acquired certain connections with that state of a similar degree to those resulting from residence. As to those connections, the Court has held that it is for the executing judicial authority to make an overall assessment of various objective factors including the length, nature and conditions of his presence and the family and economic connections which the person has with the executing Member State.[58] In the Wolzenburg case, the CJEU confirmed the validity of the requirement of a continuous period of five years' residency for "residents" in order to fulfill the objective of reintegration into society, but it rejected the necessity of the existence of administrative formalities, making the rights protection of residents in foreign countries more objective and substantive.[59]

4.2.2.2 The ability to execute sentence after applying the nationality exception

In the Daniel case, the Netherlands asked the CJEU whether it must apply the ground for non-execution of an EAW in favor of persons residing in the Netherlands. The CJEU held that the mere fact that that Member State declared itself "willing" to execute the sentence could not be regarded as justifying a refusal: any refusal to execute an EAW must be preceded by the executing judicial authority's examination of whether it is actually possible to execute the sentence in accordance with its domestic law. In the event that the executing Member State finds that it is in fact impossible to undertake to execute the sentence, it falls to the executing judicial authority to execute the EAW and, therefore, to surrender the requested person to the issuing Member State.[60]

58. Case C-66/08, *Szymon Kozlowski* [2008] ECR I-06041, ¶48–49.
59. Case C-123/08, *Dominic Wolzenburg* [2009], ECR I-09621, ¶51–53.
60. Case C-579/15, *Daniel Adam Poplawski* [Judgment of the Court, 29 June 2017], ¶22.

4.3 The reasons for the choice of surrender of nationals in the EAW system

4.3.1 The adoption of the Convention on the Transfer of Sentenced Persons 1983

In 1983 the Council of Europe adopted the Convention on the Transfer of Sentenced Persons. In 1997 an additional protocol was added. The Preamble to the Convention states that cooperation should further the ends of justice and the social rehabilitation of sentenced persons. In 1987, the European Communities adopted an Agreement on the Application among the Member States of the European Communities of the Council of Europe Convention on the Transfer of Sentenced Persons. It provides that for the purpose of applying the Convention on Transfer, each Member State shall regard as its own national the national of another Member State whose transfer is deemed to be appropriate and in the interest of the persons concerned, taking into account their habitual and lawful residence in its territory.[61]

All of these conventions and agreements did the preparatory work for the surrender of nationals under the EAW Framework Decision. The general principle is that the warrant must be executed even if it concerns a national. However, it may be preferable for the requested person (national or permanent resident) to serve his sentence in the state where he was arrested; in that case, the executing state will be able, with the person's consent, to decide to execute the sentence on its territory rather than executing the warrant.[62]

4.3.2 The concept of EU citizenship contributes to the surrender of nationals

The concept of EU citizenship was officially introduced by the Maastricht Treaty of 1992, also known as the Treaty on the European Union (TEU). It states that citizenship of the Union is hereby established, and every person holding the nationality of a Member State shall be a citizen of the Union.[63] The establishment of European citizenship made the excision of traditional grounds of refusal such as the non-extradition of nationals acceptable. This finds support in a draft preamble paragraph of the proposal for the EAW Framework Decision. It states that since the European arrest warrant is based on the idea of citizenship of the Union, the exception for a country's nationals, which has existed under traditional extradition arrangements,

61. Agreement on the Application among the Member States of the European Communities of the Council of Europe Convention on the Transfer of Sentenced Persons, art. 2.
62. See Deen-Racsmany and Blekxtoon, "The Decline of the Nationality Exception," n 6.
63. See Treaty on European Union 1992, art. 8(1).

should not apply within the common area of freedom, security, and justice. A citizen of the Union should face prosecution and sentence wherever he or she has committed an offence within the territory of the European Union, irrespective of his or her nationality.[64]

By prohibiting "any discrimination on grounds of nationality", it requires Member States to place EU citizens, in situations governed by EU law, on equal footing with their nationals.[65] So all Member States' nationals enjoy the same EU citizenship identity, contributing to the decline of the exception for nationals in the new surrender system. There is trust that whether nationals are tried or punished domestically or in other EU countries, they will be treated as their own nationals and receive the fair trial. The EU citizenship concept also means that both nationals and residents who have close connections with host Member States through living there for some period should be protected equally.[66] Both "nationals" and "residents" can have grounds for requested Member States to reject the execution of EAWs issued for executing sentences, or ask for guarantees when an EAW is issued for prosecution.

The concept of EU citizenship led the trend of surrender of nationals in the EU.[67] But the development path which created and guaranteed the effectiveness of EU citizenship also matters. With more than 50 years' economic and political integration, a sense of common identity has been built around the EU, responding to freedom of movement.[68] Therefore, in a sense, the surrender of nationals between Member States equates to surrender of EU citizens in one "sovereign country", the EU.

64. EAW FD, Preamble, Point 12.
65. Treaty establishing the European Community, art. 18.
66. See Tony Marguery, "EU Citizenship and European Arrest Warrant: The Same Rights for All?" *Utrecht Journal of International and European Law* 27, no. 73 (2011): 84.
67. See Marguery, "EU Citizenship" 84, n66. See also Stephen Coutts, *Citizenship, Crime and Community in the European Union* (Oxford: Hart, 2019), 1–24.
68. See Willem Maas, "The Origins, Evolution, and Political Objectives of EU Citizenship," *German Law Journal* 15, no. 5 (2014): 798.

5 Surrender of national (resident) choices in mainland China, Hong Kong, and Macau

5.1 To surrender nationals (residents) should be the basic principle

5.1.1 Surrender between mainland China, Hong Kong, and Macau occurs in one country

The nationality exception in the traditional extradition system is mainly based on sovereignty theory, such as the nationality jurisdiction and the protection obligation of a country to its nationals.[69] In the European arrest warrant system, one of the grounds for the surrender of nationals is that all EU Member States have submitted part of their sovereignty to the EU, and none of them enjoy full sovereignty when cooperating with other EU Member States. The sovereignty ground for the nationality exception has been broken.

This concept has a more absolute existence in mainland China, Hong Kong, and Macau, as the three regions politically and legally belong to one country, the PRC. Surrender of fugitive offenders within the PRC is not an issue of international judicial cooperation. It is domestic judicial cooperation in criminal matters.[70] Hong Kong (Macau) and mainland China do not engage in country-to-country relations and Hong Kong (Macau) residents are not Hong Kong (Macau) nationals.[71] The power to govern local residents belongs not only to the three regions respectively, but also to the Central Government. Protecting local residents is not only the obligation of the three regions, but also of the PRC. Surrender of fugitive offenders between mainland China, Hong Kong, and Macau becomes a purely domestic issue, not one between sovereign countries. This is more so than in the EU. Accordingly, the surrender of nationals (residents) in a China arrest warrant system should be enforced more completely than in the EAW.

---

69. See the above section 3.
70. See Miguel Manero de Lemos and Teresa Lancy Robalo, "Judicial Cooperation in Criminal Matters in the Special Administrative Regions of Hong Kong and Macau: Through the Lens of 'One Country, Two Systems' and the Surrender of Fugitives to Mainland China," *Porto Alegre* 5 (2019): 756.
71. See Ng Kang-chung, "Hong Kong Trials for Offences in Mainland China Will Not Work, Top Legal Scholar Albert Chen Says," *South China Morning Post*, June 3, 2019, https://www.scmp.com/news/hong-kong/law-and-crime/article/3012942/hong-kong-trials-offences-mainland-china-will-not-work.

5.1.2 Common Chinese nationality

Relying on the one country fact and the China's Nationality Law, the majority of Hong Kong residents, Macau residents, and mainland Chinese share the same Chinese nationality.[72] This compares with the EU where, no matter if German, French, or Dutch, all share common EU citizenship. The EU offers the experience that a citizen of the Union should face being prosecuted and sentenced wherever he or she has committed an offence within the territory of the European Union irrespective of his or her nationality. In the common Chinese nationality zone, including mainland China, Hong Kong, and Macau, a resident who commits a crime in one region and is investigated or tried in the same region can be regarded as in his or her home region. If the ground to refuse surrender of nationals for trial is mainly based on emotional arguments,[73] then common Chinese nationality will offer Hong Kongers, Macanese, and Mainlanders the same emotional and spiritual support to face trial in another region but within the same country.

Even foreigner permanent residents of Hong Kong and Macau, living in China's two SARs, can still enjoy "China citizenship" in name. This identity is mainly based on their place of residence, which is China, broadly speaking. In fact, they also enjoy political and civil rights recognized in the Basic Laws. Hence, "China citizenship" can still function as a basis for surrender. Like the "EU citizenship", the establishment of a common "Chinese nationality" identity or a broader "China citizenship" identity not only functions to remove discrimination among requested persons based on different identities, but also promotes mutual respect between the judicial authorities of the three regions.

5.1.3 Integration promotes mutual understanding and trust

One reason for the nationality exception in the traditional extradition system is that, for people who live in one country and are unfamiliar with the culture, language, law, and people of the other country, will be disadvantaged by being judged abroad.[74] This problem has been overcome in the EU with increased regional integration and increased movement of people across borders. The degree of the nationality

72. The majority of Hong Kong and Macau residents have Chinese nationality; only a small portion are foreigners. The Hong Kong data can be seen in the 2016 Population By-census, "Nationality and Ethnicity", last revised July 20, 2017, https://www.bycensus2016.gov.hk/en/bc-ne.html; the Macau data can be seen in DSEC, "Intercensos 2016 Resultados Globais," May 2017, https://www.dsec.gov.mo/getAttachment/bfa0112a-eaf3-49a9-9168-b5add46e9d65/C_ICEN_PUB_2016_Y.aspx.

73. See Ivan A. Shearer, "Non-extradition of Nationals: A Review and a Proposal," *Adelaide Law Review* 2 (1966): 294.

74. See Costa, *Extradition Law*, 554, n 2.

exception can vary with specific levels of political integration and for the convenience of movement. This is evident in that many states have completely relinquished their classical nationality exceptions in exchange for security advantages that have started to be perceived as indispensable in such an integrated area.[75]

The same phenomenon is forming in mainland China, Hong Kong, and Macau. The three regions are close to each other geographically, and most of the people living in the three regions have the same ancestors and have families or kinships across the border. They share the same, or at least similar, language and culture. All of these factors offer basis for further integration. What's more, since Hong Kong and Macau came back to the PRC, formal and official cooperation between the three regions have increased. The social, cultural, economic, and political integration has progressed. In brief, the basis for surrender of the residents is well-founded.

5.1.4 Surrender of residents has been practiced in mainland China

Without an agreement on the surrender of persons between mainland China, Hong Kong, and Macau, neither Hong Kong nor Macau has surrendered persons back to mainland China, but mainland China has surrendered Hong Kong and Macau residents upon request of the Hong Kong or Macau police. For instance, on February 6, 2018, the police in Guangdong arrested fleeing Hong Kong offender Zhan Weijian and sent him back to Hong Kong. Reportedly, mainland China has handed over 300 criminals to Hong Kong[76] and also some to Macau.[77] This practice offers experience for the three regions in achieving closer cooperation in future.

5.1.5 No legal prohibition on the surrender of residents within one country

In the European arrest warrant system, in order to implement the surrender of nationals principle, some countries have to amend their constitutions.[78] There is no similar need in mainland China, Hong Kong, and Macau. As explained earlier, mainland China and Macau refuse to extradite (surrender) Chinese nationals or residents to foreign countries. The Hong Kong Fugitive Offenders Ordinance does not prohibit surrender of residents, but the practice may vary from agreement to agreement in

75. See Costa, *Extradition Law*, 557, n 2.
76. Grenville Cross, "Fugitive Surrender: Rights and Responsibilities," *China Daily*, June 12, 2019, https://www.chinadailyhk.com/epaper/pubs//chinadaily/2019/06/12/07.pdf.
77. See Gao Tong, "Macau and Mainland Push the Judicial Cooperation in Criminal Matters," The State Council Information Office of the People's Republic of China, April 18, 2014, http://www.scio.gov.cn/37236/37256/Document/1586882/1586882.htm.
78. Like Germany, Poland and other civil law countries discussed in above section 4.2.1.

order to protect Chinese nationals. Regarding China domestic surrender, there are no clues in the laws that the surrender of nationals (residents) should be prohibited. All three regions recognize territorial jurisdiction, particularly prioritized by Hong Kong. All of this offers a basis for surrendering fugitive offenders to the region where the crimes take place and recognizing the surrender of residents as a basic principle.

In brief, the principle of surrender of residents can be more completely realised in the China domestic surrender system than in the EAW system. At the same time, based on the identity of the resident, there can be an optional ground to refuse surrender or to ask for guarantees. A proposed design follows.

5.2 Optional refusal ground and guarantee based on resident identity

The legal systems in the three regions are different from and independent of each other. The law and judicial system with which Hong Kong residents are familiar are different from those known to Macau residents and mainland Chinese. Refusing surrender or asking for guarantees on some conditions supports humanitarian objectives and can help criminals to better integrate into society after serving a sentence. In particular, although the majority of Hong Kong and Macau residents are Chinese, there are still a great number of foreigners in Hong Kong and Macau. Sending these non-Chinese permanent residents back to Hong Kong or Macau to serve sentences or detention orders is meaningful.

The ability to execute a sentence after refusing surrender also needs consideration. After national security laws were legislated in mainland China, Macau, and Hong Kong, the three regions have had a similar basis on which to crack down on national security crimes. Other serious crimes have also been combated in concert in the three regions. Common legislation offers a basis for the executing region to execute a sentence imposed by the requesting region after refusing surrender of a requested person for social integration purpose. At the same time, if the sentence cannot be executed in the requested region for legal or practical reasons, surrender may not be refused only on the basis of nationality or residency, as will be further discussed below.

5.3 The design of the residents surrender mechanism between mainland China, Hong Kong, and Macau

Based on the controversy over the traditional nationality exception principle, the development of the nationality exception principle in the European arrest warrant system, and the reality in mainland China, Hong Kong, and Macau, the design of the nationality (resident) exception principle in China arrest warrant should be updated. See Table 7.1 on page 144.

The surrender of residents should be the general principle, and the traditional nationality (residents) exception should not be applied for prosecution purposes. At the same time, the identity of permanent residents (including foreigners and Chinese) in Hong Kong and Macau as well as for mainland Chinese can be an optional ground to refuse surrender, if the China arrest warrant is issued for executing a sentence or detention order. Based on the identity of permanent residents or Chinese nationals, guarantees can be requested to send them back to the requested region to serve sentence after trial.

In the above situation the requested region should undertake to execute the punishment locally. The requested person can have the right to inform the judge if he or she wants to stay or not, but the final decision should be made by the judge in the requested region. Some criteria should be followed when the judge makes the decision, which may include if the requested persons' social connection with the requested region is close enough, how long they have stayed there, if families are there, if the person is too old to adjust to new surroundings, and if there is a serious language problem. If the requested person does not mind serving sentence in the requesting region, or volunteers to be surrendered, the surrender cannot be refused or asked for guarantee by the requested region only based on the resident identity of the requested person. In addition, referring to the CJEU jurisprudence, if the requested region finds that after refusing the surrender of the requested person based on their identity that it cannot execute the sentence imposed by the requesting region for some legal or practical reason, to surrender is the better choice.[79]

Additionally, the European Union has utilized a document on the transfer of sentenced persons in the Member States which provides justifications and enables the Member State to execute the sentence after refusing a European arrest warrant on the ground of social integration.[80] This is also inspiring to mainland China, Hong Kong, and Macau. An agreement on the transfer of sentenced prisoners between mainland China, Hong Kong, and Macau should be considered seriously.[81] It not only will contribute to judicial cooperation in transferring sentenced prisoners but will also speed up cooperation in surrender of fugitive offenders indirectly.

79. See Case C-579/15, n 60.
80. See Jannemieke Ouwerkerk, "Are Alternatives to the European Arrest Warrant Underused? The Case for an Integrative Approach to Judicial Cooperation Mechanisms in the EU Criminal Justice Area?" *European Journal of Crime, Criminal Law and Criminal Justice* 29, no. 2 (2021): 87.
81. At this moment, an Agreement on the Transfer of Sentenced Prisoners between Hong Kong and Macau has been been in place.

Table 7.1: Identity of the requested person in the China arrest warrant (CAW) system

Identity of the requested person	CAW issuing region	CAW executing region	CAW issuing purpose	Mandatory refusal ground	Optional refusal ground	Guarantees
Mainland Chinese	Hong Kong or Macau	Mainland China	Prosecute	No	No	May ask for guarantee "sent back for service sentence after trial"
			Execute sentence or detention order	No	Mainland can execute the sentence or detention order	
Hong Kong permanent residents	Mainland China or Macau	Hong Kong	Prosecute	No	No	May ask for guarantee "sent back for service sentence after trial"
			Execute sentence or detention order	No	Hong Kong can execute the sentence or detention order	
Macau permanent residents	Mainland China or Hong Kong	Macau	Prosecute	No	No	May ask for guarantee "sent back for service sentence after trial"
			Execute sentence or detention order	No	Macau can execute the sentence or detention order	
Persons with other identity	Any of the three regions	Any of the three regions	Prosecute	No	No	No
			Execute sentence	No	No	No

6 Conclusion

The nationality exception principle is more and more controversial with continuing globalization. The European arrest warrant has gone further on the issue. In the China domestic surrender system, the nationality (residents) exception is a bad fit and open to criticism.

Under the "one country, two systems" policy, the surrender of residents for trial should be the principle, but the requested persons can be sent back to their home region to serve sentence for social integration purpose. When surrender is requested for the purpose of executing a sentence, the identity of the requested person may be relied on to refuse surrender, but the requested region has the obligation to execute the sentence locally. At the same time, other relevant practical circumstances of the requested person and the requested region should be taken into consideration before the requested region makes the final decision. When better integration is achieved, surrender of residents can be the general rule. No optional refusal or guarantees should be allowed on the sole basis of a resident's identity.

8

The Exception for Death Penalty Offenders

1 Introduction

The surrender of death penalty offenders is another controversial issue for the China domestic surrender system.[1] Both Hong Kong and Macau have abolished the death penalty, but mainland China retains it both in law and in practice. In 2011, mainland China abolished the death penalty for thirteen offences,[2] and in 2015, after the 9th amendment to the Criminal Law, the death penalty was abolished for another nine offences.[3] At present, the death penalty can still be imposed for forty-six criminal offences.[4]

1. See Marsha Wellknown Yee, "Hong Kong's Legal Obligation to Require Fair Trial for Rendition," *Columbia Law Review* 102, no. 5 (2002): 1373.
2. The offences include: trafficking in cultural relics; trafficking in precious metals; trafficking in precious animals and articles made of precious animals; trafficking in ordinary cargos and articles; receipt fraud; financial certificate fraud; credit card fraud; issuing false VAT invoices for the use of cheating on export rebates and tax-deductible invoices; forging or selling forged VAT invoices; larceny; imparting criminal methods; robbing ancient cultural ruins and ancient tombs; and excavation of ancient human fossils and ancient vertebrate fossils.
3. The offences include: trafficking in weapons and ammunitions; trafficking in nuclear materials; trafficking in fake currencies; counterfeiting currencies; illegal fund collection; organizing prostitution; forcing prostitution; hindering the implementation of military duties; and spreading rumors during wartime.
4. Including: seven offences endangering national security such as splitting the nation, rebellion, espionage, and financing enemies; fourteen offences endangering the public order such as arson, explosion, breaking electric equipment, and breaking public transport tools; two offences endangering the order of the socialist market economy such as manufacturing and selling fake medicines, and manufacturing and selling toxic and hazardous food; five offences breaching civil and personal rights such as murder, international assault, rape, kidnapping, and robbery; three offences breaching social management order such as, organizing an armed mass prison raid, smuggling, selling, and transporting and producing drugs; two offences endangering national defense rights such as

Globally, the trend has been to abolish death penalty and non-extradition of death penalty offenders is an indirect way to push for the abolition of the death penalty in other countries.[5] The European Union has completely abolished the death penalty, and before it did so it practiced non-extradition of death penalty offenders. Whether to surrender death penalty offenders in the China domestic surrender system is an important question.

In this chapter, firstly, I analyze present disputes over the application of the death penalty in mainland China, Hong Kong, and Macau. Secondly, I explore the penalty's abolition and the non-extradition of death penalty offenders from the UN perspective. Thirdly, I study the case of the European Union. Fourthly, I offer justification for the non-surrender of death penalty offenders in the China domestic surrender system.

2 Death penalty divergence in the three regions

2.1 *Hong Kong has abolished the death penalty*

The Hong Kong Bill of Rights states that every human being has the inherent right to life, which shall be protected by law, and no one shall be arbitrarily deprived of his life.[6] It also specifies that anyone sentenced to the death penalty shall have the right to seek a pardon or commutation of the sentence.[7] It stipulates that nothing in its text may be invoked to delay or to prevent the abolition of capital punishment in Hong Kong.[8] In 1993, Hong Kong legislatively abolished the death penalty for all crimes. Before this, it had not carried out a death sentence for decades: the last was in 1966.[9]

---

breaking ammunition equipment, military instructions, and military telecommunications; providing unqualified ammunition equipment and military instruction; two bribery offences including corruption and taking bribes; and ten offences regarding soldiers breaching duties including violating orders during wartime, hiding and falsely reporting military intelligence, and giving in.

5. See William A. Schabas, "Indirect Abolition: Capital Punishment's Role in Extradition Law and Practice," *Loyola of Los Angeles International and Comparative Law Review* 25, no. 3 (2003): 581.
6. Hong Kong Bill of Rights, art. 2(1).
7. Hong Kong Bill of Rights, art. 2(4).
8. Hong Kong Bill of Rights, art. 2(6).
9. Yongqiang Feng, "Retrace Hong Kong Abolition the Death Penalty: Violent Crime Is Not Increased in Past 20 Years," The Rule of Law Weekend, April 29, 2013, http://news.sina.com.cn/c/sd/2013-04-29/025626983311.shtml. See also David T. Johnson, "Asia's Declining Death Penalty," *Journal of Asian Studies* 69, no. 2 (2010): 337.

2.2 *Macau has abolished the death penalty*

Macau ratified the International Covenant on Civil and Political Rights (ICCPR) in 1976 as a part of Portugal. When it returned to the PRC in 1999, the Basic Law of Macau dictated that the convention was to be applied.[10] Hence, Macau is also obligated to respect the right to life. Macau abolished the death penalty in law in 1976, though it had ceased carrying it out in the 1930s. Moreoever, there is no prospect of the reintroduction of the death penalty in Macau. The Macau Criminal Code of 1995 specifies that no death penalty can be imposed.[11]

2.3 *Mainland China retains the death penalty*

On October 5, 1998, mainland China signed the ICCPR, but to date it has yet to ratify it. One major obstacle to ratification is that China still applies the death penalty in both law and practice, in forty-six categories of offences.[12] The scale of executions is impossible to discern because the total number of death penalty executions is kept secret.

In summary, mainland China, Hong Kong, and Macau differ in their approaches to the death penalty. This divergence affects how the surrender or non-surrender of death penalty offenders is viewed in the three legal systems. But recommendations should also be based on the international tendency towards the death penalty and extradition. The experience of the European Union can also be referenced.

3 The extradition of death penalty offenders around the world

3.1 *Global promotion of death penalty abolition*

3.1.1 The theoretical and practical grounds for abolishing the death penalty

The death penalty has long been the harshest method to punish criminals.[13] Execution methods vary from beheading, hanging, and lethal injection to shooting.[14]

10. Basic Law of Macau, art. 40.
11. See Macau Penal Code, art. 39(1).
12. See supra, n 4.
13. See Mark A. Costanzo and Lawrence T. White, "An Overview of the Death Penalty and Capital Trials: History, Current Status, Legal Procedures, and Cost," *Journal of Social Issues* 50, no. 2 (1994): 1.
14. See Amnesty International, "Death Penalty in 2019: Facts and Figures," April 21, 2020, https://www.amnesty.org/en/latest/news/2020/04/death-penalty-in-2019-facts-and-figures/.

In modern times, the death penalty has come to be regarded as the ultimate cruel, inhuman, and degrading punishment.[15] Voices for its abolition continue to grow.

The first reason is that the death penalty is irreversible, and mistakes happen.[16] Execution is the ultimate irrevocable punishment, and the risk of executing an innocent person can never be eliminated. Since 1973, for example, more than 160 prisoners sent to death row in the United States have later been exonerated or released from death row, while others have been executed despite serious doubts about their guilt.[17]

The second reason is that death penalty does not deter crime. Punishment is utilitarian and countries who execute commonly cite the death penalty as a way to deter people from committing crimes, but this claim has been repeatedly discredited.[18] There is no evidence that the death penalty is any more effective in reducing crime than any other punishment, like life imprisonment.[19]

The third reason is that the death penalty is often used within skewed justice systems. In many cases, people have been executed after being convicted in grossly unfair trials, on the basis of torture-tainted evidence, and with inadequate legal representation.[20] This situation can occur in any death penalty country, from China to the United States to Libya or Saudi Arabia. Moreover, in some countries death sentences are the mandatory punishment for certain offences, and judges are not allowed to consider the circumstances of the crime before sentencing.[21]

---

15. Amnesty International, "The Death Penalty: A Cruel, Inhuman and Arbitrary Punishment," May 1, 1995, ASA/22/03/95, https://www.refworld.org/docid/3ae6a9dd4.html.
16. See Chris Jones, "Death Penalty: A Human Rights Issue for South Africa" in *Human Rights in the Contemporary World*, ed. Trudy Corrigan (London: IntechOpen, 2022), https://www.intechopen.com/chapters/74995.
17. Indeed, even in a rule-of-law country like the US, such mistakes can happen. Countries where the rule of law is not so well developed which retain the death penalty make even more mistakes. In China, there were cases where innocent people were executed before the actual murderers later surfaced.
18. See Michael L. Radelet and Ronald L. Akers, "Deterrence and the Death Penalty: The Views of the Experts," *Journal of Criminal Law and Criminology* 87, no. 1 (1996): 1.
19. See Phoebe Ellsworth, Craig Haney, and Mark Costanzo, "SPSSI Statement on the Death Penalty," SSPPI Newsletter online, April 2001 (original statement dated February 9, 2001), https://www.spssi.org/index.cfm?fuseaction=page.viewpage&pageid=1461.
20. See Chris Richardson, *Violence in American Society: An Encyclopedia of Trends, Problems, and Perspectives* (Santa Barbara: ABC-CLIO, 2020), 299.
21. There are still at least 28 countries that maintain a mandatory death penalty for specified offences. These are Afghanistan, Brunei, Equatorial Guinea, Guinea, Guyana, Iran, Jordan, Kuwait, Libya, Malaysia, Mauritania, Myanmar, Niger, Nigeria, Pakistan, the Palestinian Authority, Qatar, Saudi Arabia, Singapore, Sri Lanka, Sudan, Syria, Tanzania, Thailand, Trinidad, United Arab Emirates, Yemen, and Zambia.

The fourth reason is that the death penalty is discriminatory.[22] The weight of the penalty is disproportionately carried by those with disadvantaged socio-economic backgrounds and by those who belong to racial, ethnic, and/or religious minorities. This can arise from, for example, limited access to legal representation or greater disadvantage in their experience of the criminal justice system. For example, in the US, black people are more likely to receive death penalty sentences than white people. In China, death penalty offenders at the grassroots level will be executed by means of shooting, but death penalty offenders from upper levels of society can receive lethal injections.[23]

The fifth reason is that the death penalty can be used as a political tool. Authorities in some countries, such as Iran and Sudan, use the death penalty to punish political opponents.[24] For these reasons, the international community has adopted several instruments that ban the use of the death penalty, detailed below.

3.1.2 The legal basis for the abolition of the death penalty

The ICCPR stipulates that every human being has the inherent right to life, that this right shall be protected by law, and that no one shall be arbitrarily deprived of life.[25] The sentence of death shall not be imposed for crimes committed by persons below eighteen years of age and shall not be carried out on pregnant women.[26] But the ICCPR also permits parties to make reservations. The US, for example, has raised the reservation that its government may impose capital punishment on any person other than a pregnant woman, including persons below the age of eighteen.[27] There are also some densely populated countries, like China, which signed the convention but did not ratify it, so the force of Article 6 is compromised in practice.

The Second Optional Protocol to the ICCPR promoted the trend toward abolition. It states that the death penalty's abolition contributes to the enhancement of human dignity and the progressive development of human rights, and that all measures of death-penalty abolition should be considered to be progress in the enjoyment of the right to life.[28] It then specifies that no one within the jurisdiction

22. See Kaspar Lippert-Rasmussen, "Punishment and Discrimination," in *Punishment and Ethics*, ed. J. Ryberg and J.A. Corlett (London: Palgrave Macmillan, 2010), 169.
23. See Zou Bing, "On the Standardization of Lethal Injections in China," *Asian Social Science* 8, no. 6 (2012): 83.
24. See Amnesty International, "Death Penalty," accessed November 1, 2022, https://www.amnesty.org/en/what-we-do/death-penalty/.
25. International Covenant on Civil and Political Rights, art. 6(1).
26. International Covenant on Civil and Political Rights, art. 6(5).
27. International Covenant on Civil and Political Rights.
28. Second Optional Protocol to the International Covenant on Civil and Political Rights, Preamble.

of a state party to the protocol shall be executed,[29] and that each state party shall take all necessary measures to abolish the death penalty within its jurisdiction.[30] Reservations relating to war crimes can be made.[31] But seldom do parties make this reservation: only Brazil, Chile, EI Salvador, Azerbaijan, and Greece retain it, though Azerbaijan and Greece have abolished the death penalty in all circumstances.[32]

The American Convention on Human Rights, which emphasizes the right to life, restricts the application of the death penalty within a narrower scope. It stipulates that in countries that have not abolished the death penalty, the death penalty may be imposed only for the most serious crimes.[33] In no case shall capital punishment be inflicted for political offences or related common crimes.[34] This convention also excludes certain age groups from the application of the death penalty by declaring that capital punishment shall not be imposed upon persons who, at the time the crime was committed, were under eighteen or over seventy years of age; nor shall it be applied to pregnant women.[35]

Like the ICCPR, the American Convention on Human Rights also takes the optional protocol approach to abolishing the death penalty.[36] This protocol seeks to abolish the death penalty and does not allow reservations to be made. It asserts that state parties to the protocol shall not apply the death penalty to any person subject to their jurisdiction.[37] It also provides that no reservation may be made to the protocol. However, at the time of ratification or accession, the state parties to this instrument could declare that they reserved the right to apply the death penalty during wartime in accordance with international law for extremely serious crimes of a military nature.[38]

The African Charter on Human and People's Rights is a regional human rights instrument intended to promote and protect human rights and basic freedoms on the African continent.[39] Currently, fifty-four states have signed and ratified the

29. Second Optional Protocol to the International Covenant on Civil and Political Rights, art. 1(1).
30. Second Optional Protocol to the International Covenant on Civil and Political Rights, art. 1(2).
31. Second Optional Protocol to the International Covenant on Civil and Political Rights, art. 2.
32. Regarding the details, see https://en.wikipedia.org/wiki/Second_Optional_Protocol_to_the_I, accessed November 1, 2022.
33. American Convention on Human Rights, art. 4(2).
34. American Convention on Human Rights, art. 4(4).
35. American Convention on Human Rights, art. 4(5).
36. See Eric Neumayer, "Death Penalty Abolition and the Ratification of the Second Optional Protocol," *International Journal of Human Rights* 12, no. 1 (2008): 3.
37. American Convention on Human Rights, art. 1.
38. American Convention on Human Rights, art. 2.
39. See Fatsah Ouguergouz, *The African Charter of Human and People's Rights: A Comprehensive Agenda for Human Dignity and Sustainable Democracy in Africa* (Leiden: Brill, 2003), 19.

charter.[40] It states that human beings are inviolable, and every human being shall be entitled to integrity of their person and respect for their life. No one may arbitrarily be deprived of this right.[41] The normative impact of the African charter has been significant in urging states to adopt a moratorium on the death penalty and support the trend towards abolition in Africa.[42]

Until now, more than two-thirds of the countries in the world have abolished the death penalty in law or in practice.[43] The non-extradition of death penalty offenders is also widely used as an indirect way to globally.[44]

3.2 The non-extradition of death penalty offenders in global practice

Since the late nineteenth century, extradition treaties have contained clauses by which state parties may refuse extradition for capital offences in the requesting state without a satisfactory assurance that the death penalty will not be imposed. Such provisions can be found as early as 1889 in the South American Convention, in the 1892 extradition treaty between the United Kingdom and Portugal, in the 1908 extradition treaty between the United States and Portugal,[45] and in the 1912 treaty prepared by the International Commission of Jurists.[46] In 1981 the Inter-American Convention on Extradition was adopted by the Organization of American States; it specifies that state parties shall not grant extradition when the offence in question is punishable in the requesting state by the death penalty unless the requested state has previously obtained from the requesting State, through diplomatic channels, sufficient assurances that the death penalty will not be imposed on the person sought or that, if such penalties is imposed, it will not be enforced.[47]

---

40. African Commission on Human and People's Rights, "State Parties to the African Charter," accessed November 1, 2022, https://www.achpr.org/statepartiestotheafricancharter.
41. African Charter on Human and People's Rights, art. 4.
42. African Commission on Human and People's Rights, "Impact of the African Charter on Domestic Human Rights in Africa," accessed November 11, 2021, http://www.achpr.org/instruments/achpr/impact-on-domestic-human-rights/.
43. See Amnesty International, "Abolitionist and Retentionist Countries as of July 2018," ACT 50/6665/2017, July 2018, https://nonews.co/wp-content/uploads/2019/10/AARC2018.pdf.
44. See Craig R. Roecks, "Extradition, Human Rights, and the Death Penalty: When Nations Must Refuse to Extradite a Person Charged with a Capital Crime," *California Western International Law Journal* 25, no. 1 (1994): 189.
45. Portugal is also the first country recorded by Amnesty International to have abolished the death penalty for all crimes, in 1976.
46. See Williams A. Schabas, "Nationality, Double Jeopardy, Prescription and the Death Sentence as Bases for Refusing Extradition," *International Review of Penal Law* 62 (1991): 259–80. See also Williams A. Schabas, "Human Rights Safeguards and International Cooperation in Extradition: Striking the Balance," *Criminal Law Forum* 3 (1992): 191–224.
47. Inter-American Convention on Extradition, art. 9.

The Model Treaty on Extradition specifies that extradition may be refused if the offence for which extradition is requested carries the death penalty under the law of the requesting state, unless that state gives such assurance as the requested state considers sufficient that the death penalty will not be imposed or, if imposed, will not be carried out.[48] In resolution 2005/59, adopted on April 20, 2005, the UN Commission on Human Rights requested: "States that have received a request for extradition on a capital charge to reserve explicitly the right to refuse extradition in the absence of effective assurances from relevant authorities of the requesting State that the death penalty will not be carried out" and called upon "states to provide such effective assurances if requested to do so, and to respect them".[49] So the non-extradition of death penalty offenders is also encouraged from the UN perspective.

Although the trend has been to abolish the death penalty, and the non-extradition of death penalty offenders has been applied globally, the EU is currently the only world region where the death penalty has been abolished completely.[50] Hence the death penalty is no longer an obstacle to surrender in the European Union. A closer analysis of the history of death penalty abolition and of the non-surrender of death penalty offenders in the EU can offer experience to mainland China, Hong Kong, and Macau as they consider the death penalty issue in their surrender system.

From a global perspective, human rights protection has greatly influenced the abolition of the death penalty, the non-extradition of death penalty offenders is implemented to protect human rights, and this story in Europe is more complete and fulfilled than in any other region of the world.[51] The EU countries not only ratified all relevant UN human rights protection conventions, the region has constructed its own human rights protection mechanism and set a higher standard for human rights protection.[52] Having reached the zero death penalty stage, the EU maintains the position of non-extradition of death penalty offenders.

---

48. See Model Treaty on Extradition, art. 4(d).
49. See UN Commission on Human Rights, "Human Rights Resolution 2005/59: The Question of the Death Penalty," April 20, 2005, https://www.refworld.org/docid/45377c730.html.
50. See Sangmin Bae, "International Norms, Domestic Politics, and the Death Penalty: Comparing Japan, South Korea, and Taiwan," *Comparative Politics* 44, no. 1 (2011): 41.
51. See Ved P. Nanda, "Bases for Refusing International Extradition Requests: Capital Punishment and Torture," *Fordham International Law Journal* 23, no. 5 (1999): 1369. See also Robert Gregg, "The European Tendency Toward Non-Extradition to the United States in Capital Cases: Trends, Assurances, and Breaches of Duty," *University of Miami International and Comparative Law Review* 10, no. 1 (2002): 113.
52. See Christian Behrmann and Jon Yorke, "The European Union and the Abolition of the Death Penalty," *Pace International Law Review Online Companion* 4, no. 1 (2013): 1.

4 The extradition of death penalty offenders in the European Union

4.1 *The death penalty abolished in the EU*

4.1.1 The grounds for abolishing the death penalty in the EU

The abolition of the death penalty is an important part of European history.[53] As to the penalty's inability to deter crime, one study found that the absence of the death penalty had "not in any way contributed to an increase in the number of such crimes which were formerly punished by death".[54] Regarding the execution of innocent people, Lafayette famously said in the French Assembly: "I shall ask for the abolition of the punishment of death until I have the infallibility of human judgment demonstrated to me".[55] Regarding the punishment's brutalizing effect on society, the opinion has been ventured that the death penalty in Germany, for example, can actually add psychological stimulus to crimes of violence.[56] But abolition has only been a clear trend since the end of the Second World War when human rights became a priority. James Megivern notes that the old argument used to justify the theoretical legitimacy of the state's right to execute has been repeated by defenders of capital punishment, but that it would never sound the same after Hitler.[57] Europeans and others who have recently and vividly experienced terrible abuses of state power may see more reasons to remove the death penalty from the state's arsenal of sanctions.[58]

53. The reasons for abolishing death penalty globally are explained in the above section 3.1.
54. Carl Torp, "The Abolition of Capital Punishment in Denmark," in *The Abolition of the Death Penalty in Holland and Scandinavia,* 2nd ed., ed. S. Margery Fry (London: Howard League for Penal Reform, 1928), p. 5. Similar remarks are also made by Simon van der Aa, at p. 8 and Victor Almquist, at p. 15.
55. See Charles Lucas, *Receuil des Debats . . .* (1831), 32, pt. II, quoted in Hugo Adam Bedau, "The Case against the Death Penalty," accessed November 1, 2022, http://deathpenalty.narod.ru/nauka/Thecas2.htm. In the 1928 Howard League Report, Denmark similarly acknowledged "the now commonly accepted view that capital punishment is irreparable" and that "later it may be discovered that sentence was passed unjustly." See Great Britain House of Commons, *Report from the Select Committee on Capital Punishment* (London: HMSO, 1930), 222, quoted in Jon Yorke, "The Council of Europe and the Death Penalty: The Relationship of State Sovereignty and Human Rights" (PhD thesis, University of Warwick, 2008), 6, 97.
56. Hans-Heinrich Jescheck, "Modern Criminal Policy in the Federal Republic of Germany and the German Democratic Republic," in *Crime, Criminology and Public Policy: Essays in Honor of Sir Leon Radzinowicz,* ed. Roger Hood (London: Heinemann, 1974), 511.
57. James Megivern, *The Death Penalty: An Historical and Theological Survey* (Mahwah, NJ: Paulist Press, 1997), 282.
58. Carol S. Steiker, "Capital Punishment and American Exceptionalism," in *American Exceptionalism and Human Rights,* ed. Michael Ignatieff (Princeton: Princeton University Press, 2005), 83.

Gradually, each government, from Northern Europe through the rest of Western Europe, accepted that it no longer had the right to impose the punishment.[59]

4.1.2 The legal basis for abolition of the death penalty

On the basis that everyone's right to life is a basic value in a democratic society and that the abolition of the death penalty is essential for the protection of this right and for full recognition of the inherent dignity of all human beings, Protocol 13 to the ECHR on the abolition of the death penalty in all circumstances was adopted by the Council of Europe in 2002. It stipulates that the death penalty shall be abolished; no one shall be condemned to such penalty or executed.[60]

In fact, the European Union had committed to abolishing the death penalty completely two years before the adoption of Protocol 13. The Charter of Fundamental Rights of the European Union (CFR) provides that everyone possesses the right to life and no one shall be condemned to the death penalty or executed.[61] Regarding extradition, it stipulates that no one may be removed, expelled, or extradited to a state where there exists a serious risk that he or she would be subject to the death penalty, torture, or any other inhuman or degrading treatment or punishment.[62]

All of the European Union countries abolished the death penalty by 2002 when the European arrest warrant (EAW) Framework Decision was adopted. This explains why there is no wording on the death penalty issue in grounds for mandatory and optional non-execution of the warrant.

4.2 Non-extradition of death penalty offenders in the EU

4.2.1 The traditional extradition stage

The 1957 European Convention on Extradition stipulates that if an offence for which extradition is requested is punishable by death under the law of the requesting party, and if in respect of such offence the death penalty is not provided for by the law of the requested party or is not normally carried out, extradition may be refused unless the requesting party gives such assurance as the requested party considers sufficient that the death penalty will not be carried out.[63] The same clause appears in Europe's

59. See Jon Yorke, "The Council of Europe and the Death Penalty: The Relationship of State Sovereignty and Human Rights" (PhD thesis, University of Warwick, 2008), 88, http://wrap.warwick.ac.uk/4106/1/WRAP_THESIS_Yorke_2008.pdf.
60. 2002 Protocol 13 to the Convention for the Protection of Human Rights and Fundamental Freedoms concerning the Abolition of the Death Penalty, art. 1.
61. Charter of Fundamental Rights of the European Union, art. 2.
62. Charter of Fundamental Rights of the European Union, art. 19.
63. European Convention on Extradition 1957, art. 11.

subsequent extradition-related conventions, even by the time of the EAW when the death penalty had been abolished.

4.2.2 The European arrest warrant (EAW)

By the time of the European arrest warrant, all Member States of the EU had abolished the death penalty. Thus, death penalty wording does not appear in the grounds for mandatory or optional non-execution of an EAW. However, the preamble to the EAW FD still contains language regarding the extradition of death penalty offenders. The preamble states that no person should be removed, expelled, or extradited to a state where there is a risk that he or she would be subjected to the death penalty, torture, or other inhuman and degrading treatment or punishment.[64] This wording actively responds to the CFR. When the requested person faces the death penalty in a third country, the requesting state should offer the guarantee that it will not impose or execute the death penalty if imposed.

4.2.3 Case law from the European Court of Human Rights (ECtHR)

The ECtHR has repeatedly stated that the extradition or expulsion of a person to a third country in which that person might face the death penalty would give rise to violations of the right to life and of the prohibition of torture and inhumane or degrading treatment or punishment.[65] Since the Soering case, the court has considered that states must require firm diplomatic assurances from retention countries that persons to be extradited or expelled will not be sentenced to death.[66]

The case of *Rrapo v. Albania* concerned the extradition of an applicant to the United States and the possible imposition of a capital sentence. The court assessed the quality of assurances given and whether in light of the requesting state's practices they could be relied upon. The court found that the assurances given in this case were specific, clear, and unequivocal, and that there were no reported breaches of an assurance given by the United States to a contracting state.[67] Therefore, the applicant's extradition would not give rise to a breach of Articles 2 and 3 of the ECHR and Article 1 of Protocol 13 due to risk of the death penalty being imposed.

A recent judgment, *AI Nashiri v. Poland*, concerned a Saudi Arabian national currently detained in Guantanamo Bay due to suspicion of involvement in terrorist activities. The ruling court held that judicial execution involves the deliberate

64. EAW FD, Preamble, Point 13.
65. *Bader and Kanbor v. Sweden*, application no. 13284/04 [Judgment of ECtHR, November 8, 2005]; *Jabari v. Turkey*, application no. 40035/98 [Judgment of ECtHR, July 11, 2000].
66. *Soering v. the United Kingdom*, application no. 14038/88 [Judgment of ECtHR, July 7, 1989].
67. *Rrapo v. Albania*, application no. 58555/10 [Judgment of ECtHR, September 25, 2012].

and premeditated destruction of a human being by state authorities; whatever the method of execution, the extinction of life involves some physical pain; the foreknowledge of death at the hands of the state must inevitably give rise to intense psychological suffering; and that the imposition and use of the death penalty negates fundamental human rights recognized by the Member States of the Council of Europe.[68]

In summary, the EU approach to the non-extradition of death penalty offenders is closely related to the choice to abolish the death penalty in the region. The rule of non-extradition of death penalty offenders not only functions within the region but also influences external relations between the EU, Member States of the EU, and third countries.[69] The complete abolition of the death penalty in the EU is also an important measure to enhance human rights protection and to promote abolition in other regions.[70]

5 The surrender of death penalty offenders between mainland China, Hong Kong, and Macau

5.1 Choice of external extradition (surrender) in death penalty situation

5.1.1 Hong Kong's surrender option with foreign countries regarding the death penalty

In the Hong Kong Fugitive Offenders Ordinance (FOO), the death penalty is an optional ground for refusal of surrender if the requested person is Chinese, and this discretion is given to the Chief Executive.[71]

Hong Kong has concluded surrender agreements with twenty countries.[72] Within these countries, India, Indonesia, Malaysia, the United States, and Singapore

68. *Al Nashiri v. Poland*, no. 28761/11 [Judgment of ECtHR, 24 July 2014], ¶577.
69. See Robert Gregg, "The European Tendency toward Non-Extradition to the United States in Capital Cases: Trends, Assurances, and Breaches of Duty," *University of Miami International and Comparative Law Review* 10, no. 1 (2002): 113. See also Laura Teuber, "Extradition and Human Rights: A Look at the EU-US and Germany-US Extradition Agreements and Their Consistency with Each Other and with Human Rights" (Bachelor's thesis, University of Twente, S1009184), 16–31.
70. See Eric Neumayer, "Death Penalty: The Political Foundations of the Global Trend toward Abolition," *Human Rights Review* 9, no. 2 (2008): 241.
71. See Fugitive Offenders Ordinance, pt. 2, ss. 13(4) and 13(5).
72. These countries include Australia (1997), Canada (1997), the Czech Republic (2015), Finland (2013), Germany (2009), India (1997), Indonesia (1997), Ireland (2009), Korea (2007), Malaysia (2001), the Netherlands (1997), New Zealand (1998), the Philippines (1997), Portugal (2004), Singapore (1998), South Africa (2011), Sri Lanka (2003), the UK (1998), and the US (1998). The

still retain the death penalty, and in the surrender agreements signed between them and Hong Kong, the death penalty can be a ground for refusal to surrender. The Hong Kong and India Surrender Agreement specifies that if the offence of a fugitive offender requested under the agreement is punishable according to the law of the requesting party with the death penalty, and if in respect of such an offence the death penalty is not provided for by the law of the requested party, surrender may be refused unless the requesting party gives such assurance as the requested party considers sufficient that the death penalty will not be imposed, or if imposed it will not be carried out.[73] A similar clause can be found in the agreements between Hong Kong and Indonesia[74] and between Hong Kong and the US.[75] The surrender agreement between Hong Kong and Singapore specifies that surrender may be refused if the requested party believes the surrender might place that party in breach of its obligations under an international treaty.[76] As Hong Kong has ratified the ICCPR, this convention can be relied upon in refusing the surrender of death penalty offenders. The surrender agreement between Hong Kong and Malaysia lacks any clause on the surrender of death penalty offenders, but it does allow refusal on humanitarian grounds,[77] which could include the death penalty.

Hong Kong also has concluded surrender agreements with sixteen other countries where the death penalty has been abolished. Non-surrender on death penalty grounds is also written into these agreements, including with New Zealand, the Netherlands, South Africa, the Philippines, South Korea, the Czech Republic, Canada, the United Kingdom, and Germany.[78]

The surrender agreement between Hong Kong and Portugal specifies that if the offence for which the surrender of a fugitive is requested is punishable according to the law of the requesting party by death, surrender shall be refused.[79] A similar clause can be found in the surrender agreements with Finland and Ireland.[80] Differences in

---

details can be seen in Department of Justice, "List of Surrender of Fugitive Offenders Agreements," November 9, 2020, https://www.doj.gov.hk/en/external/table4ti.html.

73. Surrender Agreement between Hong Kong and India, art. 5.
74. See Surrender Agreement between Hong Kong and Indonesia, art. 5.
75. See Surrender Agreement between Hong Kong and US, art. 4.
76. See Surrender Agreement between Hong Kong and Singapore, art. 6.
77. See Surrender Agreement between Hong Kong and Malaysia, art. 9.
78. See article 4 of the Surrender Agreement with South Africa; article 6 of the Surrender Agreement with the Philippines; article 4 of the Surrender Agreement with South Korea; article 5 of the Surrender Agreement with the Czech Republic; article 4 of the Surrender Agreement with Canada; article 4 of the Surrender Agreement with the New Zealand; article 4 of the Surrender Agreement with the Netherlands; article 4 of the Surrender Agreement with the UK; and article 4 of the Surrender Agreement with Germany.
79. Surrender Agreement between Hong Kong and Portugal, art. 4(1).
80. See Surrender Agreement between Hong Kong and Finland, art. 5; Surrender Agreement between Hong Kong and Ireland, art. 4.

wording on the death penalty issue will not lead to different results in reality, as all these countries as well as Hong Kong have abolished the penalty.

5.1.2 Macau's surrender choice with foreign countries regarding the death penalty

We can see Macau's position on non-surrender of death penalty offenders from its Law on Mutual Legal Assistance in Criminal Matters. It states that the legal assistance sought may be refused if it would lead to cruelty, including if the relevant facts are punishable with a death penalty sentence, but that cooperation shall not be precluded if the requesting party offers an undertaking that the penalty shall not be imposed or enforced, or if the requesting state accepts the conversion of the penalty by a Macau court in accordance with Macau law to one applicable to the crime for which the person was convicted.[81]

Macau has also concluded surrender agreements with Portugal and South Korea. In the Macau and Portugal surrender agreement, the death penalty constitutes a mandatory ground for refusal of surrender, and no assurance is needed.[82] In the agreement with South Korea, the death penalty also establishes a ground on which to refuse surrender, though it can be granted with sufficient assurances.[83]

5.1.3 Mainland China's extradition choices with foreign countries vis-á-vis the death penalty

Although mainland China has not abolished the death penalty, it has chosen the non-extradition approach in concluding extradition treaties with foreign countries. In the China Extradition Law, there is no wording on the non-extradition of death penalty offenders. But the extradition treaties mainland China has concluded reveal that it accepts the non-extradition of death penalty offenders.

To date, mainland China has concluded more than fifty extradition treaties. Many of these treaty partners have abolished the death penalty, like Spain, Portugal, Italy, and Belgium. Some have retained it, like Thailand, Pakistan, and Iran. The extradition treaties with the latter three contain no wording on the non-extradition of death penalty offenders.

But extradition treaties that China has concluded with countries that ban the death penalty recognize the non-extradition of such offenders. The extradition treaty with Spain, regarding mandatory grounds on which to refuse extradition, includes

81. See Macau Law of Judicial Cooperation in Criminal Matters, art. 7.
82. See Surrender Agreement between Macau and Portugal, art. 6(5).
83. See Surrender Agreement between Macau and South Korea, art. 4.

where under to the law of the requesting party the requested person may be subject to death penalty for the offence for which they are requested, unless the requesting party offers sufficient guarantee that the death penalty will not be imposed, or if imposed not carried out.[84] A similar clause appears in the extradition treaty with Australia.[85]

The extradition treaty with Italy does not directly stipulate non-extradition for death penalty offences, but it recognizes that a penalty prohibited by the requested party is a mandatory ground to refuse extradition.[86] In the extradition treaty with Portugal, there is also no direct clause on non-extradition for the death penalty, but going against the basic principles of the law of the requested party is a mandatory ground to refuse extradition.[87] Portugal can rely on this ground to refuse the extradition of a death penalty offender.

When it comes to the China domestic surrender system, I argue that non-surrender on death penalty offences should be the principle.

5.2 Domestic surrender and the death penalty

5.2.1 From the perspective of the "one country, two systems" policy

5.2.1.1 "One country" and the death penalty

The impetus behind restricting or abolishing the death penalty does not necessarily come from a sovereign country itself; it can be motivated by external forces.[88] The analysis of the death penalty abolition at the UN level and in the European Union showed that the decision is not made only by individual states. From this perspective, the restriction or abolition of the death penalty is an issue above the sovereignty of a state, driven by the mandates of international humanitarian law.[89] This view is supported by the fact that the UN and the EU chose to abolish the death penalty mainly for the sake of human rights protection.[90]

84. See Extradition Treaty between China and Spain, art. 3(8).
85. See Extradition Treaty between China and Australia, art. 3(6).
86. See Extradition Treaty between China and Italy, art. 3(7).
87. See Extradition Treaty between China and Portugal, art. 3(8).
88. See Jennifer Leigh Thomas, "The Influence of European Union Policy on Capital Punishment in the United States Judicial System" (Master's thesis, Western Kentucky University, 2012), https://digitalcommons.wku.edu/cgi/viewcontent.cgi?referer=&httpsredir=1&article=1377&context=stu_hon_theses.
89. See Gérard Niyungeko, "The Implementation of International Humanitarian Law and the Principle of State Sovereignty," *International Review of the Red Cross* 31, no. 281 (1991): 105.
90. See Robert Johnson, "Reflection of the Death Penalty: Human Rights, Human and Dignity, and Dehumanization in the Death House," *Seattle Journal for Social Justice* 13, no. 2 (2014): 583.

When it comes to mainland China, Hong Kong, and Macau, one region retains the death penalty while the other two ban it. That they belong to the same country is not a good argument that Hong Kong and Macau should accept or tolerate the existence of the death penalty in mainland China and surrender offenders to it. Human rights protection is substantively superior to a "sovereignty" argument which has only a symbolic meaning in this domain. The non-surrender of death penalty offenders does not mean that mainland China caves in to Hong Kong and Macau; it instead expresses a position or attitude from mainland China that demonstrates its efforts to protect human rights in a second-best way despite its inability to promptly abolish the death penalty.

5.2.1.2 *"Two systems" and the death penalty*

Before all EU countries abolished the death penalty, they applied the principle of non-extradition of death penalty offenders as discussed above. This approach can be regarded as respecting the distinction of legal systems on human rights protection in the death penalty issue. In another word, different legal systems choose to respect human rights in different ways. While some legal systems choose to abolish the death penalty directly, others choose to offer guarantees not to impose the penalty in the name of judicial cooperation. This demonstrates mutual understanding and mutual respect.

Similarly for mainland China, Hong Kong, and Macau, in their surrender system, mainland China can offer guarantees to Hong Kong and Macau regarding the imposition of the death penalty or its execution as a way for mainland China to meet its obligation on human rights protection. This obligation has been fulfilled by Hong Kong and Macau by abolishing the penalty completely. One criticism goes to the "unequal treatment" of local criminals and those surrendered by Hong Kong and Macau to mainland China, since the former may be executed and the latter may suffer life imprisonment at worst. However, whether "different treatment" should be called "unequal treatment" is debatable. After all, imposing the death penalty locally and offering guarantees to refrain from executing a surrendered person are both decisions based in law. The law does not grant favor to any person but rather serves different situations. From another perspective, the imposition of the death penalty and its execution in mainland China are mitigated by the surrender requirement.

5.2.2 The international stance on the death penalty

From UN, Inter-American, and EU practices we see that the abolition of the death penalty and the non-extradition of death penalty offenders have been pushed at both international and regional levels. As closely related regions, mainland China, Hong

Kong, and Macau should follow this tendency and take a positive position on the issue. In particular, mainland China should realize that the whole world applauds the death penalty's abolition and recognizes the legitimacy of non-extradition of death penalty offenders. This position should be supported no matter whether mainland China is engaging with foreign countries or with other regions, like Hong Kong and Macau.

Death penalty abolitionist states have responsibilities with regard to jurisdictions which retain the death penalty. They should not facilitate the use of the penalty elsewhere through the extradition of a person they know to be at genuine risk of the death penalty.[91] Generally, abolitionist states only extradite individuals when the state requesting custody has provided assurance that the person will not be sentenced to death or executed. Since the twenty-first century, the tendency to seek assurances has evolved into a legal obligation. Even death penalty retention states have been unwilling or legally unable to transfer requested persons to places where they could receive capital punishment.[92]

5.2.3 Mainland China's stance on the death penalty

Since 2011, legislation in mainland China has widely abolished the death penalty. The first instance occurred on May 1, 2011, when it abolished the death penalty for thirteen offences. The second happened on August 29, 2015, when bans were imposed for another nine offences.[93] Currently, mainland China's policy on the death penalty seeks to protect human rights and restrict the penalty's application. I argue that the non-surrender of death penalty offenders between mainland China, Hong Kong, and Macau is an appropriate and positive response to this trend and policy position.

5.2.4 The role of non-surrender of death penalty offenders in the China domestic surrender system

In previous chapters, I analyzed the China domestic surrender situation and found that mainland China, Hong Kong, and Macau have their own concerns regarding the surrender of residents and surrender for political offences. In the cases of Hong Kong and Macau, residents do not face the death penalty locally, but they will be

91. See J. Yorke, "Europe's Inquiry in Extradition Cases: Closing the Door on the Death Penalty," *ECR* 29, no. 4 (2004): 546.
92. See Bharat Malkani, "Extradition and Non-refoulment," in *Comparative Capital Punishment*, ed. Carol S. Steiker and Jordan M. Steiker (Cheltenham: Edward Elgar, 2019), 76.
93. Regarding the concrete offences which have been abolished the death penalty, see supra, n 2, n 3 and n 4.

concerned that if they are surrendered to mainland China the death penalty may be imposed. Regarding surrender for political offences, under the double criminality principle, many politically-related offences can result in surrender to mainland China; accordingly, Hong Kong and Macau will harbor concerns about capital punishment. The non-surrender of death penalty offenders not only can function to protect human rights but also can help to reduce tensions in the entire surrender system regarding the surrender of residents and political offenders and make the surrender system more workable.

6 Conclusion

Abolishing the death penalty has long been the international trend, and the non-extradition of death penalty offenders has been widely adopted to protect human rights and push the abolition of the death penalty globally. Mainland China, Hong Kong, and Macau should follow this tendency. For mainland China, non-surrender of death penalty offenders in the surrender system with Hong Kong and with Macau can release inter-regional tension. It can also push mainland China to further abolish the death penalty in law and in practice, contributing to human rights protection.

9
The Exception for Life Imprisonment Offenders

1 Introduction

Mainland China and Hong Kong retain the punishment of life imprisonment in law and practice, while Macau has abolished it completely. Accordingly, in the China domestic surrender system, life imprisonment may be a point of conflict. In 2018, Cristina Ferreira, the former director of the Legal Affairs Bureau in Macau, perceptively remarked: "The surrender of fugitive offenders between mainland China, Hong Kong, and Macau should take both the death penalty and life imprisonment issues into account."[1]

Non-extradition or non-surrender of death penalty offenders relates closely to the trend toward abolishing the death penalty worldwide.[2] However, concerns about life imprisonment in extradition or surrender procedure are not based on the view that this punishment should be abolished completely.[3] Instead, they are based on the ideas that even life imprisonment offenders should retain the right to hope and the right to have their cases reviewed.[4] Implicit is the possibility that some offenders may remain in jail until their death after fulfilling their right to review.[5] The European Court of Human Rights (ECtHR) holds that a human right is not

1. Interview with Cristina Ferreira, previous acting department head of the International and Inter-Regional Law Department of the Macau Legal Affairs Bureau, Macau, February 2018.
2. See Eric Neumayer, "Death Penalty: The Political Foundations of the Global Trend toward Abolition," *Human Rights Review* 9, no. 2 (2008): 241.
3. See Dirk Van Zyl Smit, "Outlawing Irreducible Life Sentences: Europe on the Brink?" *Federal Sentencing Reporter* 23, no. 1 (2010): 39.
4. See William A. Schabas, *The European Convention on Human Rights: A Commentary* (Oxford: Oxford University Press, 2015), 187.
5. See Stephen Gieger, "*Trabelsi v. Belgium*: Extradition of Terrorist Suspects and Aversion to Whole-Life Prison Sentences," *Tulane Journal of International and Comparative Law* 23 (2015): 576.

violated if a lifetime prisoner has the right under domestic law to be considered for release but is refused because he or she may continue to pose a danger to society.[6] Life imprisonment is also a concern for the China domestic surrender system.

In this chapter, firstly, I explore the domestic legislation on life imprisonment in mainland China, Hong Kong, and Macau, to ascertain the options for a surrender agreement. Secondly, I analyze experiences globally to show the tendency on this issue. Thirdly, I discuss the EU and EAW practices on life imprisonment in that region's surrender system. Fourthly, I conclude on how the life imprisonment issue can be solved in the China arrest warrant system.

2 Life imprisonment in the three regions

2.1 Life imprisonment in mainland China

The application of life imprisonment in domestic law strongly influences the position of life imprisonment in a jurisdiction's extradition or surrender system. If the use of life imprisonment with the possibility of parole has been applied, such a jurisdiction will prefer to request a guarantee as to life imprisonment in its extradition or surrender procedure. To decide upon the role of life imprisonment in the China domestic surrender system, we should first analyze life imprisonment in the three regions.

Life imprisonment is a severe penalty in mainland China, but the sentence can be commuted or prisoners paroled.[7] The China Criminal Law specifies that the punishment of a criminal sentenced to public surveillance, criminal detention, fixed-term imprisonment, or life imprisonment may be commuted. The conditions include that while serving the sentence he or she conscientiously observes prison regulations, accepts education and reform through labor, and expresses true repentance or performs meritorious services. The sentence can also be commuted if a criminal performs any of the following major meritorious services: preventing another person from conducting major criminal activities; informing against major criminal activities conducted inside or outside prison and verified through investigation; having inventions or important technical innovations to his or her credit; coming to the rescue of another in everyday life at the risk of losing one's own life; performing remarkable service in fighting against natural disasters or curbing major

6. See Case *Vinter and Others v. the UK*, applications nos. 66069/09, 130/10 and 3896/10 [Judgment of ECtHR, July 9, 2013], ¶108.
7. See Shu Hongshui 舒洪水, "Lun zhongshen jianjin de biyaoxing he tixihua goujian: yi kongbu zhuyi, jiduan zhuyi fanzui fangkong wei shijiao" 论终身监禁的必要性和体系化构建-以恐怖主义、极端主义犯罪防控为视角 [Study on the necessity and systematic construction of life sentences—from the perspective of prevention and combating terrorism], *Falü kexue* 法律科学 3 (2018): 152.

accidents; or making other major contributions to the country and society.[8] After commutation, the term of punishment actually to be served by those sentenced to life imprisonment may not be less than ten years.[9]

Moreover, the China Criminal Law stipulates that a criminal sentenced to life imprisonment who has served not less than ten years[10] may be granted parole. The conditions are that he or she conscientiously observes prison regulations, accepts education and reform through labor, expresses true repentance and will no longer cause harm to society. In special circumstances, upon verification and approval by the Supreme People's Court, the above requirements may be disregarded, but no parole may be granted to recidivists or to criminals who are sentenced to life imprisonment for crimes of violence, such as homicide, bombing, robbery, rape, and kidnap.[11]

Persons convicted of the most heinous forms of corruption or bribery can receive life imprisonment without the possibility of commutation or parole. However, the prerequisite for this penalty is that the convicted person receives a suspended death penalty; after two years' suspension, life imprisonment without commutation or parole will be imposed.[12] As this research has already proposed the refusal of surrender for death penalty offenders, it will not propose the application of life imprisonment without commutation or parole in the China domestic surrender system.

In practice, the majority of the life imprisonment sentences can be commuted, and seldom are prisoners imprisoned until death.[13] In law and practice, mainland China applies life imprisonment with the possibility of conditional release. This forms a basis for cooperation between mainland China, Hong Kong, and Macau on life imprisonment issues.

---

8. China Criminal Law, art. 78.
9. China Criminal Law, art. 78.
10. According to the Regulation on the Legal Application of Addressing Cases of Commutation and Parole by Supreme People's Court, the years of actual imprisonment after which life-imprisonment criminals can be paroled should not be less than thirteen years.
11. See China Criminal Law, art. 83.
12. See China Criminal Law, art. 383(3).
13. See Li Jun 黎军 and Yang Wentao 杨文滔, "Sixing xianzhi jianxing zhidu de chubu jianzhi: jiyu zhongji fayuan de sifa shijian de kaocha" 死刑限制减刑制度的初步检视-基于中级法院的司法实践的考察 [Preliminary examination of the system of death-penalty restriction and commutation: A study based on the judicial practices of intermediate courts], in *Jianshe gongping zhengyi shehui yu xingshi falü shiyong wenti yanjiu* 建设公平正义社会与刑事法律适用问题研究 [Research on the construction of a fair and just society and the application of criminal law], ed. Wan Exiang 万鄂湘 (Beijing: Renmin faxue chubanshe, 2012), 1211.

2.2 *Life imprisonment in Hong Kong*

Hong Kong maintains life imprisonment, but the sentence can be commuted and the prisoner conditionally released. The Long-term Prison Sentences Review Ordinance regulates such commutation and release under the authority of the Long-term Prison Sentences Review Board.[14] Pursuant to this Ordinance, the sentence of a prisoner serving a long-term prison sentence including a mandatory life sentence[15] is to be referred for review as soon as practicable after the fifth anniversary of the date of the start of the sentence and as soon as practicable after each subsequent second anniversary of that date.[16] If a prisoner is serving a discretionary life sentence[17] or is detained at executive discretion, the sentence is to be referred for review as soon as practicable after the relevant date and as soon as practicable after each subsequent second anniversary of that date.[18] After review, the Board can make a recommendation to Hong Kong's Chief Executive for commutation or the conditional release of a life sentence offender. In general, only after serving twenty years of a life sentence can offenders be conditionally released, and only if they comply with the conditions specified in the ordinance.

2.3 *Life imprisonment in Macau*

There is no life imprisonment in Macau. The highest sentence is twenty-five years, but if the offender commits several serious crimes that threshold can be raised to thirty-five years.[19] The law also specifies that the death penalty cannot be established, nor can life imprisonment or indeterminate imprisonment.[20]

In summary, mainland China and Hong Kong still apply life imprisonment whereas Macau has abolished it completely. For the surrender of fugitive offenders between them, this distinction should be taken into consideration. The international position on life imprisonment also offers options.

---

14. See Hong Kong Long-Term Prison Sentences Review Ordinance, ss. 5 and 7.
15. According to s. 4 of this Ordinance, a mandatory life sentence means a sentence of imprisonment for life; indeed, the only sentence that could be imposed for the relevant offence was life imprisonment.
16. See Hong Kong Long-Term Prison Sentences Review Ordinance, s. 11(2).
17. According to s. 4 of this ordinance, a discretionary life sentence means (a) a sentence of imprisonment for life in which the maximum sentence that could be imposed for the relevant offence is life imprisonment; and (b) a sentence of imprisonment for life under section 2 of the Offences against Person Ordinance (Cap. 212) regarding a person convicted of murder who is under eighteen years of age at the time of the offence.
18. See Hong Kong Long-Term Prison Sentences Review Ordinance, s. 11(3).
19. See Macao Penal Code, art. 41.
20. See Macau Penal Code, art. 39.

3 Life imprisonment and international extradition

3.1 Life imprisonment and human rights protection

3.1.1 The International Covenant on Civil and Political Rights (ICCPR)

Although the ICCPR contains no direct clause on life imprisonment, there are some hints on this issue which emphasize the rights protection of offenders.[21] The convention highlights the offender's right to review; in other words, everyone convicted of a crime shall have the right to have their conviction and sentence reviewed by a higher tribunal according to law.[22] The review of a life imprisonment sentence is part of the review of sentence referred to in this clause.[23]

3.1.2 Recommendations from the UN Congress on the Prevention of Crime and the Treatment of Offenders

In 1980, the Sixth UN Congress on the Prevention of Crime and the Treatment of Offenders recognized that long-term imprisonment, especially life imprisonment, did not serve the desired purposes unless adequate measures were provided to bring such prisoners back into the mainstream of social life in an appropriate condition.[24] The Eighth Congress on the Prevention of Crime and the Treatment of Offenders in 1990 requested the Committee on Crime Prevention and Control to examine the legal position regarding the rights and duties of prisoners serving life sentences and the various systems for reviewing their suitability for conditional release. It also requested the committee to give special consideration to assessment procedures and decision-making in cases of life sentences and to examine the need for life sentences.[25]

21. See Nadia Bernaz, "Life Imprisonment and the Prohibition of Inhuman Punishment in International Human Rights Law: Moving the Agenda Forward," *Human Rights Quarterly* 35, no. 2 (2013): 470.
22. International Covenant on Civil and Political Rights, art. 14(5).
23. See Dirk Van Zyl Smit, "Life Imprisonment and the Right to Hope," *Penal Reform International Blog*, July 24, 2013, https://www.penalreform.org/blog/life-imprisonment-hope/.
24. See Secretariat for the Sixth UN Congress, "Deinstitutionalization of Corrections and Its Implications for the Residual Prisoner" (Working Paper on the Prevention of Crime and the Treatment of Offenders, NCJ No. 77041, 1980), accessed November 1, 2022, https://www.ojp.gov/ncjrs/virtual-library/abstracts/deinstitutionalization-corrections-and-its-implications-residual.
25. See Report of the Secretary-General, "Criminal Justice Policies in Relation to Problems of Imprisonment, Other Penal Sanctions and Alternative Measures: Research on Alternatives to Imprisonment" (Eighth UN Congress on the Prevention of Crime and the Treatment of Offenders, A/CONF.144/13, June 1, 1990), 19–24, https://www.unodc.org/documents/congress//Previous_Congresses/8th_Congress_1990/016_ACONF.144.13_Report_Crim_Justice_Policies_in_Relation_to_Problems_of_Imprisonment_Other_Penal_Sanctions_Alter_Measures.pdf. See also Report of the Secretary-General, "Criminal Justice Policies in Relation to Problems of

On December 17, 2015, the UN General Assembly adopted the United Nations Standard Minimum Rules for the Treatment of Prisoners. These specify that the purpose of a sentence of imprisonment or similar measure depriving a person of liberty is primarily to protect society against crime and reduce recidivism; those purposes can be achieved only if the period of imprisonment is used to ensure, so far as possible, the reintegration of such persons into society upon release so that they can lead a law-abiding and self-supporting life.[26] Putting offenders into jail for the remainder of their lives deters the reintegration of offenders into society. This series of UN instruments recommends reviews of life imprisonment and conditional release.

3.1.3 Theoretical justification for prohibition of life imprisonment

The argument for prohibiting life imprisonment is related to the understanding of punishment as a means of rehabilitation. The detention of an offender for life means a clear rejection of the objective of reintegrating the convicted person into society.[27] Life imprisonment without parole is a cruel, inhuman, and degrading punishment which harms human dignity; it violates the proportionality principle and breaches the right to rehabilitation.[28]

From a functional perspective, life imprisonment without parole is without benefit. According to criminological research, adolescents and young adults commit most crimes and crime rates steadily decline after the age of thirty;[29] this putting offenders into life imprisonment without parole is useless in deterring crime. Interviews with prison insiders show that it takes prisoners only a few years to come

Imprisonment, Other Penal Sanctions and Alternative Measures: Alternatives to Imprisonment and the Reduction of the Prison Population" (Eighth UN Congress on the Prevention of Crime and the Treatment of Offenders, A/CONF.144/12, May 28, 1990), 19–22, https://www.unodc.org/documents/congress//Previous_Congresses/8th_Congress_1990/015_ACONF.144.12_Crim_Justice_Policies_in_Relation_to_Problems_of_Imprisonment_Other_Penal_Sanctions_Alter_Measures.pdf. See also Report of the Secretary-General, "Implementation of the Standard Minimum Rules for the Treatment of Prisoners" (Eighth UN Congress on the Prevention of Crime and the Treatment of Offenders, A/CONF.144/1, July 19, 1990), 27–30, https://www.unodc.org/documents/congress//Previous_Congresses/8th_Congress_1990/014_ACONF.144.11_Implementation_of_the_Standard_Minimum_Rules_for_the_Treatment_of_Prisoners.pdf.

26. See the United Nation Standard Minimum Rules for the Treatment of Prisoners, Rule 4(1).
27. See Giovanna Maria Frisso, "The Abolition of Life Imprisonment in Brazil and its Contradictions," in *Life Imprisonment and Human Rights*, ed. Dirk van Zyl Smit and Catherine Appleton (Oxford: Hart, 2016), 309.
28. See Esther Gumboh, "The Penalty of Life Imprisonment under International Criminal Law," *African Human Rights Law Journal* 11 (2011): 77–79.
29. See Vanessa Maaskamp, "Extradition and Life Imprisonment," *Loyola of Los Angeles International and Comparative Law Review* 6 (2003): 758.

to realization and understand of what they have done; life imprisonment without parole does not encourage them to think more deeply.[30]

However, as the global tendency has been to abolish the death penalty, life imprisonment including without parole has been regarded as a replacement, justified by the three general purposes of retribution, general deterrence, and incapacitation.[31] In practice, life imprisonment remains widely applied in law and practice, and life imprisonment without parole also exists in a minority of countries.

3.2 Life imprisonment in practice

Around the world, nearly thirty countries or regions have abolished life imprisonment completely, including Honduras, Panama, Mexico, Bolivia, Kosovo, Montenegro, Serbia, Slovenia, Cape Verde, and Macau.[32] Compared to the death penalty,[33] countries abolishing life imprisonment are fewer. Countries applying life imprisonment with the possibility of parole constitute the majority. In more than a hundred countries where life imprisonment is applied, around fourteen practice life without parole. These include Afghanistan, Cambodia, Egypt, Indonesia, Israel, Jordan, Laos, and Morocco.[34] Around ten countries apply life imprisonment without parole to certain crimes, including Argentina, Austria, India, Italy, Japan, Malaysia, Singapore, South Korea, the US, and Uzbekistan.[35]

3.3 Life imprisonment in extradition

3.3.1 UN Model Treaty on Extradition

The Revised Model Treaty lists the death penalty as an optional ground to refuse extradition and states that some countries may wish to apply the same restriction on a life or indeterminate sentence.[36] This offers a legal basis for states to refuse extradition where there is a possibility of life imprisonment without parole.

---

30. See "Life Imprisonment," *Prison Insider*, published April 13, 2016, https://www.prison-insider.com/en/articles/l-emprisonnement-perpetuel.
31. See Sarah Browning, Eric Jensen, and Waid Courtney, "Life Imprisonment as a Penal Policy," *International Journal on Basque Studies* 55 (2010): 25.
32. See "Life Imprisonment," Wikipedia, accessed November 1, 2022, https://en.wikipedia.org/wiki/Life_imprisonment#Reform_or_abolition.
33. According to data from Amnesty International, more than 100 countries have abolished the death penalty to date. See "Death Penalty in 2020: Facts and Figures," Amnesty International, accessed November 1, 2022, https://www.amnesty.org/en/latest/press-release/2021/04/death-penalty-in-2020-facts-and-figures/.
34. See "Life Imprisonment," n 32.
35. See "Life Imprisonment," n 32.
36. See Revised Manual on the Model Treaty on Extradition, art. 4.

3.3.2 Inter-American Convention on Extradition

This regional convention provides that state parties shall not grant extradition when the offence in question is punishable in the requesting state by the death penalty, life imprisonment, or degrading punishment, unless the requested state has previously obtained from the requested state, through diplomatic channels, sufficient assurance that none of the above-mentioned penalties will be imposed on the person sought, or that if such penalties are imposed they will not be enforced.[37] The reason for this clause is that a lot of American countries have abolished life imprisonment completely, and few of the remaining countries apply life imprisonment without parole.

3.3.3 Bilateral extradition treaties

Although extradition treaties which include provisions for non-life imprisonment assurances from the requesting state are much fewer than extradition treaties which provide for death penalty assurances, we still find this provision in some bilateral treaties.

The treaty on extradition between Australia and the Republic of Venezuela, for example, provides that extradition may be refused where the offence for which extradition is requested is punishable by life imprisonment under the laws of the requesting state and where a similar punishment for that offence is not contained in the law of the requested state.[38] However, extradition may proceed if "the requesting State undertakes that a life sentence, if imposed, will not result in a period of deprivation of liberty exceeding 30 years being served."[39] The US-Venezuela extradition treaty provides that extradition may be declined for crimes punishable by death or life imprisonment.[40] However, the executive authority of each party may grant extradition for such offences "upon receipt of satisfactory assurance that in case of conviction the death penalty or imprisonment for life will not be inflicted."[41] Spain's extradition treaties with Panama[42] and Paraguay[43] provide that extradition shall not be granted unless the requesting state guarantees that the death penalty shall not be imposed upon the offender and that life imprisonment shall be commuted to the immediately lesser punishment.

---

37. Inter-American Convention on Extradition, art. 9.
38. Treaty on Extradition between Australia and the Republic of Venezuela, art. VII(b).
39. Treaty on Extradition between Australia and the Republic of Venezuela, art. VII(b).
40. Treaty on Extradition between the United States and Venezuela, art. IV.
41. Treaty on Extradition between the United States and Venezuela, art. IV.
42. Treaty on Extradition between the Kingdom of Spain and the Republic of Panama, art. 4(8).
43. Treaty on Extradition between the Kingdom of Spain and the Republic of Paraguay, art. 5(7).

From extradition treaties which include a life imprisonment clause, we see that such provisions exist between countries where at least one has abolished life imprisonment without parole or life imprisonment *per se*. Even in the case of countries in which life imprisonment without parole has been abolished, one can still find inconsistent approaches towards life imprisonment in extradition. The extradition treaties between Spain and India[44] and Spain and the US[45] do not provide for assurances in cases of life imprisonment. Summarily, in regional extradition convention or bilateral extradition treaties we find that requesting assurance as to life imprisonment is common. But the tendency is more evident in the European arrest warrant system on the basis of human rights protection.[46]

4 The European arrest warrant and life imprisonment

4.1 Life imprisonment and human rights protection in the EU

4.1.1 European Convention on Human Rights

The ECHR specifies that no one shall be subjected to torture or to inhuman or degrading treatment or punishment.[47] This has been widely interpreted as precluding life sentences.

In the case of *Vinter and Others v. the UK*, three applicants had been given "whole life orders" meaning that they could not be released without the discretion of the UK's Justice Secretary, who would do so only on compassionate grounds (for example, in cases of terminal illness or serious incapacitation). They complained that their imprisonment for life amounted to inhuman and degrading treatment as they had no hope of release. The Grand Chamber of the ECtHR held that there had been a violation of Article 3 of the ECHR. The court considered that for a life sentence to remain compatible with Article 3 it had to be reducible; in other words, there had to be a prospect of the prisoner's release and the possibility of a review of the sentence.[48] The court noted that there was clear support in European and international law and practice for that principle, with most of the ECHR contracting states not actually imposing life sentences at all or, if they did impose them, providing for a review after a set period (usually 25 years' imprisonment).[49]

---

44. Treaty on Extradition between Kingdom of Spain and Republic of India, art. 11.
45. Treaty on Extradition between Kingdom of Spain and US, art. VII.
46. See Martin Bose, "Harmonizing Procedural Rights Indirectly: The Framework on Trials in Absentia," *North Carolina Journal of International Law* 37, no. 2 (2011): 489.
47. European Convention on Human Rights, art. 3.
48. Case *Vinter and Others v. the UK*, applications nos. 66069/09, 130/10 and 3896/10 [Judgment of ECtHR, July 9, 2013], ¶109.
49. Case *Vinter and Others v. the UK*, ¶68–75.

4.1.2 Charter of Fundamental Rights of the European Union

Reference can also be made to the CFR. It resonates with the ECHR, stipulating that no one shall be subjected to torture or to inhuman or degrading treatment or punishment.[50] It also holds that no one may be removed, expelled, or extradited to a state where there is a serious risk that he or she would be subjected to the death penalty, torture or other inhuman or degrading treatment or punishment.[51] These articles respond positively to Article 3 of the ECHR and offer further legal basis for the protection of potential life imprisonment offenders.

4.1.3 Other relevant EU documents

The Recommendation of the Committee of Ministers to Member States on conditional release[52] strongly recommends governments to legislate for conditional release if they have not already done so. It states that in order to reduce the harmful effects of imprisonment, and to promote the resettlement of prisoners under conditions that seek to guarantee safety of the outside community, the law should make conditional release available to all sentenced prisoners including life-sentence prisoners.[53] It also suggests that the minimum or fixed period should not be so long that the purpose of conditional release cannot be achieved,[54] and that if the decision-making authority decides not to grant conditional release it should set a date for reconsidering the question. In any case, prisoners should be able to reapply to the decision-making authority as soon as their situation has substantially changed to their advantage.[55]

A report from the European Committee for the Prevention of Torture and Inhuman or Degrading Treatment or Punishment (CPT) also takes the position that life sentence without parole is problematic.[56] The CPT considers that a prison sentence which offers no possibility of release precludes one of the essential

50. Charter of Fundamental Rights of the European Union, art. 4.
51. Charter of Fundamental Rights of the European Union, art. 19(v2).
52. See Recommendation (2003) 22 of the Committee of Ministers to member states on conditional release.
53. See Recommendation (2003) 22 of the Committee of Ministers to member states on conditional release, art. 4(a).
54. See Recommendation (2003) 22 of the Committee of Ministers to member states on conditional release, art. 6.
55. See Recommendation (2003) 22 of the Committee of Ministers to member states on conditional release, art. 21.
56. See European Committee for the Prevention of Torture and Inhuman or Degrading Treatment or Punishment (CPT), "Situation of Life-sentenced Prisoners, Extract from the 25th General Report of the CPT," CPT/Inf (2016) 10-part, accessed November 1, 2022, https://rm.coe.int/16806cc447.

justifications of imprisonment itself, the possibility of rehabilitation.[57] While punishment and public protection are important elements of a prison sentence, excluding from the outset any hope of rehabilitation and return to the community effectively dehumanizes the prisoner.[58]

In the 27 European Union countries, four have abolished life imprisonment completely, namely Croatia, Portugal, Spain, and Slovenia. Five other countries apply life imprisonment without parole, including Austria, Bulgaria, Hungary, Italy, and Malta. The remaining 18 countries apply life with parole.[59]

4.2 Cases from the European Court of Human Rights

In the case of *Laszlo Magyar v. Hungary,* the ECtHR held that there had been a violation of ECHR Article 3 due to the applicant's life sentence without eligibility for parole. It was not persuaded that Hungarian law allowed life prisoners to know what they had to do to be considered for release and under what conditions. In addition, the law did not guarantee proper consideration of changes in the lives of prisoners and their progress towards rehabilitation. Therefore, the court concluded that the sentence of the applicant could not be regarded as reducible, which amounted to a violation of Article 3.[60]

In the case of *T.P. and A.T. v. Hungary,* the applicants alleged that despite new legislation, which introduced an automatic review of whole life sentences by means of a mandatory pardon procedure after forty years, their sentences remained inhumane and degrading as they effectively had no hope of release.[61] The court held that there had been a violation of ECHR Article 3. It found that waiting forty years for one's first clemency hearing was too long and that, in any case, there was a lack of sufficient safeguards in the remainder of the procedure provided by the new legislation.[62] The court was therefore unpersuaded that, at the time of judgment, the applicants' life sentences could be regarded as providing them with the prospect of release or a possibility of review, and the legislation was therefore not compatible with Article 3.[63]

In brief, most European countries have reached consensus on conditional life imprisonment. This actively responds to human rights protection requirements

57. See CPT, "Situation," 4, n 56.
58. See CPT, "Situation," 4, n 56.
59. The relevant data should be found in "Life Imprisonment," accessed November 1, 2022, https://en.wikipedia.org/wiki/Life_imprisonment.
60. See Case *Laszlo Magyar v. Hungary,* no. 73593/10 [Judgment of ECtHR, May 20, 2014].
61. See Case *T.P. and A.T.V. Hungary,* nos. 37871/14 and 73986/14 [Judgment of ECtHR, October 4, 2016].
62. See Case *T.P. and A.T.V. Hungary,* ¶45, 49.
63. See Case *T.P. and A.T.V. Hungary,* ¶50.

in Europe and also makes guarantees as to life imprisonment in the surrender of offenders feasible.

4.3 *Life imprisonment and the surrender of fugitive offenders in the European arrest warrant system*

4.3.1 Before the European arrest warrant's Framework Decision

Before the EAW Framework Decision, an attempt had been made to provide for guarantees on life imprisonment in the European Convention on Extradition of 1957. This Convention provided that extradition may be refused unless the requesting party gave such assurance as may be considered satisfactory that the death penalty would not be carried out.[64] Portugal raised a reservation to this article, indicating that it would not grant extradition of persons who could face "a life-long sentence or detention order." The reservation was rejected by several governments (Germany, Austria, Switzerland, Belgium, and the Russian Federation), which considered it to be incompatible with the meaning and purpose of the Convention.

4.3.2 The European arrest warrant period

The EAW Framework Decision makes clear provision for the life imprisonment issue. It states that execution of a European arrest warrant by an executing judicial authority may, according to the law of the executing Member State, be subject to the condition that if the offence on the basis of which the EAW has been issued is punishable by a custodial life sentence or a lifetime detention order, the execution of the warrant may be subject to the condition that the issuing Member State has provisions in its legal system for review of the penalty or measures imposed, upon request or at the latest after twenty years, for the application of measures of clemency for which the person is entitled to apply under the law or practice of the issuing Member State, aiming at non-execution of such penalty or measure.[65]

4.4 *Application of the life imprisonment clause with third countries*

In the case of Nizar Trabelsi, the ECtHR ruled that while life sentences were not inherently disproportionate, Belgium did violate ECHR Article 3 by extraditing the

64. See European Convention on Extradition 1957, art. 11.
65. See EAW FD, art. 5(2).

offender to a country where a conviction could carry an irreducible life sentence.[66] The court also held that in extradition cases, the assessment of the reducibility of a life sentence liable to be served by an applicant in the requesting state must be made before his arrival. The court also found that Belgium failed to honor its convention commitments by extraditing Trabelsi before the court's final judgment on the case.[67]

We can see that EU human rights law on life imprisonment can intervene directly in extradition between EU Member States and third countries. The US and other countries where life imprisonment is applied will be affected, including China. In the following section, I analyze the inspirations that can be drawn from global trends and EU practice for the China domestic surrender system.

5 Life imprisonment in surrender between mainland China, Hong Kong, and Macau

5.1 Life imprisonment and extradition (surrender) in extradition (surrender) agreements with foreign countries

5.1.1 Life imprisonment in extradition between mainland China and foreign countries

The China Extradition Law is silent on the life imprisonment issue. Most of the extradition treaties concluded between mainland China and other countries do not refer to it. However, it is taken into consideration in the extradition treaties between mainland China and Spain and between mainland China and Portugal.

The extradition treaty between mainland China and Portugal provides that the requesting Member State should offer a letter of request stating the conviction and penalty that may be imposed on the offender, the likely prospects for the prosecution or punishment, and the rules relating to early release.[68] The extradition treaty between mainland China and Spain contains a similar clause, which more clearly states that if the requested offender will be sentenced to life imprisonment, the requesting party should submit the legal regulations on commutation.[69] Thus, although requirements on the life imprisonment issue in mainland China's extradition are new and rare, they do exist in some treaties.

66. See Case *Trabelsi v. Belgium*, application no. 140/10 [Judgment of ECtHR, 4 September 4, 2014], ¶137–38.
67. See Case *Trabelsi v. Belgium*, ¶151–54.
68. See Extradition Treaty between Mainland China and Portugal, art. 7(1).
69. See Extradition Treaty between Mainland China and Spain, art. 7(3).

5.1.2 Life imprisonment in surrender between Hong Kong and foreign countries

The Hong Kong Fugitive Offenders Ordinance (FOO) says nothing as to life imprisonment, like the China Extradition Law. In the surrender agreement concluded with Spain, however, the issue is addressed. The agreement stipulates that the requested party may refuse assistance if the request relates to an offence which is punishable according to the law of the requesting party with life imprisonment or carries a prison sentence of undetermined duration, unless the requesting party gives such assurance as the requested party considers sufficient that these penalties will not be imposed, or if imposed that they will not be carried out.[70] A similar clause appears in the surrender agreement between Hong Kong and Portugal.[71]

Portugal and Spain have abolished life imprisonment and, according to the ECtHR, their extraditing fugitive offenders to a place where actual life imprisonment exists violates basic human rights.[72] These countries' arrangements with Hong Kong thus offer some guarantees as to the application of life imprisonment.

5.1.3 Life imprisonment in surrender between Macau and foreign countries

The Macau Law on Judicial Cooperation in Criminal Matters asserts that judicial cooperation should be refused if the request will lead to a permanent or indefinite penalty of liberty deprivation or security punishment.[73] Macau's surrender agreement with Portugal contains a clear statement that surrender may be refused if the requested person will face life imprisonment.[74]

In summary, all three China regions adopt the similar position that guarantees on life imprisonment can be required in extradition or surrender with foreign countries. Such guarantees should also be made in the China domestic surrender system.

---

70. See Agreement between the Hong Kong Special Administrative Region of the People's Republic of China and Spain Concerning Mutual Legal Assistance in Criminal Matters, art. 3(4).
71. See Surrender Agreement between Hong Kong and Portugal, art. 4(2).
72. See the cases in section 4.2 above.
73. See Macau Law in Judicial Cooperation in Criminal Matters, art. 7(6).
74. See Surrender Agreement between Macau and Portugal, art. 7(6).

5.2 *The choice for the three regions on life imprisonment*

5.2.1 The global trend

As explained in the first part of this chapter, although not many countries have abolished life imprisonment worldwide, life imprisonment with conditional release has become the norm. This has been supported by international human rights conventions and has greatly influenced international extradition practice.[75] Particularly in the European Union, the ECHR and ECtHR not only require parole for life imprisonment in the European arrest warrant mechanism, but also stress the necessity of parole availability in EU Member States' extradition with third countries. Mainland China, Hong Kong, and Macau should follow this trend, which will also help mainland China to cooperate more effectively with the countries of Europe in extradition matters.

5.2.2 Conflict of penalty in the three regions

Compared to guarantees on the death penalty in the surrender of persons between mainland China, Hong Kong, and Macau, there should be fewer obstacles for the three regions to reach consensus on guarantees on life imprisonment. Macau has abolished life imprisonment while mainland China and Hong Kong apply life imprisonment with parole and conditional release. Therefore, giving guarantees on life imprisonment in surrender between the three regions will not alter the present legal state at all. This should be easy for mainland China, Hong Kong, and Macau to accept.

5.2.3 Previous experience in mainland China and Hong Kong of extradition (surrender) with foreign countries

In the Macau Law on Judicial Cooperation in Criminal Matters, analyzed above, guarantees as to life imprisonment are clearly required. Likewise, in mainland China's extradition treaties with Spain and with Portugal, guarantees on life imprisonment are stipulated. In the surrender agreement between Hong Kong and Spain, and Hong Kong and Portugal, Hong Kong can also offer guarantees on life imprisonment. Such guarantees can also be expected in a surrender agreement between mainland China, Hong Kong, and Macau.

75. See Marko Milanovic, "Extradition and Life Imprisonment" *Cambridge Law Journal* 69 (2009), 248. See also Lewis Graham, "Extradition, Life Sentences and the European Convention," *Judicial Review* 25, no. 3 (2020): 228.

6 Conclusion

From this chapter, we see that although not so many countries have abolished life imprisonment, most of them have mitigated the sentence with parole and other conditions for release mainly due to growing concern for human rights protection and growing uncertainty about the effectiveness of life imprisonment. This tendency has deeply influenced international extradition. More and more countries ask for guarantees on life imprisonment in extradition cases, especially in the European arrest warrant system. Mainland China, Hong Kong, and Macau should follow this international trend, putting a life imprisonment guarantee clause into their surrender arrangement. Their own criminal laws on life imprisonment and their extradition or surrender practices with foreign countries offer precedents for this choice.

10
The Application of the Human Rights Ground

1 Introduction

Human rights protection is an important consideration for the China domestic surrender system. In international extradition, the lack of human rights protection is generally a mandatory ground to refuse cooperation.[1] This concerns the actual rights of the offenders and also represents the breadth and depth of cooperation between the requesting and requested parties.[2] The China domestic surrender system must apply the human rights ground, not only responding to the "one country, two systems" policy but also protecting the rights of fugitive offenders in line with international standards.

In this chapter, firstly, I compare a China domestic surrender system with international extradition to analyze what human rights protection model the mainland China, Hong Kong, and Macau need. Secondly, I analyze how human rights have been protected in the European arrest warrant system. Thirdly, I explore if and how the European arrest warrant approach can be introduced to establish the China arrest warrant system.

1. This is generally the case in international extradition treaties, regional extradition conventions, bilateral extradition treaties and domestic extradition laws, as detailed in this chapter.
2. See Robert J. Currie, "Human Rights and International Mutual Legal Assistance: Resolving the Tension," *CLF* 11, no. 2 (2000): 1.

2 Human rights protection in the surrender of fugitive offenders between mainland China, Hong Kong, and Macau

The China domestic surrender system shares similarities with international extradition but also has its own characteristics, including as to the position and function of human rights protection. The surrender of fugitive offenders and extradition are for the same purpose, namely transferring the requested persons back to the requesting jurisdiction for prosecution or for enforcement of penalty under the request of the latter.[3] As such, the China domestic surrender system should follow comparable basic procedures and conditions as in the international extradition.

In the China domestic surrender system, the main participants include the requesting region, the requested region, and the individual concerned, as in the case of extradition.[4] The former two parties are generally represented by their executive or judicial authorities.[5] The basic obligation to protect human rights should attach to the requesting and the requested regions, as in international extradition. But how the obligation is shared or distributed between the requesting and requested regions will be defined by the nature of the China arrest warrant system.

International extradition takes place in different states, where sovereignty matters, whereas surrender between mainland China, Hong Kong, and Macau occurs within one sovereign state. Hence, the surrender procedure between mainland China, Hong Kong, and Macau may have international law origins but should be based on and guided by domestic legal concerns.[6] This central feature diverts the China domestic surrender system substantively from the traditional extradition system in terms of the human rights protection.

In extradition, the concerned states, namely the requesting and requested states, are mainly bound by extradition agreements and international human rights standards or traditions relating to extradition. No other moral or legal obligations with a constitutional origin force the requested state to grant extradition in spite of human rights concerns. The core interests of the concerned states are separate and independent from each other, and refusing or granting the extradition is influenced by their own national interests.

---

3. See Julia Jansson, *Terrorism, Criminal Law and Politics: The Decline of the Political Offence Exception to Extradition* (London: Routledge, 2020), 40.
4. See M Cherif Bassiouni, *International Extradition: United States Law and Practice* (Oxford: Oxford University Press, 2014), 2.
5. See Steven Lubet, "Extradition Reform: Executive Discretion and Judicial Participation in the Extradition of Political Terrorists," *Cornell International Law Journal*15, no. 2 (1982): 247.
6. See Thomas Bress, "Some Phases of Uniform Interstate Extradition," *St. John's Law Review* 10, no. 2 (1936): 272.

However, in the China domestic surrender system, the factors influencing rights protection are not exactly the same. The three regions have the obligation to protect individual human rights in accordance with extradition traditions as well as international human rights conventions. But they also share the common obligation to safeguard the common interests of the PRC, including to promote the human rights cause in the country. As president Xi Jinping stated, "the Hong Kong people should contribute to the great rejuvenation of the Chinese nation"[7] and "the essence of the great rejuvenation of the Chinese nation is to promote human rights development".[8] Promoting the human rights cause can be regarded as a moral obligation of mainland China, Hong Kong, and Macau under the "one country" framework. To fulfil this obligation does not mean to sacrifice individual human rights; instead it requires human rights protection to be fulfilled in a more comprehensive, constructive, reflective, and interactive way.

In brief, human rights protection in the China domestic surrender system is not only the end for requested persons but also the means to promote the human rights cause of the whole country. Under these double aims, this chapter suggests that the traditional way to protect human rights in extradition—by using human rights as a mandatory ground to refuse extradition—should be rejected and more sophisticated and tailored human rights protection methods should be adopted. Compared to traditional extradition, the China surrender system requires more dialogue and communication between the requesting and requested regions, and more effective involvement of the requested region. The process of negotiation and dialogue may also lead to internal changes, which is more consonant with the peaceful nature of human rights.[9] On these requirements, the European arrest warrant can offer some inspiration.

7. Zhonggong zhongyang wenxian yanjiushi 中共中央文献研究室, ed., *Xijinping guanyu shixian zhonghua minzu weida fuxing de zhongguomeng lunshu zhaibian* 习近平关于实现中华民族伟大复兴的中国梦论述摘编 [Excerpts from Xi Jinping's discussion on realizing the Chinese dream of the great rejuvenation of the Chinese nation] (Beijing: Zhonggong zhongyang wenxian chubanshe, 2013), 57.
8. Zhonggong zhongyang dangshi he wenxian yanjiuyuan 中共中央党史和文献研究院, ed., *Xijinping guanyu zunzhong he baozhang renquan lunshu zhaibian* 习近平关于尊重和保障人权论述摘编 [Excerpts from Xi Jinping's discussion on respecting and protecting human rights] (Beijing: Zhongyang wenxian chubanshe, 2012), 164.
9. Daria Jarczewska, "Do Human Rights Challenge State Sovereignty?" *E-international Relations*, March 15, 2013, https://www.e-ir.info/2013/03/15/do-human-rights-challenge-state-sovereignty/.

3 The human rights ground in the EAW system

3.1 Human rights law in the EU

3.1.1 European Convention on Human Rights (ECHR)

The ECHR enumerates a series of human rights to be protected within the jurisdictions of the contracting parties. As to torture, it specifies that no one shall be subjected to torture or to inhuman or degrading treatment or punishment,[10] which responds to the basic human rights protection requirement in European extradition conventions and the EAW Framework Decision.

On the right to liberty and security, the ECHR states that no one shall be deprived of his liberty save for the lawful arrest or detention of a person effected for the purpose of bringing him before a competent legal authority on reasonable suspicion of having committed an offence or when it is reasonably considered necessary to prevent his committing an offence or fleeing after having done so.[11] This regulation can also be applied to the extradition or surrender procedure.

The right to a fair trial lists a series of discrete rights that should be protected in the course of criminal procedure. The ECHR specifies that in the determination of civil rights and obligations or of any criminal charge, everyone is entitled to a fair and public hearing within a reasonable time by an independent and impartial tribunal established by law; judgment shall be pronounced publicly, although the press and the public may be excluded from all or part of the trial in the interest of morals, public order or national security in a democratic society, where the interests of juveniles or the protection of the private life of the parties so require, or to the extent strictly necessary in the opinion of the court in special circumstances where publicity would prejudice the interests of justice.[12] Thus, the right to be heard and a limited right to privacy in criminal proceedings are confirmed.

The ECHR also provides that all persons charged with a criminal offence shall be presumed innocent until proved guilty according to the law.[13] It lists a series of rights which should be enjoyed by persons charged with an offence, including: to be informed promptly, in detail and in a language which he understands, of the nature and cause of the accusation against him; to have adequate time and facilitates for the preparation of his defence; to defend himself in person or through legal assistance of his own choosing or, if he has insufficient means to pay for legal assistance, to be given it free when the interests of justice so require; to examine or have examined

10. European Convention on Human Rights, art. 3.
11. European Convention on Human Rights, art. 5(1)(c).
12. European Convention on Human Rights, art. 6(1).
13. European Convention on Human Rights, art. 6(2).

witnesses against him and to obtain the attendance and examination of witnesses on his behalf under the same conditions as witnesses against him; and to have the free assistance of an interpreter if he cannot understand or speak the language used in court.[14] This confirms further concrete rights including the rights to be informed, to prepare a defence, to legal representation, to examine witnesses, and to an interpreter.

3.1.2 Charter of Fundamental Rights of the European Union (CFR)

The Charter repeats the general human rights protection, including that no one shall be subjected to torture or to inhuman or degrading treatment or punishment.[15] On rights protection in the event of removal, expulsion, or extradition, it stipulates that no one may be removed, expelled or extradited to a state where there is a serious risk that he or she will be subjected to the death penalty, torture or other inhuman or degrading treatment or punishment.[16]

The Charter also confirms the right to an effective remedy and right to a fair trial by specifying that everyone whose rights and freedoms guaranteed by the law of the Union are violated has the right to an effective remedy before a tribunal in compliance with the conditions laid down in this article; everyone is entitled to a fair and public hearing within a reasonable time by an independent and impartial tribunal previously established by law; everyone shall have the possibility of being advised, defended and represented; and legal aid shall be made available to those who lack sufficient resources, in so far as such aid is necessary to ensure effective access to justice.[17]

On the principles of legality and proportionality of criminal offences and penalties, the Charter stipulates that no one shall be held guilty of any criminal offence on account of any act or omission which did not constitute a criminal offence under national law or international law at the time when it was committed.[18] Nor shall a heavier penalty be imposed than that which was applicable at the time the criminal offence was committed; if, subsequent to the commission of a criminal offence, the law provides for a lighter penalty, that penalty shall be applicable.[19] The severity of penalties must not be disproportionate to the criminal offence.[20] All of these rights are also protected in the European extradition and surrender procedures, explained in the following case study.

---

14. European Convention on Human Rights, art. 6(3).
15. Charter of Fundamental Rights of the European Union, art. 4.
16. Charter of Fundamental Rights of the European Union, art. 19.
17. Charter of Fundamental Rights of the European Union, art. 47.
18. Charter of Fundamental Rights of the European Union, art. 49(1).
19. Charter of Fundamental Rights of the European Union, art. 49(2).
20. Charter of Fundamental Rights of the European Union, art. 49(3).

In addition, after the Resolution of the Council on a Roadmap for Strengthening Procedural Rights of Suspected or Accused Persons in Criminal Proceeding in 2009, a series of directives were made to protect the rights to translation, information, access to a lawyer and others. The enactment of these directives was a positive response to the implementation of the European arrest warrant, as the protections were already written into the EAW Framework Decision in 2002.

3.2 The protection of human rights in Member States

Under these human right instruments, human rights protection in the EU is strong overall, but in some countries and some fields human rights violations are nonetheless recorded. This is evident in cases from the European Court of Human Rights (ECtHR). Member States among the top ten worst violators of the ECHR from 2014 to 2017 included Romania, Greece, Hungary, Bulgaria, Italy, and Croatia.[21] Article 3 of the ECHR, in prohibiting torture and inhuman or degrading treatment or punishment, mainly concerns detention and prison conditions. The ECtHR consistently ranks Article 3, along with Article 2 (the right to life), as one of the most fundamental rights.[22] The majority of violations of Article 3 occur in the context of detention.[23] Human rights violations are evident in some Member States; there is no guaranteed parity of human rights fulfilment across Member States. But human rights are neither a mandatory nor optional refusal ground in the EAW system. This is explained in the following CJEU judgments.

3.3 The human rights ground from European extradition to the EAW

The human rights clause in the European Convention on Extradition 1957specifies that extradition shall not be granted if the requested party has substantial grounds for believing that a request for extradition for an ordinary criminal offence has been made for the purpose of prosecuting or punishing a person on account of his race, religion, nationality or political opinion, or that that person's position

21. See Emily Barley, Lisl Biggs-Davison, and Chris Alderton, "Human Rights abuses in European Arrest Warrant Member States," p. 9, Due Process in Association with Center for Research into Post-Communist Economies, October 2018, https://www.adb.org/sites/default/files/publication/606551/adbi-wp1140.pdf.
22. Council of Europe, "The Prohibition of Torture: A Guide to the Implementation of Article 3 of the European Convention on Human Rights," Human Rights Handbooks No. 6 (2003) 19, accessed November 2, 2022, https://rm.coe.int/168007ff4c.
23. Council of Europe, "The Prohibition of Torture," 22, n 22.

may be prejudiced for any of these reasons.[24] The same requirement appears in the Additional Protocol to the European Convention on Extradition 1975 and Convention on Extradition between Member States 1996. A change took place with the EAW Framework Decision.

Unlike the previous extradition conventions, the human rights ground is not written into the EAW Framework Decision as a mandatory or optional refusal ground. A series of preliminary rulings of the CJEU explains the new position and role of human rights in the European arrest warrant system.

3.4 Human rights protection and the European arrest warrant in the CJEU

3.4.1 Right to an effective judicial remedy

The CJEU's position on the right to an effective judicial remedy appears in the case of Melloni. The CJEU held that the Charter of Fundamental Rights of the European Union did not allow the surrender of a person convicted in absentia to be made conditional upon a national (constitutional) rule requiring the conviction to be open to review in the issuing Member State. The CJEU opined that the right of the accused to appear in person at his trial was an essential component of the right to a fair trial, but it was not an absolute right and could be waived provided that certain safeguards were met; for instance, the waiver was established in an unequivocal manner, attended by minimum safeguards commensurate to its importance, and did not run counter to any important public interest.[25]

The court also held that Framework Decision 2009/299[26] effected a harmonization of the conditions of execution of an EAW in the event of a conviction rendered in absentia, as allowing a Member State to make the surrender conditional upon the fulfilment of a requirement not foreseen under Framework Decision 2002/584[27] would cast doubt on the uniformity of the standard of fundamental rights protection as defined in the EAW FD, undermine the principles of mutual

24. European Convention on Extradition 1957, art. 3(1) and art. 3(2).
25. See Case C-399/11, *Stefano Melloni v. Ministerio Fiscal* [Judgment of the Court, 26 February 2013], ¶49.
26. The full name of the Framework Decision is "Council Framework Decision 2009/299/JHA on Amending Framework Decision 2002/584/JHA, 2005/214/JHA, 2006/783/JHA, 2008/909/JHA and 2008/947/JHA, thereby enhancing the procedural rights of persons and fostering the application of the principle of mutual recognition to decisions rendered in the absence of the person concerned at the trial."
27. Namely the European arrest warrant Framework Decision.

trust and recognition which the EAW FD purports to uphold, and would therefore compromise its efficacy.[28]

3.4.2 Fair trial and judicial independence

Judicial independence is a key element of the right to a fair trial. The CJEU case of L.M. addressed this issue.[29] The accused contested his surrender on the ground that it would expose him to a real risk of a flagrant denial of justice in contravention of his right to a fair trial. The requested court referred the question to the CJEU, asking if it were necessary for the executing judicial authority to make any further assessment.

The CJEU responded with a two-stage examination process for a breach of human rights. The first step is "systemic assessment": the executing authority must assess, on the basis of material that is objective, reliable, specific and properly updated concerning the operation of the system of justice in the issuing Member State, whether there is a real risk, connected with a lack of independence of the courts of that Member State on account of systemic or generalized deficiencies there, of the fundamental right to a fair trial being breached.[30] It said that requested Member States should not automatically reject an EAW; it is for the European Council to determine a breach in the issuing Member State of the principles set out in TEU Article 2 with a view to the application of the EAW mechanism being suspended in respect of that Member State.[31]

The second step is the "specific assessment": the authority must assess specifically and precisely whether, in the particular circumstances of the case, there are substantial grounds for believing that, following surrender to the issuing Member State, the requested person will run a risk of human rights violation. In the course of such an assessment, the executing judicial authority must, in particular, examine to what extent the systemic or generalized deficiencies are liable to have an impact at the level of that state's courts with jurisdiction over the proceedings to which the requested person will be subject; if the examination shows that the deficiencies are liable to affect those courts, the executing judicial authority must also assess whether there are substantial grounds for believing that the person will run a real risk of breach of his fundamental right to an independent tribunal and, therefore, of the essence of his fundamental right to a fair trial, having regard to his personal situation, as well as to the nature of the offence for which he is being prosecuted and the factual context that forms the basis of the EAW; the executing authority must

28. See Case C-399/11, ¶58–63.
29. See Case C-216/18 PPU, LM, [Judgment of the Court, July 25, 2018].
30. See Case C-216/18, ¶61.
31. See Case C-216/18, ¶72–73.

also take into account the information provided by the issuing authority on the basis of EAW FD Article 15(2).[32]

3.4.3 Detention conditions and human rights protection

In the M.L. case, where M.L. was requested to be surrendered to Hungary from Germany, the CJEU offered detailed analysis on the prison condition evaluation in the execution of the European arrest warrant.[33] The CJEU ruled that the objective of the EAW FD was to facilitate and accelerate surrenders, that Member States are required to comply with the time limits of the EAW FD, and that an obligation to assess the detention conditions in all the prisons in which the person might be detained is clearly excessive.[34] Thus, the executing authority is solely required to assess the detention conditions in the prisons in which, according to the information available to them, it is actually intended that the person concerned will be detained, including on a temporary or transitional basis.[35]

The CJEU also pointed out that assurances given by the authorities of the issuing Member State should be taken into account. The executing judicial authority and the issuing judicial authority may, respectively, request information or give assurances concerning the actual and precise conditions in which the person concerned will be detained in the issuing Member State, and an assurance provided by the competent authorities of the issuing Member State is a factor which the executing judicial authority cannot disregard: when an assurance has been given, or at least endorsed, by the issuing judicial authority, the executing judicial authority must rely on it.[36]

3.4.4 Some conclusions from the CJEU case study

The above cases make the CJEU's position on human rights scrutiny in the EAW system clear. Firstly, priorities are to fulfill the mutual recognition principle and to realize swift surrender; secondly, some non-absolute rights, such as the right of defence, can be remedied after the surrender, while other rights, like the right to be heard, should be protected from the outset in the requested state; thirdly, official assurance from the issuing Member State plays an important role where there is a dispute on human rights protection. The China arrest warrant system can take guidance from these developments.

32. See Case C-216/18, ¶68–77.
33. Case C-220/18 PPU, ML [Judgment of the Court, July 25, 2018].
34. Case C-220/18, ¶82–84.
35. Case C-220/18, ¶87–89.
36. Case C-220/18, ¶108–12.

4 Human rights protection in the surrender procedure between mainland China, Hong Kong, and Macau

4.1 The application of the human rights ground with other countries

4.1.1 The human rights ground in extradition between mainland China and other countries

China's Extradition Law provides that extradition should be refused if the requested person will be prosecuted or punished for his or her race, religion, nationality, sex, political opinion or identity, or the requested person will encounter unfair treatment in judicial proceedings.[37] The human rights ground is a mandatory ground to refuse extradition. The Law further specifies that extradition shall be refused if the requested persons suffered or will suffer torture or other cruel, inhuman or degrading treatment or punishment.[38] It provides that extradition should be refused if the extradition is requested in the circumstances of conviction based on trail in absentia, but there is an exception if the requesting country guarantees that the surrendered person will be retried if he or she can appear in court.[39] In most of the extradition treaties the mainland China has concluded with other countries,[40] the human rights ground is a mandatory ground to refuse extradition, with an option for guarantees concerning absentee trials.[41] Exceptions based on guarantees were seldom applied in the older treaties signed by the mainland China, but after the Extradition Law of 2000 the exception based on guarantee regarding trial in absentia became accepted as a general principle.

4.1.2 The human rights ground in surrender between Hong Kong and other countries

In the Hong Kong Fugitive Offenders Ordinance, a similar approach to human rights protection is taken as in the China Extradition Law. The Ordinance provides

37. See China Extradition Law, art. 8(4).
38. See China Extradition Law, art. 8(7).
39. See China Extradition Law, art. 8(8).
40. In all extradition treaties mainland China has concluded with other countries, the human rights ground is a mandatory ground to refuse extradition, but before 2000 when the Extradition Law was enacted some extradition treaties did not make stipulatiojn on this, such as the Extradition Treaty between China and Uzbekistan.
41. This kind of guarantee request can be found in the extradition treaties with Cambodia, Laos, Spain, Portugal, France, Australia, Indonesia, Argentina, Barbados, the latest extradition treaties signed between mainland China and the other countries, and most of the treaties signed after the China Extradition Law.

that a person shall not be surrendered to a prescribed place, or committed to or kept in custody for the purposes of surrender, if it appears to an appropriate authority that the request for surrender (though purporting to be made on account of a relevant offence) is in fact made for the purpose of prosecuting or punishing him on account of his race, religion, nationality or political opinions; or that he might, if surrendered, be prejudiced at his trial or punished, detained or restricted in his personal liberty by reason of his race, religion, nationality or political opinions.[42] It also specifies that the person shall not be surrendered if the offence in respect of which surrender is sought was prosecuted in his absence and a conviction obtained and the person has not had an opportunity of being tried in his presence for that offence and, if surrendered, would not have an opportunity of being re-tried in his presence for that offence.[43] The human rights ground appears in all the surrender agreements Hong Kong has concluded with other countries.

4.1.3 The human rights ground in surrender between Macau and other countries

Macau's Law on Judicial Cooperation in Criminal Matters provides that judicial cooperation should be refused if the evidence is sufficient to believe that the objective of the request for judicial cooperation is to perpetrate or punish a person on the ground of his or her nationality, blood relationship, race, ideology, education degree, economic situation, social situation, or membership of a community.[44] It also specifies that a request for judicial cooperation should be refused if relevant procedures do not satisfy or comply with international conventions applying to Macau.[45] As Macau has signed the same human rights conventions as Hong Kong, it can be concluded that Macau shares Hong Kong's position on human rights protection in the surrender domain. The human rights ground is also written into its surrender agreements with Portugal[46] and South Korea.[47]

In summary, all three regions make human rights a mandatory ground to refuse extradition or surrender. But how the human rights ground can be used in a China arrest warrant system is open to question. In the European arrest warrant system, human rights protection is neither a mandatory nor optional ground to refuse surrender. Instead, under the mutual recognition principle, the human rights ground can be applied to refuse surrender only in exceptional cases. Compared to

42. See the Fugitive Offenders Ordinance, s. 5(1)(c).
43. See the Fugitive Offenders Ordinance, s. 5(1)(b).
44. See the Macau Law on Judicial Cooperation in Criminal Matters, art. 7(1)(2).
45. See the Macau Law on Judicial Cooperation in Criminal Matters, art. 7(1)(1).
46. See the Surrender Agreement between Macau and Portugal, art. 6(4).
47. See the Surrender Agreement between Macau and South Korea, art. 5(5).

the traditional application of the human rights ground, this prioritises the judicial cooperation. The EAW model is a good example for mainland China, Hong Kong, and Macau. This research will next analyze the possible obstacles to introducing the approach.

4.2 Possible problems with the EAW approach

4.2.1 Lack of uniform human rights protection in the three regions

The EU and its Member States have strong political will to protect human rights. All Member States have joined the ECHR and CFR and there are other specific directives on procedural rights protection. These legal instruments offer a baseline for human rights protection in the Member States and account for removing the human rights ground as a mandatory or optional refusal ground in the EAW system.

In mainland China, Hong Kong and Macau, we do not find common human rights conventions which can govern the three regions in the way that the ECHR and CFR do in the European Union. Without such legal basis, it is possible that human rights protection in one region will be endangered by another region. The lack of a common legal basis for human rights protection harms the mutual trust.

4.2.2 Unbalanced human rights protection in the three regions

Compared to Hong Kong and Macau's legal infrastructure for the protection of human rights, mainland China obviously lags behind. There is no human rights bill in place. Mainland China signed but still has not ratified the ICCPR. As well as the divergence in human rights laws, in practice, more human rights violations are reported to occur in mainland China. For instance, prison conditions in mainland China are problematic. There are reports that prisoners live in crowded collective cells, with one cell accommodating ten to twenty persons or more,[48] with no private living space, no individual beds for prisoners, and poor conditions for undisturbed sleep.[49] There are also cases in which police officers use torture to extract evidence.[50] These are serious concerns for the application of the human rights ground in the China arrest warrant system.

---

48. See Dai Yanling 戴艳玲, *Zhongguo jianyu zhidude gaige yu fazhan* 中国监狱制度的改革与发展 [The reform and development of China prison system] (Beijing: Zhongguo gong'an daxue chubanshe, 2004), 272.
49. See Dai, *Zhongguo*, 276, n 48.
50. See Li torture case, Criminal (2010) 51 People's Court of Shandong Province Rizhao Economic Development Region, accessed November 2, 2022, http://www.faxin.cn/lib/cpal/AlyzContent.aspx?gid=C1185943.

4.2.3 No uniform institution of judicial control

At the European level, the European Court of Human Rights is the judicial organization that safeguards human rights.[51] As detailed above, the Court can offer preliminary rulings on human rights protection in the EAW system. The CJEU regulates the EAW system, clearly classifying the relationship between mutual recognition and human rights protection. However, there is no such judicial organization to exercise the jurisdiction over mainland Ching, Hong Kong, and Macau. This may affect human rights protection in the China domestic surrender system.

4.3 Potentials solutions

4.3.1 International conventions and Basic Laws as a legal basis

Firstly, China (mainland China) is also a contracting party to most of the international human rights conventions that Hong Kong and Macau have joined. These include the International Convention against Torture and Other Cruel, Inhuman or Degrading Treatment or Punishment; the International Convention on the Elimination of All Forms of Racial Discrimination; the Convention on the Elimination of All Forms of Discrimination against Women; and the Convention on the Rights of the Child. Thus, there is common legal basis from an international perspective for the three regions to be aware that they share a position on human rights protection.

Secondly, domestically speaking, the two Basic Laws also offer guarantees on human rights protection. The Basic Law of Hong Kong and the Basic Law of Macau are the most important legal sources of human rights protection in Hong Kong and Macau. The Basic laws were drawn up by delegates from mainland China, Hong Kong, and Macau, demonstrating the willingness and position of all the Chinese people on human rights protection. Moreover, the Basic Laws are enacted on the basis of the national Constitution which covers mainland China as well. All of these common conventions and constitutional instruments offer ways to solve the human rights problem in China domestic surrender.

51. See chapter 2 on the role of judicial authorities in the surrender of fugitive offenders.

4.3.2 The improvement of law in China (mainland China) offers a legal guarantee

In China's Constitution, Criminal Law, Criminal Procedure Law, and other relevant legislation, human rights protection is confirmed. All of these laws can be relied on to protect the rights of the requested persons in the surrender procedure.

The Constitution of the People's Republic of China confirms that all citizens are equal before the law and that the PRC respects and protects human rights.[52] Human rights protection has also been incorporated into the Criminal Law and Criminal Procedure Law. The Criminal Law affirms the principle of legality by stating that for acts that are explicitly criminal acts in law, the offenders shall be convicted and punished in accordance with law; otherwise, they shall not be convicted or punished.[53] The Criminal Law also recognizes the proportionality principle by stipulating that the degree of punishment shall be commensurate with the crime committed and criminal responsibility borne by the offender.[54] The Criminal Procedure Law confirms the presumption of innocence by stating that prior to a judgment rendered by the people's court, no one may be convicted.[55] China has ratified the Convention against Torture and other Cruel, Inhuman or Degrading Treatment or Punishment, and the Criminal Procedure Law also stipulates that the use of torture to extract confessions is strictly prohibited, as are threats, enticement, trickery and other illegal methods of gathering evidence.[56] The confessions of suspects or defendants obtained by the use of torture or other illegal methods, and witness testimony or victim statements gathered by the use of illegal methods such as violence or threats, shall be excluded.[57] In relation to a fair trial, the independence and the transparency of judicial organs are required by law. The Criminal Procedure Law stipulates that the people's courts should comply with the law to independently exercise the power of adjudication; the people's procuratorates should comply with the law to independently exercise prosecution powers; and neither of them shall be interfered with by administrative organs, social groups or individuals.[58]

Additionally, the Prison Law, Public Prosecutor's Law, People's Court Law, and the interpretations and other documents issued by the Supreme People's Court and the Supreme Public Prosecutor's Office all guarantee human rights protection in criminal proceedings. Specifically, in order to protect judicial independence and avoid

52. Constitution of the People's Republic of China, art. 33.
53. Criminal Law, art. 3.
54. Criminal Law, art. 5.
55. Criminal Procedure Law, art. 12.
56. Criminal Procedure Law, art. 52.
57. Criminal Procedure Law, art. 56.
58. Criminal Procedure Law, art. 5.

the intervention of the external or internal senior officials, the Central Leading Team for Comprehensively Deepening Reform approved the Regulation on Recording, Notification and Accountability of Officials' Intervening in Judicial Activities and/or Handling Specific Cases in 2015. Following that, the Supreme People's Court and the Supreme Public Prosecutor's Office issued the Implementation Measures to Fulfil the Regulation and also the Implementation Measures to Fulfil the Regulation on Recording and Notification of Judicial Organ Staff's Intervention in Handling Cases. A series of cases has been reported since the enactment of the Regulation.[59]

4.3.3 Unbalanced human rights protection can be overcome through concrete judicial protection

Although the ECHR, the CFR, and other directives protect human rights in the EU, human rights protection is unbalanced in Member States, as discussed above.[60] Similarly, in China, mainland China's human rights credit is not as high as that of Hong Kong and Macau. From this perspective, EAW solutions can inspire the construction of the China domestic surrender system.

Regarding the authority in charge of surrender, as in the European arrest warrant system, the China arrest warrant system should be also under the full control of judicial authorities, mainly judges. This is a dramatic departure from traditional extradition where the executive authority exercises power and political interventions occur. Judicial authorities, mainly judges, in mainland China, Hong Kong, and Macau can independently and objectively make decisions relating to the issuance as well as the execution of China arrest warrants, offering multi-level judicial protection to requested persons.[61]

4.3.4 A Standing Committee or joint court can provide further guarantees

There is no overarching court above mainland China, Hong Kong, and Macau like the CJEU in the European Union. This has been identified as an obstacle to effective human rights protection in the China arrest warrant system. However, a joint court could function similarly. The Supreme People's Court in mainland China, the Court of Final Appeal in Hong Kong, and the Court of Final Appeal in Macau can operate together to settle disputes over surrender. At the same time, inspired by the role of

59. Chen Guangzhong 陈光中 et al., ed., *Zhongguo xiandai sifa zhidu* 中国现代司法制度 [China modern judicial system] (Beijing: Beijing daxue chubanshe, 2020), 217.
60. See above section 3.2 on the practice of human rights protection in Member States.
61. See chapter 2 on the role of judicial authorities in the surrender of fugitive offenders.

the European Council in deciding whether human rights are systematically violated in Member States, I suggest that the Standing Committee of the National Peoples' Congress (NPCSC) could decide whether human rights were violated systematically in a region and whether surrender requests could be rejected automatically.

4.4 *The design of human rights protection in surrender between mainland China, Hong Kong, and Macau*

4.4.1 Two-level protection

The protection of a requested person's rights mainly focuses on whether his or her judicial rights can be fulfilled in the requesting region after surrender, while at the same time relevant rights should also be realized in the requested region. The China arrest warrant system could feature two levels of judicial protection, one at the requesting stage (in the requesting region) and one at the execution stage (in the requested region). At the requesting stage, judicial protection starts by issuing domestic judicial decisions and continues to issue a China arrest warrant. At the execution stage, rights protection by the requested region begins by scrutinizing the human rights situation in the requesting region to monitoring rights' actual fulfillment after surrender. The requested region should also take steps to realize the rights of requested persons in its own region. Intensive exchange and dialogue are needed throughout the surrender process. See Figure 10.1.

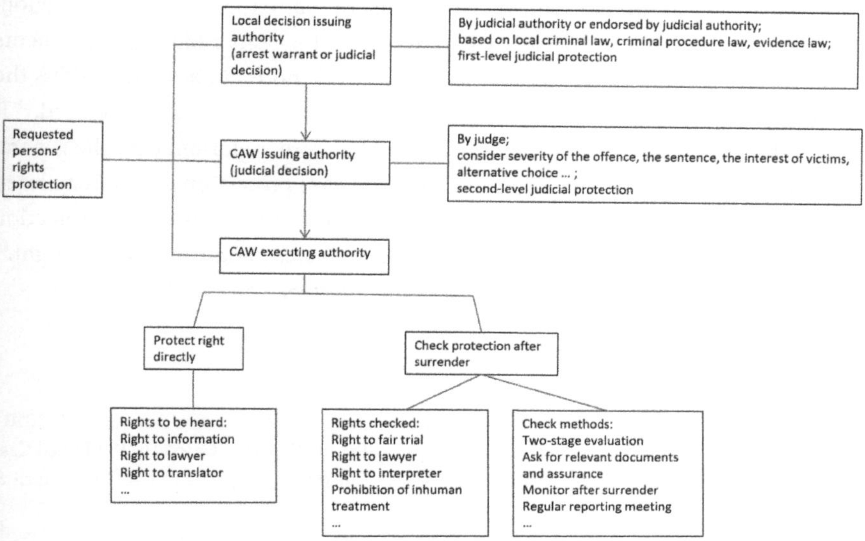

Figure 10.1: Human rights protection in the China arrest warrant system

4.4.2 Two-step evaluation

There should be sophisticated evaluation of the rights protection of a requested person before his or her surrender. In the traditional extradition system, where the human rights ground is used as a mandatory or optional refusal ground, the evaluation is not binding and can be simple and symbolic. However, in the China arrest warrant system, the evaluation work should be more tailored and sophisticated. Evidence of systemic or generalized deficiencies concerning the independence of the judiciary in the requesting region cannot be used as a substantial ground for believing that that person will run a real risk of losing his or her fundamental right to a fair trial.[62] The human rights evaluation should be more focused on the concrete situation of the specific case and the specific individual concerned. When faced with human rights complaints or concerns about the requesting region, the requested court should conduct a two-step human rights evaluation.

The first step should be a "systemic" assessment. The requested judicial authority must assess, on the basis of material that is objective, reliable, specific and properly updated concerning the judicial system of the requesting region, whether there is a real risk in a systemic and generalized way that certain human rights will be breached, such as the right to a fair trial. Whether the answer is affirmative or negative, this evaluation alone cannot be relied on to refuse or accept the surrender request.

For the second step evaluation, the requested authority must assess specifically and precisely whether, in the particular circumstances of the case, there are substantial grounds for believing that, following the surrender to the issuing region, the rights of the requested person will be at risk. At this step, additional documents or information can be requested by the requested authority in order to address the concern, and if the risk still cannot be eliminated surrender may be refused.[63] It should be accepted that the specific assessment is more important than the general assessment, since the latter addresses the risk of rights protection in a more tailored way. Additionally, mainland China is a large region, and human rights protection varies from big cities to small villages, from east to west, and from right to right.[64] Evaluation work should therefore be detailed, objective, and specific.

62. Joined Case C-354/20 and C-412/20 PPU, *L and P* [Judgment of the Court, December 17, 2020].
63. The two evaluative steps have been well developed in the EAW system: Case 216/18 (Joined Case C-404/15 and Case C-659/15 PPU, *Aranyosi and Caldararu* [Judgment of the Court, April 5, 2016].
64. Chen Su 陈甦 et al., eds., *Fazhi lanpishu: Zhongguo fazhi fazhan baogao No. 18* 法治蓝皮书：中国法治发展报告 No. 18 [Blue book of rule of law: Annual report on rule of law in China No. 18] (Beijing: Shehui kexue wenxian chubanshe, 2020), 174–276.

4.4.3 Assurances play a role

Assurances can also be used to guarantee human rights protection in the surrender process. Assurance or guarantee are commonly used in extradition.[65] They allow the requested state to fulfill its obligations under human rights law without sabotaging cooperation; they are also more acceptable to the requesting state, as a request for assurances in respect of an individual's treatment is less judgmental of its criminal justice system than outright refusal of an extradition request.[66] The assurance can be coordinated with the human rights evaluation. For instance, if the requested authorities find that prison conditions in the requesting region will violate the human rights of the requested person, besides evaluating if prison conditions in the region where the requesting authority is located have the same problem(s), the requested court can seek an assurance from the requesting authority that the requested person will not suffer from poor prison conditions. If there is a risk of torture, the relevant assurance can also be sought. If there is a risk that the requested person will have the death penalty imposed, the requested authority can seek assurance from the requesting court or prosecutors that the death penalty will not be imposed or executed. If the requested person is tried in absentia, the requested authority can seek assurance that when the person is surrendered, he or she will be granted a re-trial.

There have been cases where a Mainland authority gives an assurance to a foreign authority that the concerned person will not be subjected to the death penalty or to a term of imprisonment in excess of a certain number of years, and the Mainland authorities have kept to their promise.[67] Further, in relation to torture, fair trial, and appropriate prison conditions, relevant regulations appear in China's Criminal Law, Criminal Procedure Law, and Prison Law. There are bases on which the assurance of the requesting authorities can be relied upon. Offering assurances is also an important method for helping the requesting region, such as mainland China, to address loopholes on human rights protection in its judicial system and to push the relevant organs to make progress in the future. Assurances are a form of positive dialogue and interaction between different legal systems, and should be

---

65. Within the EAW system, there have been specific regulations on the use of guarantees: see European Arrest Warrant Framework Decision, art. 5. The Court of Justice of the European Union also emphasizes the importance of assurances given by the requesting Member State: Case C-306/09, I.B. [2010] ECR-I 10341.
66. John Dugard and Christine Van Den Wyngaert, "Reconciling Extradition with Human Rights," *American Journal of International Law* 92 (1998): 207.
67. Jingjing Huang, "Lai Changxing Gets Life for Smuggling and Bribery," *Global Times*, May 19, 2012, accessed November 2, 2022, https://www.globaltimes.cn/content/710251.shtml; see also Laurie Chen, "After 13 Years on the Run, China's Most-Wanted Fugitive Jailed for Graft," *South China Moring Post*, October 13, 2017, https://www.scmp.com/news/china/policies-politics/article/2115279/after-13-years-run-chinas-most-wanted-fugitive-jailed.

supported and fully utilised. Moreover, after surrender, necessary monitoring can be undertaken by the requested authority or its agents.

4.4.4 Monitoring functions

In traditional extradition cases, consular and diplomatic officials of requested states regularly monitor trials involving their own nationals. They might attend and report on trials involving extradited persons and request the right to visit such persons after sentence in the same way that they can visit their own nationals in prison.[68] For mainland China, Hong Kong, and Macau, there are no so-called diplomatic officials in each other's regions as the three regions belong to one country; however, they have offices in each other's region which function similarly to diplomatic organs. For instance, Hong Kong has set up a series of Economic and Trade Offices in mainland China, and immigration divisions are set up in these offices to provide practical assistance to Hong Kong residents in mainland China.[69] On the one hand, these offices can be entrusted by the relevant judicial authorities to monitor trials or the enforcement of punishments in the requesting region. On the other hand, the judicial organs also have judiciary administrators who can take on this duty.

Through the development of technology, monitoring via video conference and other modern methods is also possible. Such monitoring should provide feedback to the requested judicial authorities in a timely manner, especially when enforcement in the requesting regions clearly diverges from assurances given. That should prompt further dialogue between the two regions, followed by any revision of actions by the requesting region. In addition, before the surrender of a requested individual, lawyers from the issuing side should have been engaged who can also contribute to monitoring.

4.4.5 Rights fulfilled in the requested region

Generally, human rights protection in surrender or extradition focuses on the fulfilment of rights in the requesting region post-surrender/extradition. Seldom do we find provisions that impose specific and direct obligations on the requested states or regions to protect the rights of requested individuals. The lack of obligations imposed on a requested state or region can be justified from the perspective that the main criminal proceedings, including trial or enforcement of punishment, will be executed in the requesting region and the pure surrender or extradition process is

68. See Dugard and Van Den Wyngaert, "Reconciling Extradition," 208, n 66.
69. Constitutional and Mainland Affairs Bureau, "Hong Kong Offices in the Mainland and Taiwan," accessed November 2, 2022, https://www.cmab.gov.hk/en/issues/new_official.htm.

not a full criminal trial.[70] Hence, there are some specific rules to protect due process, but they are generally not required in the surrender or extradition process, and these rights are expected to be fulfilled in the requesting region post-surrender, including the presumption of innocence and the legal burden of proof of beyond reasonable doubt.

However, as the surrender procedure *per se* involves the deprivation of the liberty of the requested person, certain procedural rights should be protected in the requested region, including the right to be heard, the right to interpretation and translation, the right to information, the right of access to a lawyer, and the right to legal aid.[71] The requested person also has the right to consent the surrender, which should be carried out under effective judicial protection. Since these rights are mainly fulfilled in the requested region, implementation should be in accordance with the law of the requested region and where necessary joint documents should be issued to guarantee a minimum level of protection. Further, because these rights are specifically protected in the surrender procedure, it is suggested that they be written into the China arrest warrant document, whether it is an agreement, arrangement, or takes some other form.[72]

4.4.6 Regular reporting meetings

The China arrest warrant system should provide for regular reporting meetings on human rights protection. This research suggests that relevant judicial authorities, legislators, and executive officials in charge of judicial matters should meet regularly to address human rights protection issues in the surrender procedure. Such meetings would allow judicial authorities, the main players in the surrender system, to express their opinions, particularly concerns and criticisms relating to human rights protection in requesting regions post-surrender. There would then be opportunities for legislators and executive officials to reflect on the surrender system and make revisions where necessary.

70. Neil Boister, "Global Simplification of Extradition: Interviews with Selected Extradition Experts in New Zealand, Canada, the US and EU," *Criminal Law Forum* 29 (2018): 327.

71. This series of rights has been well protected under the EAW system by the executing Member States. Mainland China, Hong Kong, and Macau should refer to this. See the Commission Notice-Handbook on how to issue and execute a European arrest warrant [2017] OJC 335/01.

72. To date, the "rights of the requested individuals" have not been written into the Chinese extradition law or the extradition treaty between China and foreign states; nor have they been found in surrender agreements between Hong Kong and other states.

5 Conclusion

Human rights protection is an important aspect of the China domestic surrender system. Despite the human rights ground generally being used as a mandatory refusal ground in international extradition, the European arrest warrant experience can inspire mainland China, Hong Kong, and Macau to choose different approach. Human rights protection in the China arrest warrant system should be more constructive, interactive, responsive, and effective. Judicial protection of human rights should be guaranteed in both requesting region and requested region; two steps of human rights evaluation by the requested region should be made before surrender, and assurance asked for where necessary; after surrender, monitoring by the requested region can be facilitated; and regular reporting meetings can be held for better human rights protection.

11
Conclusion

Figure 11.1 combines in the form of a diagram all of the principles and procedures which can be applied in a China arrest warrant system based on the European arrest warrant experience.

To comply with the "one country, two systems" policy and requirement for human rights protection, the design of the China domestic surrender system, for domestic surrender of fugitive offenders between mainland China, Hong Kong, and Macau, can be inspired by the European arrest warrant experience. The main characteristics of the China arrest warrant system include its basis in the mutual recognition principle and the direct control of judicial authorities. It should not apply the political offences exception, while the application of other principles including double criminality, the nationality exception, and the human rights

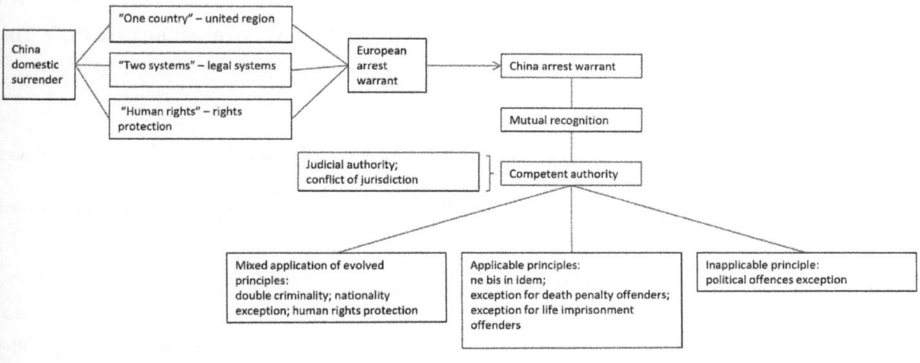

Figure 11.1: The China arrest warrant system

ground will echo the European arrest warrant model. The approach to *ne bis in idem*, death penalty offenders, and life imprisonment offenders will comply with international standards.

The mutual recognition principle, as the cornerstone of the European arrest warrant, was introduced from the EU internal market to the criminal field.[1] Mutual recognition should also function as the basic principle in the China arrest warrant system. The European experience shows that the mutual recognition principle can be flexible, non-automatic, functional, and resilient in hard situations.[2] These characteristics of mutual recognition are the basis for its application to the China domestic surrender system.

This research suggests that the judicial authorities should be in charge of the China arrest warrant system.[3] From the European arrest warrant experience, depoliticizing surrender speeds up the surrender process and contributes to human rights protection. In the China arrest warrant system, under "one country, two systems," mainland China, Hong Kong, and Macau are not foreign states. But the substantive involvement of executive authorities will lead to unnecessary political conflicts, as have occurred in international extradition. Additionally, a decisive role for executive authorities increases the risk of external intervention in the surrender process. Executive authorities will share the human rights scrutiny power which will be exercised primarily by the judicial authorities for the sake of human rights protection.[4]

The conflict of criminal jurisdiction between mainland China, Hong Kong, and Macau is an obstacle to surrender cooperation. An institution comparable to Eurojust can be established to take charge of conflict settlement.[5] A legal document like the European Framework Decision on the Settlement of Criminal Jurisdiction can also be drafted for the China arrest warrant system. As to the criteria for settling conflicts of criminal jurisdiction, this research proposes that settlement should be based on the territorial principle, as in the European arrest warrant mechanism.[6] If the preparation for a crime and the actual act occur in different regions, the region which suffers the majority of the loss should enjoy criminal jurisdiction. This

---

1. See S. Lavenex, "Mutual Recognition and the Monopoly of Force: Limits of the Single Market Analogy," *Journal of European Public Policy* 14 (2007): 764.
2. See chapter 1; see also Christine Janssens, *The Principle of Mutual Recognition in EU Law* (Oxford: Oxford University Press, 2013).
3. See chapter 2.
4. See Case on Ramanjit Singh KCMP 139 of 2018, ¶237.
5. See chapter 3.
6. As to this see European Law Institute, "Report of the European Law Institute—Draft Legislative Proposal for the Prevention and Resolution of Conflicts of Jurisdiction in Criminal Matters in the European Union," 18, accessed November 2, 2022, https://www.europeanlawinstitute.eu/fileadmin/user_upload/p_eli/Publications/Conflict_of_Jurisdiction_in_Criminal_Law_FINAL.pdf.

research also suggests if the loss of the regions does not vary widely, criminal jurisdiction should be designated to facilitate the availability of evidence and witnesses.

As to *ne bis in idem*, this principle is not only used to settle conflicts of criminal jurisdiction in the surrender procedure[7] but also functions to protect the human rights of requested persons and to safeguard the authority of final judgments.[8] The application of *ne bis in idem* has expanded from national domains to the international sphere. Although there is no international convention on this principle, its application is customary. Judging from both international and EU experience, combined with present practice in Hong Kong, Macau, and mainland China, *ne bis in idem* should be applied in the China arrest warrant system.[9]

The partial abolition of double criminality in the European arrest warrant system can be an inspiration to mainland China, Hong Kong, and Macau.[10] The principle and techniques of the European arrest warrant can be used, taking into account the legal, cultural, and social situations in the three regions. The double criminality principle can be applied in the China arrest warrant system, but several categories of offences should be listed for waiver of the double criminality check. The proportionality principle should be formally recognized and applied in the requesting region when issuing the surrender request.

This research finds that the political offences exception is controversial, not functioning effectively to protect human rights as designed,[11] and declining in the extradition sphere. Although there have been concerns over the abolition of the exception in the European arrest warrant, based on the different levels of democracy and human rights protection in EU Member States, in practice the abolition is not so problematic. This inspires the China arrest warrant system, not only in the recommendation to abolish the political offences exception but also in the measures that can be taken to achieve this.[12]

The nationality exception is also a controversial principle in international extradition. It does not necessarily protect individual rights and sometimes lets offenders

---

7. See Su Caixia 苏彩霞, *Zhongguo xingfa guojihua yanjiu* 中国刑法国际化研究 [Study on the internationalization of criminal law in China] (Beijing: Beijing daxue chubanshe, 2007), 284.
8. See John A.E. Vervaele, "The transnational ne bis in idem principle in the EU mutual recognition and equivalent protection of human rights," *Utrecht Law Review* 1, no. 2 (2005): 100. See also chapter 4.
9. See chapter 4.
10. See chapter 5.
11. J. Reuben Clark Jr., Fredrick R. Coudert, and Julian Mack, "The Nature and a Definition of Political Offence in International Extradition Discussion" *Proceedings of American Society of International Law* 3 (1909): 140. See also M. Cherif Bassiouni, *Criminal Law and Its Processes: The Law of Public Order* (New York: Thomas Press, 1969), 234.
12. See chapter 6.

simply go free.[13] The European arrest warrant has followed the international trend to limit the application of the exception, and mainland China, Hong Kong, and Macau can follow in turn. Under the reality of "one country, two systems," the surrender of residents should be the default, with the exception that requested individuals may be sent back to the requested region to serve sentences for social integration purposes. When deeper integration is achieved, the surrender of residents can be an absolute rule for the three regions without the option for refusal or guarantees based on the resident's identity.[14]

The European arrest warrant system is not concerned with the question of surrender of death penalty offenders because all Member States had abolished the death penalty when the EAW Framework Decision was enacted. Abolishing the death penalty has been the international trend and the non-extradition of death penalty offenders has been widely used as a method to protect human rights and to push for the abolition of the death penalty globally. Mainland China, Hong Kong, and Macau should follow this trend. Particularly for mainland China, the non-surrender of death penalty offenders in the China arrest warrant system not only reduces tensions with the latter two regions on the question of residents and political offences, but also pushes itself to further abolish death penalty offences.[15]

Life imprisonment is also an increasingly important topic in extradition. Although not so many countries have abolished life imprisonment, most countries which retain it provide for life imprisonment with parole. This trend in the domestic penalty setup has deeply influenced international extradition. Increasingly, countries ask for guarantees regarding life imprisonment in extradition, especially in the European arrest warrant system. Mainland China, Hong Kong, and Macau should follow the international trend and insert a life imprisonment guarantee clause into their surrender system. In fact, their own criminal laws on life imprisonment and their separate extradition or surrender practices with foreign countries also offer bases for this choice.[16]

The human rights protection in the China arrest warrant system also calls for a tailored approach. Under "one country, two systems" model, human rights protection not only functions to protect the rights of individuals but should also contribute to the improvement of human rights in the whole country. This research suggests that mainland China, Hong Kong, and Macau should not refuse surrender on the ground of human rights protection. Instead, both a systemic assessment and

13. See Rob Blekxtoon and Zsuzsanna Deen-Racsmány, "The Decline of the Nationality Exception in European Extradition?" *European Journal of Crime, Criminal Law and Criminal Justice* 13, no. 3 (2005): 318.
14. See chapter 7.
15. See chapter 8.
16. See chapter 9.

a specific assessment of the case should be carried out before a final refusal decision is made.[17]

Last but not least: this book has talked about the substantive principles, procedures, and competent authorities involved in the enforcement of the China arrest warrant system, but whether these bodies should be recognized in national legislation, by regional agreement, or elsewise also matters. Based on the fact that the China arrest warrant is a highly important "domestic extradition" system going beyond the autonomy of any of the three regions and impacting so many persons residing in the PRC, the the authority and democratic basis for its existence should be assured. Combining the example of the European arrest warrant Framework Decision functioning as one EU legal instrument, this book suggests that the China arrest warrant system can be written into the Hong Kong Basic Law and Macau Basic Law as protocol, and directly applied nationwide. This also corresponds to the fact that the Hong Kong Basic Law and Macau Basic Law are national legislation valid in all of Hong Kong, Macau, and mainland China; meanwhile, protocols to the Basic Law are of the same validity as the law per se. Considering the dilemma faced by the Hong Kong government in its unsuccessful 2019 amendment of extradition law, the establishment of the China arrest warrant system is better left to the national authorities rather than the regional authorities. In this way, the China arrest warrant as a system of "domestic extradition" will be clearly distinguished from international extradition, and mainland China, Hong Kong, and Macau's separate extradition (surrender) arrangements with other countries will not be affected.

17. See C-216/18 PPU, *LM* [Judgment of the Court, 25 July 2018], ¶60–73.

Bibliography

Journal articles

Alegre, Susie, and Marisa Leaf. "Mutual Recognition in European Judicial Cooperation: A Step too Far too Soon? Case Study-the European Arrest Warrant." *European Law Journal* 10, no. 2 (March 2004): 200–217.

Ambos, Kai. 'The German Public Prosecutor as (no) Judicial Authority within the Meaning of the European Arrest Warrant: A Case Note on the CJEU's Judgment in OG (C-508/18) and PI (C 82/19 PPU)." *New Journal of European Criminal Law* 10, no. 4 (December 10, 2019): 399–407.

Anagnostopoulos, Ilias. "Criminal Justice Cooperation in the European Union after the First Few 'steps': a Defence View." *ERA Forum* 15, no. 1 (2014): 9–24.

Anghel, Ion M. "European Union's Member States Sovereignty." *Annals Constantin Brancusi U Targu Jiu Juridical Sci Series* 2 (2010): 19–48.

Bae, Sangmin. "International Norms, Domestic Politics, and the Death Penalty: Comparing Japan, South Korea, and Taiwan." *Comparative Politics* 44, no. 1 (October 2011): 41–58.

Barbolla, Oubiña Sabela. "The European Arrest Warrant in Law and in Practice: Special Reference to the Spanish Experience." *European Journal of Legal Education* 6, no. 1 (2011): 9–29.

Basboga, Kadir. "The Role of Open Borders and Cross-border Cooperation in Regional Growth across Europe." *Regional Studies, Regional Science* 7, no. 1 (2020): 532–49.

Beale, Joseph H. "The Jurisdiction of a Sovereign State." *Harvard Law Review* 36, no. 3 (1923): 241–62.

Behrmann, Christian, and Jon Yorke. "The European Union and the Abolition of the Death Penalty." *Pace International Law Review Online Companion* 4, no. 1 (2013): 1–78.

Bernaz, Nadia. "Life Imprisonment and the Prohibition of Inhuman Punishment in International Human Rights Law: Moving the Agenda Forward." *Human Rights Quarterly* 35, no. 2 (2013): 470–97.

Black, Ann. "Double Jeopardy Revisited: Why Several Common Law Countries are Tinkering with One of the Law's Most Treasured Principles." *National Judicial Academy Law Journal* 1 (2007): 121–44.

Blekxtoon, Rob, and Zsuzsanna Deen-Racsmány. "The Decline of the Nationality Exception in European Extradition?" *European Journal of Crime, Criminal Law and Criminal Justice* 13, no. 3 (2005): 317–64.

Block, M. "Homicide Justified: The Legality of Killing Slaves in the United States and the Atlantic World." *Civil War Book Review* 19, no. 4 (2017): 1–4.

Boister, Neil. "Global Simplification of Extradition: Interviews with Selected Extradition Experts in New Zealand, Canada, the US and EU." *Criminal Law Forum* 29, no. 3 (2017): 327–75.

Bose, Martin. "Harmonizing Procedural Rights Indirectly: The Framework on Trials in Absentia." *North Carolina Journal of International Law* 37, no. 2 (2011): 489–510.

Bowett, Derek William. "Jurisdiction: Changing Patterns of Authority over Activities and Resources." *British Yearbook of International Law* 53, no. 1 (1982): 1–26.

Bradley, Curtis A. "The Juvenile Death Penalty and International Law." *Duke Law Journal* 52, no. 3 (2002): 485–557.

Braum, Stefan. "The Carles Puigdemont Case: Europe's Criminal Law in the Crisis of Confidence." *German Law Journal* 19, no. 6 (2018): 1349–58.

Bravo, Teresa. "Ne Bis in Idem as a Defence Right and Procedural Safeguard in the EU." *New Journal of European Criminal Law* 2, no. 4 (December 1, 2011): 393–401.

Bress, Thomas. "Some Phases of Uniform Interstate Extradition." *St. John's Law Review* 10, no. 2 (1936): 272–80.

Burić, Zoran. "Ne Bis in Idem in European Criminal Law—Moving in Circles?" *EU and Comparative Law Issues and Challenges Series*3 (2019): 507–20.

Cambien, Nathan. "Mutual Recognition and Mutual Trust in the Internal Market." 2017 (2) *European Papers* 2, no. 1 (2017): 93–115.

Chan, Cora. "Demise of One Country, Two Systems: Reflections on the Hong Kong Rendition Saga." *Hong Kong Law Journal* 49 (2019): 447–58.

Chen, Duanhong 陈端洪. "Lijie xianggang zhengzhi" 理解香港政治 [To understand Hong Kong Politics]. *Zhongwai faxue* 中外法学 28, no. 5 (2016): 1125–48.

Chen H.Y.A. "Constitutional Controversies in the Aftermath of the Anti-Extradition Movement 2019." *Hong Kong Law Journal* 50 (2020): 609–32.

Chen, Lan 陈岚, and Wang Lisha 王丽莎, "Lianxufan yu yishi buzaili yuanze de shiyong tantao" 连续犯与一事不再理原则的适用探讨 [Continuing offence and application of *ne bis in idem*]. *Faxue pinglun* 法学评论 3 (2006): 130–36.

Chen, Yongsheng 陈永生. "Yishi buzaili yu zhongguo quji xingshi guanxia chongtude jiejue" 一事不再理与中国区际刑事管辖冲突的解决 [*Ne bis in idem* and the settlement of conflict of criminal jurisdiction in greater China region]. *Yanjiusheng faxue* 研究生法学 1 (1988).

Chen, Yongsheng 陈永生, and Shao Cong 邵聪, "Yuan'an nanyi jiuzhengde zhidu fansi:yi shenpan jiandu chengxu weizhongdian de fenxi" 冤案难以纠正的制度反思：以审判监督程序为重点的分析 [The system reflection on the difficulty of correcting wrongly convicted cases: A focus on the trial supervision procedure]. *Bijiaofa yanjiu* 比较法研究 4 (2018): 68–88.

Clark, J. Reuben, Frederic R. Coudert, and Julian W. Mack "The Nature and a Definition of Political Offence in International Extradition Discussion." *Proceedings of American Society of International Law at Its Annual Meetings* 3 (April 23, 1909): 95–165.

Clarke, Alan. "Terrorism, Extradition and the Death Penalty." *William Mitchell Law Review* 29, no. 3 (2003): 783–808.

Conway, Gerard. "Ne Bis in Idem in International Law." *International Criminal Law Review* 3 (2003): 217–44.

Costanzo, Mark, and Lawrence T. White. "Overview of the Death Penalty and Capital Trials: History, Current Status, Legal Procedures, and Cost." *Journal of Social Issues* 50, no. 2 (1994): 1–18.

Cottim, A. "Cybercrime, Cyberterrorism and Jurisdiction: An Analysis of Article 22 of the COE Convention on Cybercrime." *European Journal of Legal Studies* 2, no. 3 (2010): 55–79.

Currie, Robert J. "Human Rights and International Mutual Legal Assistance: Resolving the Tension." *Criminal Law Forum* 11, no. 2 (2000): 143–81.

Czaputowicz, Jacek. "Sovereignty in Theories of European Integration and the Perspective of the Polish Constitutional Tribunal." *Yearbook of Polish European Studies* 17 (2014): 15–35.

Deen-Racsmány, Zsuzsanna. "Modernizing the Nationality Exception: Is the Non-extradition of Residents a Better Rule?" *Nordic Journal of International Law* 75 (2006): 29–61.

Deen-Racsmány, Zsuzsanna. "The European Arrest Warrant and the Surrender of Nationals Revisited: The Lessons of Constitutional Challenges." *European Journal of Crime, Criminal Law and Criminal Justice* 14, no. 3 (2006): 271–306.

Deere, Lora L. "Political Offenses in the Law and Practice of Extradition." *The American Journal of International Law* 27, no. 2 (April 1933): 247–70.

Dugard, John, and Christine Van Den Wyngaert. "Reconciling Extradition with Human Rights." *The American Journal of International Law* 92, no. 187 (1998): 187–212.

Fang, Quan 方泉. "Aomen yu neidi yijiao taofande falv wenti." 澳门与内地移交逃犯的法律问题 [Legal questions regarding surrender of fugitive offenders between Macau and Mainland China]. *Zhongguo xingshifa zazhi* 中国刑事法杂志 7 (2009): 117–22.

Federico, Fabbrini. "Enhanced Cooperation under Scrutiny: Revisiting the Law and Practice of Multi-Speed Integration in Light of the First Involvement of the EU Judiciary." *Legal Issues of Economic Integration* 40, no. 3 (2013): 197–224.

Feleke, Nuruye Beyan. "The Practice of US Execution of Juvenile Delinquents in Dated Times vis-à-vis International Human Rights Laws and Case Laws." *Beijing Law Review* 6, no. 4 (2015): 331–39.

Guesta, José luis de la. "Concurrent National and International Criminal Jurisdiction and the Principle 'Ne Bis in Idem.'" *Revue Internationale De Droit Pénal* 72, no. 3–4 (2001): 753–64.

Guesta, José luis de la. "Concurrent National and International Criminal Jurisdiction and the Principle 'Ne Bis in Idem': General Report." *Revue Internationale De Droit Pénal* 73, no. 3–4 (2002): 707–36.

Garcia-Mora, Manuel R. "Treason, Sedition and Espionage as Political Offenses under the Law of Extradition." *University of Pittsburgh Law Review* 26 (1964): 65.

Gardocki, Lech. "Double Criminality in Extradition Law." *Israel Law Review* 27, no. 1–2 (1993): 288–96.

Gevorgyan, Nora. "The Role, Impact and Development of the Principle of Mutual Recognition in EU Law." 67–75. http://ysu.am/files/08N_Gevorgyan_e.pdf.

Gieger, S. "*Trabelsi v. Belgium*: Extradition of Terrorist Suspects and Aversion to Whole-Life Prison Sentences." *Tulane Journal of International and Comparative Law* 23 (2014–2015): 576–87.

Glendon, Mary Ann. "The Rule of Law in the Universal Declaration of Human Rights." *Northwestern Journal of International Human Rights* 2, no. 1 (2004): 1–19.

Graham, Lewis. "Extradition, Life Sentences and the European Convention." *Judicial Review* 25, no. 3 (2020): 228–34.

Gregg, Robert. "The European Tendency toward Non-extradition to the United States in Capital Cases: Trends, Assurances, and Breaches of Duty." *University of Miami International and Comparative Law Review* 10, no. 1 (2002): 113–28.

Griffith, Gavan, and Claire Harris. "Recent Development in the Law of Extradition." *Melbourne Journal of International Law* 6, no. 1 (2005): 33–54.

Gumboh, Esther. "The Penalty of Life Imprisonment under International Criminal Law." *African Human Rights Law Journal* 11 (2011): 75–92.

Guo, Jia 郭佳. "Quji xingshi sifa xiezhuzhong shuangchong fanzui yuanze xianzhi shiyonglun" 区际刑事司法协助中"双重犯罪原则"限制适用论 [The limited application of double criminality principle in regional judicial cooperation in criminal matters] *Zhoukou Shifan xueyuan xuebao* 周口师范学院学报 34, no. 3 (2017): 95–103.

Haggenmuller, Sarah. "The Principle of Proportionality and the European Arrest Warrant." *Onati Socio-Legal Series* 3, no. 1 (2013): 95–106.

"Harvard Research in International Law: Draft Convention on Extradition." *The American Journal of International Law* 29, no. s1: 362, 363.

He, Xin. "Pressures on Chinese Judges under Xi." *The China Journal* 85 (2018): 49–74.

He, Jiahong 何家宏, and Liu Yifan 刘译矾. "Xingshi cuo'an shensu zaishen zhidu shizheng yanjiu" 刑事错案申诉再审制度实证研究 [The empirical study on the retrial system of wrongly convicted cases]. *Guojia jianchaguan xueyuan xuebao* 国家检察官学院学报 23, no. 6 (2015): 5–16, 170.

He, Hairong 何海榕. "Shenhua duiwai kaifang beijingxia zhongguo yindu mianlinde tiaozhan yuyingdui" 深化对外开放背景下中国引渡面临的挑战与应对 [The challenge and response to the China extradition under the background of deepening open policy]. *Renmin sifa* (*application*), 人民司法 (应用) 34 (2018): 76–78.

Heimrich, Chad. "European Arrest Warrants and the Independence of the Issuing Judicial Authority—How Much Independence Is Required?" *New Journal of European Criminal Law* 10, no. 4 (2019): 389–98.

Herlin, Karnell E. "European Arrest Warrant Cases and the Principles of Non-discrimination and EU Citizenship." *The Modern Law Review* 73, no. 5 (2010): 824–35.

Hu, Lusheng 胡陆生, and Li Jianghai 李江海. "Guonei butong fayu taofan yijiao wentide jiejue silu" [The thinking to solve the problem of transferring escaped criminals from different judicial region in one country]. *Faxue luntan* 法学论坛 24, no. 5 (2009): 119–24.

Huang, Yaying 黄亚英. "Lun dui benguorende yindu wenti" 论对本国人的引渡问题 [Explore the question on extradition of nationals]. *Faxue yanjiu* 法学研究 6 (1993): 69–76.

Huang, Feng 黄风, and Peng Shengjuan 彭胜娟. "Cong Zhouzhengyi an guanxia chongtu kan quji xingsu yiguan zhiduzhi goujian" 从周正毅案管辖冲突看区际刑诉移管制度之构建 [Construction the system of transfer of criminal proceedings from the conflict of regional criminal jurisdiction of Zhou Zhengyi case]. *Faxue* 法学 7 (2007): 128–34.

Hughes, Tracey. "Extradition Reform: The Role of the Judiciary in Protecting the Rights of a Requested Individual." *Boston College International and Comparative Law Review* 9, no. 2 (1986): 293–322.

"Interstate Rendition: Executive Practices and the Effects of Discretion." *The Yale Law Journal* 66 (1956): 97–120.

Imbalzano, Maria P. "In Re Mackin: Is the Application of the Political Offense Exception an Extradition Issue for the Judicial or Executive Branch?" *Fordham International Law Journal* 5, no. 2 (1981): 565–97.

Jarczewska, Daria. "Do Human Rights Challenge State Sovereignty?" *E-international Relations* (March 15, 2013): 1–5. https://www.e-ir.info/pdf/34537.

Jimeno-Bulnes, Mar. "European Judicial Cooperation in Criminal Matters." *European Law Journal* 9, no. 5 (2003): 614–30.

Johnson, David T. "Asia's Declining Death Penalty." *The Journal of Asian Studies* 69, no. 2 (2010): 337–46.

Johnson, Robert. "Reflection of the Death Penalty: Human Rights, Human and Dignity, and Dehumanization in the Death House." *Seattle Journal for Social Justice* 13, no. 2 (2014): 583–98.

Julié, William, Sophie Menegon, and Juliette Fauvarque. "From a Political to Judicial Approach to Extradition: A Case for the Consolidation of the Requesting State's Rights in Domestic Extradition Procedures." *New Journal of European Criminal Law* 12, no. 3 (2021): 464–75.

Klimek, Libor. "Surrender vs. Extradition: A Comparison Focused on Innovations of European Arrest Warrant." *International and Comparative Law Review* 11, no. 1 (2011): 145–56.

König, Julia, Paulina Meichelbeck, and Miriam Puchta. "The Curious Case of Carles Puigdemont—The European Arrest Warrant as an Inadequate Means with Regard to Political Offenses." *German Law Journal* 22, no. 2 (2021): 256–75.

Kusak, Martyna. "Common EU Minimum Standards for Enhancing Mutual Admissibility of Evidence Gathered in Criminal Matters." *European Journal on Criminal Policy and Research* 23 (2017): 337–52.

Labardini, Rodrigo. "Life Imprisonment and Extradition: Historical Development, International Context, and the Current Situation in Mexico and the US." *Southwestern Journal of Law and Trade in the Americas* 11 (2005): 1–41.

Lam, Wai-man. "Promoting Hybridity: The Politics of the New Macau Identity." *The China Quarterly* 203 (September 2010): 656–74.

Laursen, Finn. "The Lisbon Treaty: A First Assessment." *L'Europe En Formation* 4, no. 362 (2011): 45–70.

Lavenex, Sandra. "Mutual Recognition and the Monopoly of Force: Limits of the Single Market Analogy." *Journal of European Public Policy* 14, no. 5 (2007): 762–79.

Lepp, Alan W. "Note, the Death Penalty in Late Imperial, Modern, and Post-Tiananmen China." *Michigan Journal of International Law* 11, no. 3 (1990): 987–1038.

Li, Leping 李乐鹏. "Lun tebie xingzhenqu xingshi sifa guanxiaquande dulixing" 论特别行政区刑事司法管辖权的独立性 [Discussion on the independence of criminal jurisdiction of Macau]. *Yiguo liangzhi qikan* 一国两制期刊 4 (2012): 63–69.

Li, Shuo. "Legal Instruments for the Integration and Cooperation in the Guangdong-Hong Kong-Macau Greater Bay Area (GBA): Better Implementation of the SDGs." *2021 Sustainability* 13, no. 22 (2021). https://doi.org/10.3390/su132212485.

Li, Wenjian 李文健. "Zhuanxing shiqide xingsu faxue jiqi jiazhilun" 转型时期的刑诉法学及其价值论 [Study on the criminal procedure law and its value in the transformation period]. *Shehui kexue* 社会科学 4 (1997): 99–115.

Lieberman, David. "Sorting the Revolutionary from the Terrorist: The Delicate Application of the 'Political Offense' Exception in U.S. Extradition Cases." *Stanford Law Review* 59 (2006): 181–212.

Ling, Bing. "Applicability of the PRC Criminal Law in Hong Kong and the Prospect of a Rendition Agreement between Hong Kong and the Mainland." *Hong Kong Law Journal* 29 (1999): 393–421.

Lipkowitz, Noah E. "Why Countries Diverge over Extradition Treaties with China: The Executive Power to Extradite in Common and Civil Law Countries." *Virginia Journal of International Law* 60, no. 1 (2020): 440–501.

Littenberg, Michael. "The Political Offense Exception: An Historical Analysis and Model for the Future." *Tulane Law Review* 64, no. 5 (May 1990): 1195–262.

Liu, Peng 刘鹏, and Feng Weiguo 冯卫国. "Guoji yindu hezuo yuanze kuangjiaxia zhongguo quji taofan yijiao wenti yanjiu" 国际引渡合作原则框架下中国区际逃犯移交问题研究 [Study on China regional surrender of fugitive offenders under international extradition framework]. *Qiusuo* 求索 2 (2015): 103–8.

Loh, Christine. "Hong Kong's Relations with China: The Future of 'One Country, Two Systems.'" *Social Research* 73, no. 1 (2006): 293–316.

Losy, Oskar, and Anna Podolska. "The Principle of Mutual Trust in the Area of Freedom, Security and Justice: Analysis of Selected Case Law." *Adam Mickiewicz University Law Review* 8 (2018): 186–204.

Lubet, Steven. "Extradition Reform: Executive Discretion and Judicial Participation in the Extradition of Political Terrorists." *Cornell International Law Journal* 15, no. 2 (1982): 247–91.

Luchtman, Michiel. "Choice of Forum in an Area of Freedom, Security and Justice." *Utrecht Law Review* 7, no. 1 (2011): 74–101.

Luchtman, Michiel. "Transnational Law Enforcement in the European Union and the Ne Bis in Idem principle." *Review of European Administrative Law* 4, no. 2 (2011): 5–29.

Ma, Decai 马德才. Benguo guomin buyindu yuanzede fazhan qushi tanxi 兼论我国《引渡法》的完善 [Explore the development tendency of the principle of exception for nationals and discuss the perfection of the extradition Law in China]. *Jiangxi shehui kexue* 江西社会科学 31, no. 2 (2011): 165–71.

Maas, Willem. "The Origins, Evolution, and Political Objectives of EU Citizenship." *German Law Journal* 15, no. 5 (2014): 797–819.

Maaskamp, Vanessa. "Extradition and Life Imprisonment." *Loyola of Los Angeles International and Comparative Law Review* 25, no. 3 (2003): 741–66.

Malkani, Bharat. "The Obligation to Refrain from Assisting the Use of the Death Penalty." *The International and Comparative Law Quarterly* 62, no. 3 (2013): 523–56.

Mancano, Leandro. "Trust Thy Neighbour? Compliance and Proximity to the EU through the Lens of Extradition." *Yearbook of European Law* 40 (2021): 475–514.

Manero, de Lemos M., and Teresa Lancy Robalo. "Judicial Cooperation in Criminal Matters in the Special Administrative Regions of Hong Kong and Macau: Through the Lens of 'One Country, Two Systems' and the Surrender of Fugitive Offenders to Mainland China." *Porto Alegre* 5, no. 2 (2019): 737–72.

Mann, Francis A. "The Doctrine of Jurisdiction in International Law." *Recueil des Cours de L'Academie de Droit International* 111 (1964): 1–162.

Marguery, Tony. "EU Citizenship and European Arrest Warrant: The Same Rights for All?" *Merkourios* 27, no. 73 (2011): 84–91.

Martufi, Adriano, and Daila Gigengack. "Exploring Mutual Trust through the Lens of an Executing Judicial Authority: The Practice of the Court of Amsterdam in EAW proceedings." *New Journal of European Criminal Law* 11, no. 3 (2020): 282–98.

Mathisen, Gjermund. "Nordic Cooperation and the European Arrest Warrant: Intra-Nordic Extradition, the Nordic Arrest Warrant and Beyond." *Nordic Journal of International Law* 79, no. 1 (2010): 1–33.

Milanović, Marko. "Extradition and Life Imprisonment." *Cambridge Law Journal* 68, no. 2 (2008): 248–51.

Minarčíková, Eva. "EU-China Cooperation on Regional Policy." *Perspectives in Science* 7 (2016): 30–38. See also Harding, Harry. "The Concept of Greater China: Themes, Variations and Reservations." *The China Quarterly* 136 (1993): 660–86.

Montaldo, Stefano. "On a Collision Course! Mutual Recognition, Mutual Trust and the Protection of Fundamental Rights in the Recent Case Law of the Court of Justice." *European Papers* 1, no. 3 (2016): 965–96.

Mushkat, Roda. "Jurisdiction Issues in a 'Highly Autonomous Region'—The Case of Hong Kong." *International and Comparative Law Quarterly* 42, no. 1 (1993): 11–47.

Nagy, Sarah L. "Political Offense Exception to United States Extradition Policy: Aut Dedere Aut Judicare (Either Extradite or Prosecute)." *Indiana International & Comparative Law Review* 1, no. 1 (1991): 109–49.

Nanda, Ved P. "Bases for Refusing International Extradition Requests—Capital Punishment and Torture." *Fordham International Law Journal* 23, no. 5 (1999): 1369–96.

Ngearndee, Poonpol. "Mutual Legal Assistance and Extradition in Thailand." https://www.unafei.or.jp/publications/pdf/GG6/05-7_Thailand.pdf. Accessed November 5, 2022.

Nicolaidis, Kalypso. "Mutual Recognition: Promise and Denial, from Sapiens to Brexit." *Current Legal Problems* 70, no. 1 (2017): 227–66.

Nilsson, Hans G. "From Classical Judicial Cooperation to Mutual Recognition." *Revenue Internationale De Droit Pénal* 77, no. 1–2 (2006): 53–58.

Niyungeko Gérard. "The Implementation of International Humanitarian Law and the Principle of State Sovereignty." *International Review of the Red Cross* 31, no. 281 (1991): 105–33.

Ortino, Matteo. "The Role and Functioning of Mutual Recognition in the European Market of Financial Services." *International and Comparative Law Quarterly* 56, no. 2 (2007): 309–38.

Ouwerkerk, Jannemieke. "Are Alternatives to the European Arrest Warrant Underused? The Case for an Integrative Approach to Judicial Cooperation Mechanisms in the EU Criminal Justice Area?" *European Journal of Crime, Criminal Law and Criminal Justice* 29, no. 2 (2021): 87–101.

Parry, John T. "International Extradition, the Rule of Non-inquiry, and the Problem of Sovereignty." *Boston University Law Review* 90 (2010): 1973–2029.

Pérignon, Isabelle and Constance Daucé C. "The European Arrest Warrant: A Growing Success Story." *ERA Forum* 8 (2007): 203–14.

Petersen, Antje C. "Extradition and the Political Offense Exception in the Suppression of Terrorism." *Indiana Law Journal* 67, no. 3 (1992): 767–96.

Quan, Daguo 权大国. "Ouzhou daibuling duiwoguo quji taofan yijiao zhidude jiejian" 欧洲逮捕令对我国区际逃犯移交制度的借鉴 [China regional surrender of fugitive offenders: inspiration from European arrest warrant] *Xueshu Luntan* 9 (2016): 84–87.

Radelet, Michael L. and Akers Ronald L. "Deterrence and the Death Penalty: The Views of the Experts." (1996) 87 (1) *Journal of Criminal Law and Criminology* 87, no. 1 (1996): 1–16.

Ralli, Evgenia. "The Principle of Mutual Recognition Based on Mutual Trust and the Respect for Fundamental Rights: The Case of the Framework Decision on the European Arrest Warrant." European Law Institute. https://www.europeanlawinstitute.eu/fileadmin/user_upload/p_eli/YLA_Award/Submission_ELI_Young_Lawyers_Award_Evgenia_Ralli_2017.pdf accessed November 5.

Reidy, Aisling. "The Prohibition of Torture: A Guide to the Implementation of Article 3 of the European Convention on Human Rights." Human Rights Handbooks No. 6. https://rm.coe.int/168007ff4c accessed November 5.

Reyns, Charlotte. "Saving Judicial Independence: A Threat to the Preliminary Ruling Mechanism?" (2021)17 *European Constitutional Law Review* 17, no. 1 (2021): 26–52.

Roecks, Craig R. "Extradition, Human Rights, and the Death Penalty: When Nations Must Refuse to Extradite a Person Charged with a Capital Crime." *California Western International Law Journal* 25, no. 1 (1994): 189–234.

Rose, Thomas. "A Delicate Balance: Extradition, Sovereignty, and Individual Rights in the United States and Canada." *Yale Journal of International Law* 27 (2002): 193–215.

Saluzzo, Stefano. "EU Law and Extradition Agreements of Member States: The Petruhhin Case." *European Papers* 2, no. 1 (2017): 435–47.

Sanger, Andrew. "Force of Circumstance: The European Arrest Warrant and Human Rights." *Democracy and Security* 6, no. 1 (2010): 17–51.

Satzger, Helmut. "Is Mutual Recognition a Viable General Path for Cooperation?" *New Journal of European Criminal Law* 10, no. 1 (2019): 44–56.

Schabas, William A. "International Law and Abolition of the Death Penalty." *Washington and Lee Law Review* 55, no. 3 (1998): 797–846.

Schabas A. W. 'International Law and Abolition of the Death Penalty: Recent Development' (1998) 4 (2) *ILSA Journal of International Law & Comparative Law* 535.

Schabas A. W. "Indirect Abolition: Capital Punishment's Role in Extradition law and Practice." *Loyola of Los Angeles International & Comparative Law Review* 25, no. 3 (2003): 581–604.

Schwelb, Egon. "The Influence of the Universal Declaration of Human Rights on International and National Law." *Proceedings of the American Society of International Law at its Annual Meeting* 53 (1959): 217–29.

Shaihaishi Huangpuqu Renmin fayuan ketizu 上海市黄浦区人民法院课题组, "Jiceng fayuan Shenli shewai xingshi anjian jizhide wanshan." 基层法院审理涉外刑事案件机制的完善 [The perfection of foreign-related criminal cases trial in primary courts]. *Renmin sifa (Application)* 人民司法 (应用) 15 (2015): 40–44.

Shearer, Ivan A. "Non-extradition of Nationals: A Review and a Proposal." *Adelaide Law Review* 2, no. 3 (1996): 274–309.

Shu, Hongshui 舒洪水. "Lun zhongshen jianjinde biyaoxing he tixihua goujian—yi kongbu zhuyi jiduan zhuyi fanzui fangkong weishijiao." 论终身监禁的必要性和体系化构建—以恐怖主义、极端主义犯罪防控为视角 [Study on the necessity and systematic construction of life sentence—from the perspective of prevention and combating terrorism]. *Falv kexue* 法律科学 36, no. 3 (2018): 152–62.

Smit, Dirk Van Zyl. "Outlawing Irreducible Life Sentences: Europe on the Brink?" (2010)23 (1) *Federal Sentencing Reporter* 23, no. 1 (2010): 39–48.

Spinellis, Dionysios. "Global Report the Ne Bis in Idem Principle in 'Global' Instruments." *Revue Internationale De Droit Pénal* 73, no. 3–4 (2002): 1149–62.

Stamatopoulou, Elsa. "The Importance of the Universal Declaration of Human Rights in the Past and Future of the United Nation's Human Rights Efforts." *ILSA Journal of International & Comparative Law* 5, no. 2 (1999): 281–89.

Sternberg, Kenneth S. and David L. Skelding. "State Department Determinations of Political Offences: Death Knell for the Political Offense Exception in Extradition Law." *Case Western Reserve Journal of International Law* 15, no. 1 (1983): 137–72.

Storskrubb, Eva. "Mutual Trust and the Dark Horse of Civil Justice." (2018)20 *Cambridge Yearbook of European Legal Studies* 20 (2018): 179–201.

Su, Caixia 苏彩霞. "Woguo quji xingshi sifa xiezhu shiyong 'shuangchong fanzui yuanze' xinlun" 我国区际刑事司法协助适用"双重犯罪原则"新论 [The new discussion on the application of double criminality principle in the regional judicial cooperation in criminal matters] *Zhengzhi yu falü* 6 (2009): 139–45.

Sulima, Aleksandra. "The Normativity of the Principle of Mutual Trust between EU Member States within the Emerging European Criminal Area." *Wroclaw Review of Law, Administration & Economics* 3, no. 1 (2013): 72–89.

Suominen, Annika. "The Past, Present and Future of Eurojust." *Maastricht Journal of European and Comparative Law* 15, no. 2 (2008): 217–34.

Swart, Bert. "Refusal of Extradition and the United Nations Model Treaty on Extradition." *Netherlands Yearbook of International Law* 23 (1992): 175–222.

Thorhauer, Nathalie Isabelle. "Conflicts of Jurisdiction in Cross-Border Criminal Cases in the Area of Freedom, Security, and Justice: Risks and Opportunities from an Individual Rights-Oriented Perspective." *New Journal of European Criminal Law* 6, no. 1 (2015): 78–101.

Valdés, Antonio Roma. "The Mutual Recognition Principle in Criminal Matters: A Review." *ERA Forum* 16 (2015): 291–303.

Vervaele, J.A.E. "The Transnational Ne Bis in Idem Principle in the EU Mutual Recognition and Equivalent Protection of Human Rights." 2005 (1)2 *Utrecht Law Review* 1, no. 2 (2005): 100–118.

Vogel, Joachim and John Spencer. "Proportionality and the European Arrest Warrant." *Criminal Law Review* 6 (2010): 474–82.

Wang, Minyuan. "Xingshi susong faxue yanjiude zhuanxing—yixingshi zaishen wenti weilide fenxi" 刑事诉讼法学研究的转型—以刑事再审问题为例的种转 [The transformation of criminal procedure law: analyze the issue of criminal retrial]. *Faxue yanjiu* 法学研究 33, no. 5 (2011): 20–28.

Wang, Shizhou. "China Crimes against National Security." *UMKC Law Review* 82, no. 4 (2014): 1029–54.

Wang, Shuo 王硕. "Guanxia chongtu yu quji xietiao—shilun zhongguo gang'ao diqu xingshi panjue zai zhongguo neidi de shiyong" 管辖冲突与区际协调—试论中国港澳地区刑事判决在中国内地的适用 [Conflict of jurisdiction and regional coordination: study on the application of criminal judgment from Hong Kong and Macau to mainland China] *Fazhi shehui* 法治社会 4 (2018): 81–87.

Wang, Tao and Hong Liang. "II Economic Integration between Hong Kong SAR and Mainland China." International Monetary Fund. https://www.elibrary.imf.org/configurable/content/book$002f9781589062948$002fch02.xml?t:ac=book%24002f9781589062948%24002fch02.xml.

Wang, Xinqing 王新清. "Lun GangAo tebie xingzhengqu yu neidi xingshi guanxiaquande chongtu yu xietiao." 论港澳特别行政区与内地刑事管辖权的冲突与协调 [On conflict and coordination of criminal jurisdiction between mainland China and the Special Administrative Region of Hong Kong and Macau] *Faxuejia* 法学家 6 (2000): 98–106.

Wang, Zheng 王铮. "Zhixing xingshi panjuezhongde guoji sifa hezuo" 执行刑事判决中的国际司法合作 [The international judicial cooperation in executing criminal judgments] *Bijiaofa yanjiu* 比较法学研究 3 (1997): 50–64.

Wasmeier, Martin. "The Principle of Ne Bis in Idem." *Revue Internationale De Droit Pénal* 77, no. 1–2 (2006): 121–30.

Weatherill, Stephen. "Comparative Internal Market Law: The UK and the EU." *Yearbook of European Law* 40 (2021): 431–74.

Weyembergh, Anne. "Approximation of Criminal Law, the Constitutional Treaty and the Hague Programme." *Common Market Law Review* 42 (2005): 1567–97.

Williams, Sharon A. "Nationality, Double Jeopardy, Prescription and the Death Sentence as Bases for Refusing Extradition." *International Review of Penal Law* 62, no. 1–2 (1991): 261–82.

Williams, Sharon A. "The Double Criminality Rule and Extradition: A Comparative Analysis." *Nova Law Review* 15, no. 2 (1991): 581–624.

Winter, Lorena Bachmaier. "European Arrest Warrant, Double Criminality and Mutual Recognition: A Much Debated Case." *European Criminal Law Review* 8, no. 2 (2018): 152–59.

Wyngaert, Christine Van den. "The Political Offense Exception to Extradition: Defining the Issues and Searching for a Feasible Alternative." *Revue Belge De Droi't Int'le* (1983): 741–53.

Xanthopoulou Ermioni. "The Quest for Proportionality for the European Arrest Warrant: Fundamental Rights Protection in a Mutual Recognition Environment." *New Journal of European Criminal Law* 6, no. 1 (2015): 32–52.

Xiong, Qiuhong 熊秋红. "Jinzhi shuangchong weixian goujian" 禁止双重危险构建 [The Construction of Double Jeopardy]. http://iolaw.cssn.cn/zxzp/200710/t20071029_4600470.shtml.

Yakut, Bahadir. "Post-Lisbon Criminal Law Competency of the European Union." *Marmara Journal of European Studies* 17, no. 1–2 (2009): 1–52.

Yee, Marsha Wellknown. "Hong Kong's Legal Obligation to Require Fair Trial for Rendition." *Columbia Law Review* 102, no. 5 (2002): 1373–412.

Yin, Yanhong. "The Surrender of Fugitive Offenders between Mainland China, Hong Kong and Macau: Relevance of the Political Offence Exception?" *Hong Kong Law Journal* 51, no. 3 (2002): 952–83.

Yin, Yanhong. "The Surrender of Fugitive Offenders between Mainland China and Hong Kong: European Arrest Warrant Model or US Interstate Rendition Model?" *Utrecht Journal of International and European Law* 37, no. 1 (2022): 1–19.

Yin, Yanhong. "Human Rights Protection in the Surrender of Fugitive Offenders between Mainland China, Hong Kong and Macau." *Asia-Pacific Journal on Human Rights and the Law* 23, no. 3 (2022): 381–413.

Yin, Yanhong, and Irene Wieczorek. "What Model for Extradition between Hong Kong and Mainland China? A Comparison between the 2019 (Withdrawn) Amendment to Hong Kong Extradition Law and the European Arrest Warrant." *New Journal of European Criminal Law* 11, no. 4 (2020): 504–23.

Yorke, Jon. "Europe's Inquiry in Extradition Cases: Closing the Door on the Death Penalty." *European Law Review* 29, no. 4 (2004): 546–56.

Young, Simon. "The Law of the People's Republic of China on Safeguard National Security in the Hong Kong Special Administrative Region." *International Legal Materials* 60, no. 1 (2021): 1–17.

Zhao, Guoqiang 赵国强. "Lun yiguo liangzhi xiade yijiao taofan jizhi" 论"一国两制"下的移交逃犯机制 [Discussion on the surrender of fugitive offenders under "one Country, two systems] *Xingzheng* 行政 20, no. 78 (2007): 1047–1059+1197–1214+1261.

Zhao, Guoqiang 赵国强. "Guanyu neidi yu xianggang xianghu yijiao fanzui xianyirende jidian sikao" 关于内地与香港相互移交犯罪嫌疑人的几点思考 [Thinks on the surrender of fugitive offenders between Mainland and Hong Kong] *Huadong zhengfa xueyuan xuebao* 华东政法学院学报 4 (2000): 31–37.

Zhao, Guoqiang 赵国强. "Yiguo liangzhi yu guoji yindu guanli: yi Aomen yu neidi yijiao taofan wei shijiao" 一国两制与国际引渡惯例：以澳门与内地移交逃犯为视角 [One country two systems and international extradition traditions: a perspective from the surrender of fugitive offenders between Mainland and Macau] *Aomen faxue* 29, no. 3 (2015): 21–38.

Zimmermann, Frank. "Conflicts of Criminal Jurisdiction in the European Union." *Bergen Journal of Criminal Law and Criminal Justice* 3, no. 1 (2015): 1–21.

Zou, Bing. "On the Standardization of Lethal Injections in China." *Asian Social Science* 8, no. 6 (2012): 82–85.

Zoumpoulakis, Konstantinos. "From the Ground up: the Use of Minimum Rules in EU Procedural Criminal Law and the Question of Member States' Discretion" *European Papers* 5, no. 3 (2020): 1289–303.

Books

Allen, Francis A. *The Crimes of Politics: Political Dimensions of Criminal Justice*. Cambridge, MA: Harvard University Press, 1974.

Bassiouni, Mahmoud Cherif. *Criminal Law and Its Processes: The Law of Public Order*. New York: Thomas Press, 1969.

Bassiouni, Mahmoud Cherif. *International Extradition and World Public Order*. Leiden: Sijthoff, 1974.

Bassiouni, Mahmoud Cherif and Edward Wise, *Aut Dedere Aut Judicare: The Duty to Extradite or Prosecute in International Law*. Leiden: Martinus Nijhoff, 1995.

Bassiouni, Mahmoud Cherif. *International Extradition: United States Law and Practice*. 6th ed. Oxford: Oxford University Press, 2014.

Bieber, Roland, Renaud Dehousse, John Pinder and Joseph Weiler, eds. *1992: One European Market? A Critical Analysis of the Commission's Internal Market Strategy*. Baden-Baden: Nomos Verlagsgesellschaft, 1988.

Bockel, Willem Bastiaan Van. *The Ne Bis in idem Principle in EU Law*. Hague: Kluwer Law International, 2010.

Brownlie, Ian. *Principles of Public International Law*. 7th ed. Oxford: Oxford University Press, 2008.

Chen, H. Y. A. *The Changing Legal Orders in Hong Kong and Mainland China: Essays on "One Country, Two Systems."* Beijing: City University of Hong Kong Press, 2021.

Chen, Guangzhong 陈光中, Wang Wanhua 王万花, Tan Qiugui 谭秋桂 and Zeng Xinhua 曾新华, eds. *Zhongguo xiandai sifa zhidu* 中国现代司法制度 [China modern judicial system]. Beijing: Beijing University Press, 2020.

Chen, Su 陈甦, Tian He 田禾, Lv Yanbin 吕艳滨 and Wang Xiaomei 王小梅, eds. *Fazhi lanpishu: zhongguo fazhi fazhan baogao No. 18* 法治蓝皮书：中国法治发展报告 No. 18 [Blue book of rule of law: annual report on rule of law in China No. 18]. Beijing: Shehui kexue wenxian chubanshe, 2020.

Costa, Miguel João. *Extradition Law: Reviewing Grounds for Refusal from the Classic Paradigm to Mutual Recognition and Beyond.* Leiden: Brill Nijhoff, 2020.

Coutts, Stephen. *Citizenship, Crime and Community in the European Union.* Oxford: Hart 2019.

Cullen, Richard. *Hong Kong Constitutionalism: The British Legacy and the Chinese Future* Hong Kong: Routledge, 2020.

Dai, Yanling 戴艳玲. *Zhongguo jianyu zhidude gaige yu fazhan* 中国监狱制度的改革与发展 [The reform and development of China prison system]. Beijing: Zhongguo renmin gong'an daxue chubanshe, 2004.

Daillier, Patrick and Alain Pellet. *Droit international public.*7th ed. Paris: LGDJ, 2008.

Deen-Racsmány, Zsuzsanna. *Active Perspective and Non-extradition of Nationals in International Criminal Law at the Dawn of the Twenty-first Century—Adapting Key Functions of Nationality to the Requirements of International Criminal Justice.* Leiden: Leiden University Press, 2007.

Fang, Quan 方泉. *Aomen tebie xingfa gailun* 澳门特别刑法概论 [An introduction to the special criminal law of Macau]. Beijing: Shehui kexue wenxian chubanshe, 2014.

Fletcher, Maria, Robin Loof, and Bill Gilmore. *EU Criminal Law and Justice, Elgar European Law.* Cheltenham: Edward Elgar, 2008.

Fry, S. Margery, ed. *The Abolition of the Death Penalty in Holland and Scandinavia.* 2nd ed. London: The Howard League for Penal Reform, 1928.

Gao, Mingxuan 高铭瑄. *Zhongguo xingfaxue yuanli* 中国刑法学原理 [Science of China criminal law]. Beijing: Zhongguo renmin daxue chubanshe, 1993.

Graat, Joske. *The European Arrest Warrant and EU Citizenship: EU Citizenship in Relation to Foreseeability Problems in the Surrender Procedure.* Cham: Springer, 2022.

Huang, Feng 黄风. *Yindu wenti yanjiu* 引渡问题研究 [*Study on Extradition*]. Beijing: Zhongguo zhengfa daxue chubanshe, 2006.

Huang, Boqing 黄伯青. *Guoji xingshi sifa hezuo zhognde yishi buzaili yuanze* 国际刑事司法合作中的一事不再理原则 [The study on the *Ne Bis in Idem* in the judicial cooperation in criminal matters]. Shanghai: Shanghai renmin chubanshe, 2011.

Hufnagel, Saskia and Carole McCartney, eds. *Trust in International Police and Justice Cooperation.* London: Bloomsbury, 2017.

Janssens, Christine. *The Principle of Mutual Recognition in EU Law.* Oxford: Oxford University Press, 2013.

Jansson, Julia. *Terrorism, Criminal Law and Politics: The Decline of the Political Offence Exception to Extradition*. London: Routledge, 2020.

Klimek, Libor. *European Arrest Warrant*. New York: Springer, 2015.

Klip, André. *Euroepan Criminal Law: An Integrative Approach*. 2nd ed. Cambridge: Intersentia, 2012.

Kochenov, Dimitry, ed. *EU Citizenship and Federalism: The Role of Rights*. Cambridge: Cambridge University Press, 2017.

Litton, Henry. *The Dance of Folly*. Hong Kong: Kin Kwok Printing Press, 2021.

Lo, Sonny Shiu-Hing. *The Politics of Cross-border Crime in Greater China: Case Studies of Mainland China, Hong Kong and Macau*. London: Routledge, 2009.

Megivern, James J. *The Death Penalty: An Historical and Theological Survey*. Mahwah, NJ: Paulist Press, 1997.

Mitsilegas, Valsamis, Alberto di Martino and Leandro Mancano, eds. *The Court of Justice and European Criminal Law: Leading Cases in a Contextual Analysis*. Oxford: Hart, 2019.

Nie, Lize 聂立泽. *GangAo yu neidi xingshi falv bijiao yanjiu ji xingshi sifa xiezhu* 港澳与内地刑事法律比较及刑事司法协助研究 [Comparison research on criminal law and criminal judical cooperation among Hong Kong, Macau, and mainland China]. Beijing: Beijing daxue chubanshe, 2009.

Oliveira, Jorge Costa and Paulo Cardinal, eds. *One Country, Two Systems, Three Legal Orders-Perspectives of Evolution: Essays on Macau's Autonomy after the Resumption of Sovereignty by China*. New York: Springer, 2009.

Ouguergouz, Fatsah. *The African Charter of Human and People's Rights: A Comprehensive Agenda for Human Dignity and Sustainable Democracy in Africa*. Leiden: Brill 2003.

Posner, A.R. *Economic Analysis of Law*. Translated by Jiang Zhaokang 蒋兆康. Beijing: Zhongguo dabaike quanshu chubanshe,1997.

Richardson, Chris. *Violence in American Society: An Encyclopedia of Trends, Problems, and Perspectives*. Santa Barbara, CA: ABC-CLIO, 2020.

Schabas, William A. *The European Convention on Human Rights: A Commentary*. Oxford: Oxford University Press, 2015.

Shearer, Ivan Anthony. *Extradition in International Law*. Manchester: Manchester University Press, 1971.

Smit, Dirk van Zyl and Catherine Appleton, eds. *Life Imprisonment and Human Rights*. Oxford: Hart, 2016.

Steiker, Carol S. and Jordan M. Steiker, eds. *Comparative Capital Punishment: Research Handbooks in Comparative Law Series*. Cheltenham: Edward Elgar, 2019.

Su, Caixia 苏彩霞. *Zhongguo xingfa guojihua yanjiu* 中国刑法国际化研究 [Study on the internationalization of criminal law in China]. Beijing: Beijing daxue chubanshe, 2007.

Suominen, Annika. *The Principle of Mutual Recognition in Cooperation in Criminal Matters: A study of the Principle in Four Framework Decisions and in the Implementation Legislation in the Nordic Member States*. Cambridge: Intersentia, 2011.

Walsh, Wayne S.C. *Cross-Border Crime in Hong Kong*. Hong Kong: LexisNexis, 2018.

Walsh, Wayne S.C. *Cross-Border Crime in Hong Kong: Extradition, Mutual assistance, Financial Sanctions*. 2nd ed. Hong Kong: LexisNexis, 2020.

Wang, Zhongxing 王仲兴 and Guo Tianwu 郭天武. *Neidi yu xianggang xingshi sifa heuzo yanjiu* 内地与香港刑事司法合作研究 [Research on criminal judicial cooperation between Hong Kong and mainland China]. Beijing: Beijing daxue chubanshe, 2008.

Weiß, Norman and Jean-Marc Thouvenin, eds. *The Influence of Human Rights on International Law*. New York: Springer, 2015.

Wijngaert, Christine Van Den. *The Political Offence Exception of Extradition*. Deventer: Springer, 1981.

Willems, Auke. *The Principle of Mutual Trust in EU Criminal Law*. London: Hart, 2020.

Xanthopoulou, Ermioni. *Fundamental Rights and Mutual Trust in the Area of Freedom, Security and Justice: A Role for Proportionality?* Oxford: Hart, 2020.

Yang, Chunxi 杨春喜 and Yang Dunxian 杨敦先, eds. *Zhongguo xingfalun* 中国刑法论 [On China criminal law]. Beijing: Beijing daxue chubanshe, 2001.

Yue, Liling 岳礼玲 and Guo, Shuo 郭硕, eds. *Zhongguo xingshi sifa yu renquan* 中国刑事司法与人权 [Human rights and criminal justice in China]. Beijing: Falv chubanshe, 2017.

Zhao, Guoqiang 赵国强. *Jibenfa yu quji sifa xiezhu* 基本法与区际司法协助 [Basic law and regional judicial cooperation]. Beijing: Shehui kexue chubanshe, 2000.

Zhao, Linlin 赵琳琳. *Aomen xingshifa gaige yanjiu* 澳门刑事法改革研究 [European continental tradition and local consciousness: research on the reform of Macau criminal laws]. Beijing: Falv chubanshe, 2017.

Zhang, Xu 张旭. *Guoji xingfa* 国际刑法 [International Criminal Law: Present and Prospect]. Beijing: Qinghua daxue chubanshe, 2005.

Zhonggong zhongyang dangshi he wenxian yanjiuyuan 中共中央党史和文献研究院 ed. *Xijinping guanyu zunzhong he baozhang renquan lunshu zhaibian* 习近平关于尊重和保障人权论述摘编 [Excerpts from Xi Jinping's discussion on respecting and protecting human rights]. Beijing: Zhongyang wenxian chubaishe, 2013.

Zhonggong zhongyang wenxian yanjiushi 中共中央文献研究室 ed. *Xijinping guanyu shixian zhonghua minzu weida fuxingde zhongguomeng lunshu zhaibian* 习近平关于实现中华民族伟大复兴的中国梦论述摘编 [Excerpts from Xi Jinping's discussion on realizing the Chinese dream of the great rejuvenation of the Chinese nation]. Beijing: Zhongyang wenxian chubanshe, 2012.

Zhou, Daoluan 周道鸾, and Zhang Jun 张军, eds. *Xingfa zuiming jingshi* 刑法罪名精释 [Elaboration on criminal charges]. 3rd ed. Beijing: Renmin fayuan chubanshe, 2007.

Zimmer, Brenden M, ed. *Extradition and Rendition: Background and Issues*. New York: Nova Science, 2011.

Book sections

Flore, Daniel. "The Issue of Mutual Trust and the Needed Balance Between Diversity and Unity." In *The Needed Balances in EU Criminal Law: Past, Present and Future*, edited by Chloé Brière and Anne Weyembergh, 157–64. Oxford: Hart, 2018.

Frisso, Giovanna Maria. "The Abolition of Life Imprisonment in Brazil and its Contradictions." In *Life Imprisonment and Human Rights*, edited by Dirk van Zyl Smit and Catherine Appleton, 307–28. Oxford: Hart, 2016.

Hans, Heinrich Jescheck, "Modern Criminal Policy in the Federal Republic of Germany and the German Democratic Republic." In *Crime, Criminology and Public Policy: Essays in Honor of Sir Leon Radzinowicz*, edited by Roger Hood, 509–25. London: Heinemann, 1974.

Hardin, Russel. "Conceptions and Explanations of Trust." In *Trust in Society*, edited by K. S. Cook, 3–39. New York: Russell Sage Foundation, 2001.

Konstadinides, Theodore. "The Europeanisation of Extradition: How Many Light Years Away to Mutual Confidence?" In *Crime Within the Area of Freedom, Security and Justice: A European Public Order*, edited by Christina Eckes and Theodore Konstadinides, 192–223. Cambridge: Cambridge University Press, 2011.

Larsen, Lars Bay. "Afterword(s) on Mutual Recognition and the Respect for Fundamental Rights Revisited—Following the Judgment in Aranyosi and Caldararu." In *The Needed Balance in EU Criminal Law: Past, Present and Future*, edited by Chloé Brière and Anne Weymbergh, 433–42. Oxford: Hart, 2018.

Li, Jun 黎军 and Yang Wentao 杨文滔. "Sixing xianzhi zhidude chubu jianshi—jiyu zhongji fayuande sifa shijiande kaocha" 死刑限制减刑制度的初步检视—基于中级法院的司法实践的考察 [The preliminary examination on the death penalty restricted commutation: based on the investigation of the judicial practice of intermediate court]. In *Jianshe gongping Zhengyi shehui yu xingshi falv shiyong wenti yanjiu* 建设公平正义社会与刑事法律适用问题研究 [Study on building up equal and justice society and the application of criminal law], edited by Wan E'xiang 万鄂湘, 458–69. Beijing: Renmin fayuan chubanshe, 2012.

Lippert-Rasmussen, Kasper. "Punishment and Discrimination." In *Punishment and Ethics: New Perspectives*, edited by J. Ryberg and J. Corlett, 169–88. London: Palgrave Macmillan, 2010.

Malkani, Bharat. "Extradition and Non-refoulment." In *Comparative Capital Punishment*, edited by Carol S.Steiker and Jordan M. Steiker, 76–95. Cheltenham: Edward Elgar, 2019.

Massa, Anne-Sophie. "Jurisdiction in England and Wales and in the Netherlands: a comparative appraisal with a European touch." In *Substantive Criminal Law of the European Union*, edited by Klip André, 103–20. Antwerpen: Maklu, 2011.

Miettinen, Samuli. "The Evolution of Competence Distribution Between the European Union and the Member States in the Criminal Field." In *The Needed Balance in EU Criminal Law: Past, Present and Future*, edited by Chloé Brière and Anne Weymbergh, 35–64. Oxford: Hart, 2018.

Sievers, Julia. "Too Different to Trust? First Experiences with the Application of the European Arrest Warrant." In *Security Versus Justice? Police and Judicial Cooperation*, edited by Elspeth Guild and Florian Geyer, 109–28. Farnham: Ashgate, 2008.

Steiker, Carol S. "Capital Punishment and American Exceptionalism." In *American Exceptionalism and Human Rights*, edited by Michael Ignatieff, 57–89. Princeton: Princeton University Press, 2005.

Suominen, Annika. "The Sensitive Relationship Between the Different Means of Legal Integration: Mutual Recognition and Approximation." In *The Needed Balance in EU*

Criminal Law: Past, Present and Future, edited by Chloé Brière and Anne Weymbergh, 165–84. Oxford: Hart, 2018.

Young, N. M. Simon. "Old Law in New Bottles: Reintroducing National Security Legislation in Hong Kong." In *China's National Security: Endangering Hong Kong's Rule of Law*, edited by Cora Chan and Fiona de Londras, 249–71. Oxford: Hart, 2020.

Newspaper articles and weblogs

AFP. "National Security Law: Whether Macau Can be Model of Hong Kong." *BBC News*. May 28, 2020. https://www.bbc.com/zhongwen/simp/chinese-news-52817548.

Baudrihaye-Gerard, Laure. "Can Belgian, French and Swedish Prosecutors Issue European Arrest Warrant? The CJEU Clarifies the Requirement for Independence Public Prosecutors." *EU Law Analysis*. January 2, 2020. http://eulawanalysis.blogspot.com/2020/01/can-belgian-french-and-swedish.html.

Chen, Laurie. "After 13 years on the run, China's most-wanted fugitive jailed for graft." *South China Morning Post*. October 13, 2017. https://www.scmp.com/news/china/policies-politics/article/2115279/after-13-years-run-chinas-most-wanted-fugitive-jailed.

Chung, Lawrence. "Hong Kong-Taiwan Loophole Means Teen Accused of Killing Girlfriend in Taipei May Never Face Charges." *South China Moring Post*. March 17, 2018. https://www.scmp.com/news/hong-kong/law-crime/article/2137626/hong-kong-taiwan-loophole-means-teen-accused-killing.

Cross, Grenville. "Fugitive surrender: Rights and responsibilities." *China Daily*. June 12, 2019. https://www.chinadailyhk.com/epaper/pubs//chinadaily/2019/06/12/07.pdf.

Davies, Christian. "Ireland Refuses Extradition over Concern at Polish Justice Reforms." *The Guardian*. March 13, 2018. https://www.theguardian.com/world/2018/mar/13/ireland-refuses-artur-celmer-extradition-poland-justice-reforms-ecj.

Easton, Adam. "Poland Judicial Reforms: EU Takes Disciplinary Measures." *BBC News*. December 20, 2017. https://www.bbc.com/news/world-europe-42420150.

Feng, Yongqiang. "Hong Kong Abolish the Death Penalty for 20 Years." *The Rule of Law Weekend*. April 29, 2013. http://news.sina.com.cn/c/sd/2013-04-29/025626983311.shtml.

Hong, Yiyi. "Guang Dong Police Handed over One Suspect to Macau Police Which Fled to Mainland China after Murdered." *Pengpai News*. March 16, 2017. https://www.thepaper.cn/newsDetail_forward_1640835.

Huang, Jingjing. "Lai Changxing Gets Life for Smuggling and Bribery."" *Global Times*. May 19, 2012. https://www.globaltimes.cn/content/710251.shtml.

James, William, and Andy Bruce. "UK suspends Hong Kong extradition treaty, stoking China tensions." *Reuters*. July 19, 2020. https://www.reuters.com/article/uk-britain-china-diplomacy-idUKKCN24K0AS.

Jia, Yu. "Crack Down Crimes against National Sovereignty and Safeguard National Security." People's Net. August 5, 2016. http://news.jcrb.com/jxsw/201608/t20160805_1639884.html.

Jones, Chris. "Death Penalty: A Human Rights Issue for South Africa." *IntechOpen*. March 2, 2021. https://www.intechopen.com/online-first/74995.

Kang-chung, Ng. "Hong Kong Trials for Offences in Mainland China Will Not Work, Top Legal Scholar Albert Chen Says." *South China Morning Post*. June 3, 2019. https://www.scmp.com/news/hong-kong/law-and-crime/article/3012942/hong-kong-trials-offences-mainland-china-will-not-work.

Pepper, Suzanne. "The Trust Deficit: Why Hong Kongers Simply Don't Believer Gov't Reassurances Over Its China Extradition Law." *Hong Kong Free Press*. April 4, 2019. https://hongkongfp.com/2019/04/04/trust-deficit-hongkongers-simply-dont-believe-govt-reassurances-china-extradition-law/.

Ping, An. "Zhang Ziqiang Criminal Gangs Case." *People's Court News*. July 23, 2019. https://www.chinacourt.org/article/detail/2019/07/id/4200356.shtml.

ReutersStaff, "Update1-HKBillionaireLauGuiltyinMacauGraftCase." *Reuters*. March 14, 2014. https://www.reuters.com/article/hongkong-macau-lau-idUSL3N0MB2YZ20140314.

SCMP Reporters, "Hong Kong Leader Carrie Lam Announces Formal Withdrawal of the Extradition Bill and Sets Up a Platform to Look into Key Causes of Protest Crisis." *South China Morning Post*. September 4, 2019. https://www.scmp.com/news/hong-kong/politics/article/3025641/hong-kong-leader-carrie-lam-announce-formal-withdrawal.

Torode, Greg and James Pomfret. "Exclusive: Hong Kong Judges See Risks in Proposed Extradition Changes." *Reuters*. May 29, 2019. https://www.reuters.com/article/us-hongkong-politics-extradition-judges-idUSKCN1SZ09U.

UN006, "Zhang Ziqiang Was Executed on November 12th 1998." *People's Net*. November 12, 2011. http://news.sohu.com/20111112/n325374402.shtml.

Victor, Daniel, and Tiffany May. "The Murder Case that Lit the Fuse in Hong Kong." *The New York Times*. June 15, 2019. https://www.nytimes.com/2019/06/15/world/asia/hong-kong-murder-taiwan-extradition.html.

Wee, Sui-Lee. "China Hails Canada Decision to Extradite Fugitive." *REUTERS*. July 22, 2011. https://www.reuters.com/article/us-china-canada-lai-idUSTRE76L0FL20110722.

Smit, Dirk Van Zyl. "Life Imprisonment and the Right to Hope." *Penal Reform International Blog*. July 24, 2013. https://www.penalreform.org/blog/life-imprisonment-hope/.

Yin, Yanhong. "EU-UK Surrender Agreement: A Copy of the EU-Iceland and Norway One?" *European Law Blog*, March 10, 2021. https://europeanlawblog.eu/2021/03/10/eu-uk-surrender-agreement-a-copy-of-the-eu-iceland-and-norway-one/.

Zhong, Zheping, Huang Xi, and Liu Hailing. "Guangdong and Macau Police Joined Hands Cracking Down the Macau Gang Robbing the Underground Banks." *Yang Cheng Wan Bao*, November 29, 1999. http://news.sina.com.cn/china/1999-11-29/36372.html.

Reports, working papers, policy briefs, presentations, and theses

Amnesty International, "Universal Jurisdiction: The Duty of States to Enact and Implement Legislation." Accessed November 8, 2022. https://www.amnesty.org/en/documents/ior53/002/2001/en/.

Barca, Robert. "Comparative Study of Death Penalty in China and the United States: Reasons for Retention in International and Domestic Context." Master's diss., Aalborg University and University of International Relations, May 15, 2019. https://projekter.aau.dk/projekter/files/305311463/Robert_Barca_Master_s_Thesis_Final_Online.pdf.

Bondt, Wendy De. "Overcoming Offence Diversities in EU Policy Making: Needs and Feasibility Assessment." PhD diss., University of Gent, 2012. https://biblio.ugent.be/publication/2129164/file/4336026.pdf.

Brookson-Morris, Katharine. "Choosing the Right Forum: Competing Jurisdictional Competence in the Sphere of International, Transnational and National Crimes." Master's diss., University of Birmingham, February 2015. https://etheses.bham.ac.uk//id/eprint/6768/8/Brookson-Morris16MPhil.pdf.

Cacho, María, María del Carmen Rebolledo and María Teresa Vadel. "The Themis Project: Solving Conflicts of Jurisdiction in the European Union. May 2012. Accessed November 8, 2022. https://ejtn.eu/Documents/Themis%202012/THEMIS%202012%20ERFURT%20DOCUMENT/written%20paper%20Spain_Team%201.pdf.

Chau, Pak-kwan, and Stephen Lam. Research Study on the Agreement between Hong Kong and the Mainland concerning Surrender of Fugitive Offenders. March 2001. Hong Kong Research and Library Services Division and Legal Service Division. https://www.legco.gov.hk/yr00-01/english/library/erp05.pdf.

Eomois, Ele-Marit. "Role of Nationality and Residence in EU Judicial Cooperation in Criminal Matters." Master's diss., University of Tartu, 2015. https://core.ac.uk/download/pdf/79110889.pdf.

Eurojust. "Conflicts of Jurisdiction." *Eurojust News*. January 2016. https://www.eurojust.europa.eu/sites/default/files/Publications/EJNews/EurojustNews_Issue14_2016-01.pdf.

Eurojust. "Guidelines for Deciding on Competing Requests for Surrender and Extradition." Revised 2019. https://www.eurojust.europa.eu/sites/default/files/Publications/Reports/2019-10_Guidelines-competing-extradition-surrender-EAW_EN.pdf.

Eurojust. "Guidelines for Deciding 'Which Jurisdiction should Prosecute?'" Revised 2016. https://www.eurojust.europa.eu/sites/default/files/Publications/Reports/2016_Jurisdiction-Guidelines_EN.pdf

European Law Institute. "Report of the European Law Institute—Draft Legislative Proposals for the Prevention and Resolution of Conflicts of Jurisdiction in Criminal Matters in the European Union." 2017. https://www.europeanlawinstitute.eu/fileadmin/user_upload/p_eli/Publications/Conflict_of_Jurisdiction_in_Criminal_Law_FINAL.pdf.

Gao, Tong. "Aomen yu neidi jiji tuidong xingshi sifa huzhu" 澳门与内地积极推动刑事司法互助 [Macau and Mainland push the judicial cooperation in criminal matters]. The State Council Information Office of the People's Republic of China. April 18, 2014. http://www.scio.gov.cn/37236/37256/Document/1586882/1586882.htm.

Giacomelli, Giulia. "Ne Bis in Idem Profiles in EU Criminal Law." Master's diss., the Università Degli Studi Firenze, 2014. https://archiviodpc.dirittopenaleuomo.org/upload/1422126174full%20text%204917958%20GIACOMELLI.pdf.

Holmer, F. "Matter Carles Puigdemont: The Extradition for the Accusation of Embezzlement of Public Funds is Admissible: An Extradition for the Accusation of Rebellion is Inadmissible. Carles Puigdemont Remains Free." *The Press Department of the Oberlandesgericht for the State of Schleswig-Holstein*. July 12, 2018. https://www.schleswig-holstein.de/DE/Justiz/OLG/Presse/PI/201806Puigdemontenglisch.html.

Hong Kong Law Society, "Fugitive Offenders and Mutual Legal Assistance in Criminal Matters Legislation (Amendment) Bill 2019 Submission." Accessed November 8, 2022. http://video3.mingpao.com/typeset/stb/inews/20190605/20190605law.pdf.

Hong Kong Government. "Government Clarifies the Reports on Zhang Zi Qiang Case." *Press Release*. November 6, 1998. https://www.info.gov.hk/gia/general/199811/06/1106188.htm.

Hong Kong Law Reform Commission. "Double Jeopardy Consultation Paper." March 2010. https://www.gov.hk/en/residents/government/publication/consultation/docs/2010/DoubleJeopardy.pdf.

Hong Kong Legislative Committee Topic 20. "Negotiation between Mainland China and Hong Kong on the arrangement of surrender of fugitive offenders." *Press Release*. February 3, 2016. http://www.info.gov.hk/gia/general/201602/03/P201602030531.htm.

Hong Kong Legislative Committee Question 17, "Discussion between Hong Kong and Macau on the Arrangement of Surrender of Fugitive Offenders and Judicial Cooperation in Criminal Matters." *Press Release*. February 24, 2016. https://www.info.gov.hk/gia/general/201602/24/P201602240393.htm.

Hong Kong Legislative Council Question 6. "Legislation on Article 23 of Basic Law." *Press Release*. May 27, 2020. https://www.info.gov.hk/gia/general/202005/27/P2020052700520.htm.

Hong Kong Legislative Council Question 7. "Discussion of Surrender of Fugitive Offenders Arrangement between Hong Kong and Mainland." *Press Release*. May 18, 2016. https://www.info.gov.hk/gia/general/201605/18/P201605180403.htm.

Hong Kong Security Bureau Paper Prepared for Legislative Committee Panel on Security Meeting. "Arrangements with the Mainland on Surrender of Fugitive Offenders." Legislative Council. December 3, 1998. https://www.legco.gov.hk/yr98-99/english/panels/se/papers/se0312_3.htm.

Kapferer, Sibylle. "Legal and Protection Policy Research Series: The Interface between Extradition and Asylum." United Nations High Commissioner for Refugees. November 2003. https://www.unhcr.org/3fe84fad4.pdf.

Krönmark, Rebecka. "Limits of Mutual Recognition in Criminal Matters." Master's diss., Lund University, 2010. https://lup.lub.lu.se/luur/download?func=downloadFile&recordOId=1710141&fileOId=1712723.

Laura, Teuber. "Extradition and Human Rights: A Look at the EU-US and Germany-US Extradition Agreements and Their Consistency with Each Other and with Human Rights." Bachelor's diss., University of Twente, 2012. (S1009184). https://essay.utwente.nl/61772/1/BSc_L_Teuber.pdf.

Lenaerts, Koen. "The Principle of Mutual Recognition in the Area of Freedom, Security and Justice." The Fourth Annual Sir Jeremy Lever Lecture, University of Oxford, January, 30, 2015. https://www.law.ox.ac.uk/sites/files/oxlaw/the_principle_of_mutual_recognition_in_the_area_of_freedom_judge_lenaerts.pdf.

Li, Jia Chao. "Bao'an juzhang jiu 2019 nian tanfan xingshi shiyi xianghu falv xiezhu fali xiuding tiaoli can'an huijian chuanmei kaichang fayan" 保安局局长就《2019年逃犯及刑事事宜相互法律协助法例(修订)条例草案》会见传媒开场发言 [Statement Given by Secretary of HK Security Bureau on the Amendment of Hong Kong Fugitive Offender Ordinance]. *Press Release*. May 30, 2019. https://www.info.gov.hk/gia/general/201905/30/P2019053000811.htm.

Public International Law & Policy Group NL. "The Legality of Life Imprisonment: Comparative Analysis of International European and Dutch Law." Peace Negotiations Post-conflict Constitutions War Crimes Prosecution. May 2016. https://pilpnjcm.nl/wp-content/uploads/2016/09/PILPG-NL-Life-Imprisonment-Comparative-Analysis-26.05.16.pdf.

Thomas, Jennifer Leigh. "The Influence of European Union Policy on Capital Punishment in the United States Judicial System." Master's diss., Western Kentucky University, 2012. https://digitalcommons.wku.edu/cgi/viewcontent.cgi?referer=&httpsredir=1&article=1377&context=stu_hon_theses.

Winther, Dace. "Extradition, Asylum and Mutual Trust in the European Union: One Man's Terrorist is Another Man's Freedom of Fighter, yet Another Man's Asylum Seeker, yet Another Man's Fugitive." Master's diss., Lund University 2018. https://lup.lub.lu.se/luur/download?func=downloadFile&recordOId=8944578&fileOId=8944591.

Yorke, Jon. "The Council of Europe and the Death Penalty: The Relationship of State Sovereignty and Human Rights." PhD diss., University of Warwick, 2008. http://wrap.warwick.ac.uk/4106/1/WRAP_THESIS_Yorke_2008.pdf.

Yuan, Guoqiang 袁国强. "zhonghua sifa yanjiuhui chengli dahui ji shoujie zhonghua sifa yanjiu gaofeng luntan zhici" 中华司法研究会成立大会暨首届中华司法研究高峰论坛 [Speech in First Session of Chinese Justice Study Summit Forum]. July 3, 2015. https://www.doj.gov.hk/sc/community_engagement/speeches/pdf/sj20150704sc.pdf.

Table of Cases

Court of Justice of the European Union decisions

Case 120/78 *Rewe-Zentral AG v. Bundesmonopolverwaltung fÜrbranntwein* [1979] ECR 649
Case C-76/90 *Manfred Säger v. Dennemeyer & Co. Ltd* [1991] ECR I-4221
Case C-340/89 *Irene Vlassopoulou v. Ministerium für justiz, Bundes-und Europaangelegenheiten Baden-Württemberg* [1991] ECR I-2357
Cases C-187/01 and C-385/01 *Gozutok and Brugge* [2003] ECR I-1378
Case C-411/03 *SEVIC Systems* [2005] ECR I-10805
Case C-386/04 *Centro de Musicologia* [2006] ECR I-8203
Case C-303/05 *Advocaten voor de Wereld VZW v. Leden van de Ministerraad* [2007] ECR I-03633
Case C-210/06 *Cartesio* [2008] ECR I-9641
Case C-66/08 *Szymon Kozlowski* [2008] ECR I-06041
Case C-318/07 *Persche* [2009] ECR I-359
Case C-123/08 *Dominic Wolzenburg* [2009] ECR I-09621
Case C-261/09 *Gaetano Mantello* [2010] ECR I-11477
Case C-306/09 *I.B.* [2010] ECR I-10341
Case C-378/10 *VALE* [Judgment of the Court, July 12, 2012]
Case C-396/11 *Ciprian Vasile Radu* [Judgment of the Court, January 29, 2013]
Case C-399/11 *Stefano Melloni v. Ministerio Fiscal* [Judgment of the Court, February 26, 2013]
Case C-168/13 PPU *Jeremy F. v. Premier Minister* [Judgment of the Court, May 30, 2013]
Case C-237/15 PPU *Francis Lanigan* [Judgment of the Court, July 16, 2015]
Case C-463/15 PPU *Openbaar Minsterie v. A* [Order of the Court, September 25, 2015]
Case C-404/15and C-659/15PPU *Aranyosi and Caldararu* [Judgment of the Court, April 5, 2016]
Case C-486/14 Piotr *Kossowski* [Judgment of the Court, June 29, 2016]
Case C-452/16 PPU *Krzystof Maretk Poltorak* [Judgment of the Court, November 10, 2016]
Case C-477/16 PPU *Openbaar Ministerie v. Ruslanas Kovalkovas* [Judgment of the Court, November 10, 2016]
Case C-579/15 *Daniel Adam Poplawski* [Judgment of the Court, June 29, 2017]
Case C-268/17 *AY* [Judgment of Court, July 25, 2018]

Case C-216/18 PPU *LM* [Judgment of the Court, July 25, 2018]
Case C-220/18 PPU *ML* [Judgment of the Court, July 25, 2018]
Case C-508/18 and Case C-82/19 PPU *Minister for Justice and Equality v. OG and PI* [Judgment of the Court, May 27, 2019]
Case C-354/20 and C-412/20 PPU *L and P* [Judgment of the Court, December 17, 2020]
Case C-896/19 *Repubblika v. Il-Prim Ministru* [Judgment of the Court, April 20, 2021].

Advocate General opinions

Opinion on the Case C-452/16 PPU *Openbaar Ministerie v. Krzysztof Marek Poltorak* (Opinion of Advocate General, October 19, 2016)

United Nations Human Rights Committee decisions

A.P. v. Italy, CCPR/C/31/D/204/1986, Communication No. 204/1986 (Decision of UNCCPR, November 2, 1987)
Teran Jijon v. Ecuador, CCPR/C/44/D/277/1988, Communication No. 277/1988 (Decision of UNCCPR, March 26, 1992)
A.R.J. v. Australia, CCPR/C/60/D/692/1996, Communication No. 692/1996 (Decision of UNCCPR, February 6, 1996)

European Court of Human Rights judgments

Soering v. the United Kingdom, application no. 14038/88 (Judgment of ECtHR, July 7, 1989)
Jabari v. Turkey, application no. 40035/98 [Judgment of ECtHR, July 11, 2000]
Bader and Kanbor v. Sweden, application no. 13284/04 [Judgment of ECtHR, November 8, 2005]
Rrapo v. Albania application no. 58555/10 [Judgment of ECtHR, September 25, 2012]
Vinter and Others v. the UK, applications nos. 66069/09, 130/10 and 3896/10 [Judgment of ECtHR, July 9, 2013]
Laszlo Magyar v. Hungary, no. 73593/10 [Judgment of ECtHR, May 20, 2014]
Al Nashiri v. Poland, no. 28761/11 [Judgment of ECtHR, July 24, 2014]
Trabelsi v. Belgium, application no. 140/10 [Judgment of ECtHR, September 4, 2014]
Caraian v. Romania, application no. 34456/07 [Judgment of ECtHR, June 23, 2015]
EZE v. Romania, application no. 80529/13 [Judgment of ECtHR, June 21, 2016]
T.P. and A.T. v. Hungary, nos. 37871/14 and 73986/14 [Judgment of ECtHR, October 4, 2016]
Cirino and Renne v. Italy, application nos. 2539/13 and 4705/13 [Judgment of ECtHR, October 26, 2017]

International Court of Justice judgments

Legal Status of Eastern Greenland, PCIJ Series A/B. No. 53 [Judgment of the Permanent Court of International Justice, April 5, 1933]

United Kingdom judgments

Sandru v. Government of Romania [2009] EWHC2879 (Admin)

United States judgments

California v. Superior Court, 482 U.S.400, 407, 107 S.Ct.2433, 2438, 96 L.Ed.2d 332 (1987)

Macau judgments

The Macau Case on Personal Protection Order, Judge Viriato Manuel Pinheiro de Lima, Judgment on March 20, 2007, no. 12, 2007

Hong Kong judgments

Yeung Chun Pong v Secretary for Justice (2009) 12 HKCFAR 867
Case KCMP 139 of 2018, Ruling in the matter of the request for surrender of Mr. Ramanjit Singh to the Republic of India
Ubamaka Edward Wilson v Secretary for Security (2012) 15 HKCFAR 743
HKSAR v Wong Tak Keung (2015) 18 HKCFAR 158
HKSAR v Fu Man Kit (2021) 24 HKCFAR 253

Mainland China judgments

Li torture case, Criminal (2010) 51 People's Court of Shandong Province Rizhao Economic Development Region. 李某某刑讯逼供案，山东省日照市经济开发区人民法院（2010）日开刑初字第51号

Table of Legislation

European Union laws, conventions, decisions, directives, and related documents

1957 European Convention on Extradition
1996 Convention relating to Extradition between the Member States of the European Union
1975 Protocol to the European Convention on Extradition 1957
1983 Protocol 6 to the Convention for the Protection of Human Rights and Fundamental Freedoms Concerning the Abolition of the Death Penalty
2002 Protocol 13 to the Convention for the Protection of Human Rights and Fundamental Freedoms Concerning the Abolition of the Death Penalty
2003 Protocol Amending the European Convention on the Suppression of Terrorism
Agreement between the Governments of the States of the Benelux Economic Union, the Federal Republic of Germany and the French Republic on the gradual abolition of checks at their common borders
Agreement on the Application among the Member States of the European Communities of the Council of Europe Convention on the Transfer of Sentenced Persons
Agreement between the European Union and the Republic of Iceland and the Kingdom of Norway on the Surrender Procedure between the Member States of the European Union and Iceland and Norway
Charter of Fundamental Rights of the European Union
Convention on Preventing and Combating Violence Against Women and Domestic Violence 2011
Council of European Union, *Evaluation Report on the Fourth Round of Mutual Evaluations "Practical Application of the European Arrest Warrant and Corresponding Surrender Procedures between Member States" Report on Belgium* (16454/06 REV1 RESTREINT UE)
Council Decision 2002/584/JHA of 13 June 2002 on the European arrest warrant and the surrender procedures between Member States [2002] 0J L 190/1.
Council Decision 2009/299/JHA of 26 February 2009 amending Framework Decision 2002/584/JHA, 2006/783/JHA, 2008/909/JHA and 2008/947/JHA, thereby enhancing the procedural rights of persons and fostering the application of the principle

of mutual recognition to decisions rendered in the absence of the person concerned at the trial [2009] OJ L81/24.

Council Decision 2002/187/JHA of 28 February 2002 setting up Eurojust with a view to reinforcing the fight against serious crime [2002] OJ L63/1.

Council Decision 2009/948/JHA of 30 November 2009 on prevention and settlement of conflicts of exercise of jurisdiction in criminal proceedings [2009] 0JL328/42

Council Decision 2003/568/JHA of 22 July 2003 on Combating Corruption in the Private Sector [2003] OJ L192/54

Council Decision 2005/214/JHA of 24 February 2005 on the application of the principle of mutual recognition to financial penalties [2005] OJ L76/16

Council Decision 2008/978/JHA of 18 December 2008 on the European evidence warrant for the purpose of obtaining objects, documents and data for use in proceedings in criminal matters [2008] OJ L 350/72

Council Directive 2014/41/EU of 3 April 2014 regarding the European Investigation Order in criminal matters

Council Directive 2014/41/EU of 3 April 2014 regarding the European Investigation Order in Criminal Matters [2014] OJ L130/1

Council Directive 2011/95/EU of the European Parliament and the Council of 13 December 2011 on standards for the qualification of third-country nationals and stateless persons as beneficiaries of international protection, for a uniform status for refugees or for persons eligible for subsidiary protection, and for the content of the protection granted [2011] OJ L337/9

Council Directive 2013/32/EU of the Parliament and of the Council of 26 June 2013 on common procedures for granting and withdrawing international protection [2013] OJ L180/60

Council Directive 2013/33/EU of the European Parliament and the Council of 26 June 2013 laying down standards for the reception of applicants for international protection [2013] OJ L180/96

Council Regulation 604/2013/EU of the European Parliament and the Council of 26 June 2013 establishing the criteria and mechanisms for determining the Member State responsible for examining the application for international protection lodged in one of the Member States by a third country national or a stateless person (recast) [2013] OJ L180/31

Council Regulation (EU) 2018/1805 of 14 November 2018 on the mutual recognition of freezing orders and confiscation orders [2018] OJ L303/1

Council Recommendation (2003) 22 of the Committee of Ministers to member states on conditional release

Council Recommendation (2006) 2 of the Committee of Ministers to member states on the European Prison Rules

Council 17195/10 Revised Version of the European Handbook on how to issue a European Arrest Warrant [2010] Copen 275, 14.

Commission Notice, Handbook on How to Issue and Execute a European Arrest Warrant [2017] OJ C335/01

Commission, "Communication on mutual recognition" COM (2000) 495 final
Commission, "Proposal for a Council Framework Decision on the European arrest warrant and the surrender procedures between the Member State" COM (2001) 522
Commission, "Green Paper on the approximation, mutual recognition and enforcement of criminal sanctions in the European Union" COM (2004) 334 final
Commission, "The mutual recognition of judicial decisions in criminal matters and the strengthening of mutual trust between Member States" (Communication) COM (2005) 195 final
Commission, "Report on the implementation of Council Framework Decision on European Arrest Warrant" COM (2020) 270 final
Commission, "Opinion on the Draft amendments to the Law on the State Prosecutorial Council of Serbia," CDL-AD (2014) 029, §7
Commission, "Interim Opinion on the Draft Law on the State Prosecution Office of Montenegro," CDL-AD (2014) 042, §16.
Commission, "Report on the implementation of Council Framework Decision of 13 June 2002 on the European arrest warrant and the surrender procedure between Member States" COM (2020) 270 final
Commission, "Report from the Commission to the European Parliament and the Council on the implementation since 2007 of the Council Decision of 13 June 2002 on the European arrest warrant and the surrender procedures between Member States" COM (2011) 175 final
Commission, "Proposal for a Council Framework Decision on the European arrest warrant and the surrender procedures between the Member States" COM (2001) 522 final
Commission, "Green Paper on Conflicts of Jurisdiction and the Principle of Ne Bis In Idem in Criminal Proceedings" COM (2005) 696 final
European Convention on Human Rights
European Union and United Kingdom Trade and Cooperation Agreement
European Convention on the Suppression of Terrorism
Explanatory Report of 12 December 1996 on Convention on simplified extradition procedure between the Member States of the European Union [1996] OJC 375/03
Explanatory Report to the European Convention on Extradition 1957
Explanatory Report to the Additional Protocol to the European Convention on Extradition 1975
Explanatory Report to the Convention relating to extradition between the Member States of the European Union [1997] OJC 191/13
Hague Programme-Strengthening Freedom, Security and Justice in the European Union [2005] OJC53/1
Initiative of the Hellenic Republic with a View to adopting a Council Framework Decision concerning the Application of the "Ne Bis In Idem" Principle [2003] OJ C100/12
Programme of measures to implement the principle of mutual recognition of decisions in criminal matters [2001] OJC 12/10
Tampere European Council 15 and 16 October 1999 Presidency Conclusions
Treaty on the Functioning of the European Union

Treaty Establishing the European Community

United Nations, international, and regional legal documents

African Charter on Human and People's Rights
Convention on the Means of Prohibiting and Preventing the Illicit Import, Export and Transfer of Cultural Property, 1970
Convention for the Suppression of Unlawful Seizure of Aircraft
Convention for the Suppression of Unlawful Acts against the Safety of Civil Aviation
Convention on the Prevention and Punishment of Crimes against Internationality Protected Persons, including Diplomatic Agents
Extradition Agreement between Italy and US 1983
Extradition Agreement between Italy and Canada 2005
Extradition Convention of the Economic Community of West African States
International Covenant on Civil and Political Rights
International Convention for the Suppression of Terrorist Bombings
International Convention for the Suppression of the Financing of Terrorism
Inter-American Convention on Human Rights
Inter-American Convention on Extradition
Report of the Secretary-General, A/CONF.144/13 "Criminal Justice Policies in relation to Problems of Imprisonment, other Penal Sanctions and Alternative Measures-Research on Alternatives to Imprisonment" (Eighth UN Congress on the Prevention of Crime and the Treatment of Offenders, June 1, 1990), 19–24
Report of the Secretary-General, A/CONF.144/12 "Criminal Justice Policies in Relation to Problems of Imprisonment, Other Penal Sanctions and Alternative Measures—Alternatives to Imprisonment and the Reduction of the Prison Population" (Eighth UN Congress on the Prevention of Crime and the Treatment of Offenders, May 28, 1990), 19–22.
Report of the Secretary-General, A/CONF.144/1 "Implementation of the Standard Minimum Rules for the Treatment of Prisoners" (Eighth UN Congress on the Prevention of Crime and the Treatment of Offenders, July 19, 1990), 27–30.
Rome Statute of the International Criminal Court
Revised Manual on the Model Treaty on Extradition
Second Optional Protocol to the International Convention on Civil and Political Rights
Secretariat for the Sixth UN Congress, "Deinstitutionalization of corrections and its implications for the residual prisoner" (1980), Working Paper on the Prevention of Crime and the Treatment of Offenders 77041
Treaty on Extradition between Australia and the Republic of Venezuela
Treaty on Extradition between the United States and Venezuela
Treaty on Extradition between the Kingdom of Spain and the Republic of Panama
Treaty on Extradition between the Kingdom of Spain and the Republic of Paraguay
Treaty on Extradition between Kingdom of Spain and Republic of India
Treaty on Extradition between Kingdom of Spain and US

UN Convention Against Corruption
Universal Declaration of Human Rights
UN Convention on the Rights of the Child
United Nations Standard Minimum Rules for the Treatment of Prisoners
UN Model Treaty on Extradition
United Nations General Comment No. 32, International Convention on Civil and Political Rights, Article 14: Right to Equality before Court and Tribunals and to A Fair Trial

Mainland China legislation, treaties, and other documents

China Extradition Law
China Constitution Law
China Criminal Procedure Law
China Public Prosecutors Law
China Criminal Law
Extradition Treaty between China and South Korea
Extradition Treaty between China and Italy
Extradition Treaty between China and Australia
Extradition Treaty between China and Thailand
Extradition Treaty between China and Portugal
Extradition Treaty between China and Pakistan
Extradition Treaty between China and Russia
Extradition Treaty between China and Spain
Extradition Treaty between China and Uzbekistan
Extradition Treaty between China and Cambodia
Extradition Treaty between China and Laos
Extradition Treaty between China and France
Extradition Treaty between China and Argentina
Extradition Treaty between China and Barbados
Extradition Treaty between China and Belgium
Regulation on the Law Application in Addressing Cases of Commutation and Parole by Supreme People's Court

Hong Kong legislation and agreements

Agreement between Hong Kong and Macau on Transfer of Sentenced Persons
Agreement between Hong Kong and Spain Concerning Mutual Legal Assistance in Criminal Matters
Basic Law of Hong Kong
Crimes Ordinance
Criminal Procedure Ordinance
Fugitive Offenders Ordinance
Hong Kong Law on Safeguarding National Security
Hong Kong Bill of Rights

Hong Kong Long-Term Prison Sentences Review Ordinance
Offences Against the Person Ordinance
Public Cleansing and Prevention of Nuisances Regulation
Surrender Agreement between Hong Kong and New Zealand
Surrender Agreement between Hong Kong and the Netherlands
Surrender Agreement between Hong Kong and Finland
Surrender Agreement between Hong Kong and US
Surrender Agreement between Hong Kong and Canada
Surrender Agreement between Hong Kong and Portugal
Surrender Agreement between Hong Kong and India
Surrender Agreement between Hong Kong and Indonesia
Surrender Agreement between Hong Kong and Singapore
Surrender Agreement between Hong Kong and Malaysia
Surrender Agreement between Hong Kong and Germany
Surrender Agreement between Hong Kong and South Africa
Surrender Agreement between Hong Kong and Philippines
Surrender Agreement between Hong Kong and South Korea
Surrender Agreement between Hong Kong and Check Republic
Surrender Agreement between Hong Kong and UK
Surrender Agreement between Hong Kong and Ireland
Theft Ordinance

Macau legislation and agreements

Agreement on Judicial Cooperation in Civil and Criminal Matters between Macau and Cape Verde
Basic Law of Macau
Macao Law on Safeguarding National Security
Macau Criminal Procedure Law
Macau Law on Judicial Cooperation in Criminal Matters
Organic Law on Judicial Organization of Macau
Penal Code of Macau
Surrender agreement between Macau and Portugal
Surrender agreement between Macau and South Korea

United States legislation

US Constitution

German legislation

German Criminal Code
German Constitution Law

Peru legislation

Peru Code of Criminal Procedure 2004

Portugal legislation

Portuguese Constitution

Slovenia legislation

Slovenia Constitution

Dutch legislation

Dutch Criminal Code

Index

Milton Keynes UK
Ingram Content Group UK Ltd.
UKHW021401011224
451605UK00008B/73